Compatibility Breeds Success

Compatibility Breeds Success

How to Manage Your Relationship with Your Business Partner

MARVIN SNIDER

PRAEGER

Westport, Connecticut
London

Library of Congress Cataloging-in-Publication Data

Snider, Marvin.
 Compatibility breeds success : how to manage your relationship with your
 business partner / Marvin Snider.
    p.   cm.
 Includes bibliographical references and index.
 ISBN 1–56720–489–9 (alk. paper)
 1. Strategic alliances (Business) 2. Partnership. 3. Interpersonal relations.
 4. Interorganizational relations. I. Title.
HD69.S8S65   2003
658′.044—dc21   2003053561

British Library Cataloguing in Publication Data is available.

Library of Congress Catalog Card Number: 2003053561
ISBN: 1–56720–489–9

First published in 2003

Praeger Publishers, 88 Post Road West, Westport, CT 06881
An imprint of Greenwood Publishing Group, Inc.
www.praeger.com

Printed in the United States of America

The paper used in this book complies with the
Permanent Paper Standard issued by the National
Information Standards Organization (Z39.48–1984).

10 9 8 7 6 5 4 3 2 1

To the many rewarding partnerships with family, friends, clients, and especially my marital and business partner, Faye

Contents

Preface

Partnerships are a common phenomenon. They are commonly referred to as though they are a single entity—that one partnership is like another. Partnerships are as varied as the people who participate in them. This book takes a closer look at the different types and characteristics of business partnerships. My hope is that it will help people better prepare for entering a partnership and better understand what is involved in making a partnership a satisfying and productive experience.

Discussion with colleagues and a review of the literature led to the conclusion that too little has been written on relationships in partnerships. Discussion with Eric Valentine, former publisher of Quorum Books, led to the writing of this book.

The book will be of most interest to the entrepreneur already in a partnership or one who is considering entering one. Understanding the dimensions of a partnership will be useful to those considering forming one. It will help those entrepreneurs already in a partnership to improve the quality of their relationship. My view is that all relationships need to be viewed as a partnership if they are to be successful. That includes relationships not usually considered partnerships, such as those between entrepreneurs and the consultants they use—lawyers, accountants, and the like. Considering those relationships as partnerships may enhance their quality. The same may be true of the many partnerships found in complex organizations, such as those between a chief executive officer and board members and various subordinates. It may also lend added perspective to appreciating the complex partnerships in the noncorporate world of religious groups and universities. Clergy and university presidents have challenges parallel to those of a CEO in managing many levels of "partnership."

This book is divided into three parts. Part I describes the dynamics of partnerships. Each chapter discusses one of 10 dimensions that define them. Part II applies the concepts of Part I to the formation and management of a partnership. Each chapters considers a different aspect of partnership life. Part III describes two groups of partnerships: basic and collateral. The *basic* group is composed of six types of partnerships: active, silent, corporate, professional, family business, and product. *Collateral* partnerships are supportive partnerships that enable the basic partnerships to function; they are relationships with professionals—lawyers, accountants, other consultants—banks, the family, and consumers. I show how the dimensions described in Part I apply to each of these partnerships.

Two appendices augment the main text. Appendix A contains the findings from case studies of and interviews with a variety of partnerships. Further information pertaining to case examples referred to throughout this book can be found in Appendix A. Appendix B provides an instrument for monitoring the health of partnerships. Partnerships, like any relationship, are not static. Periodic assessment of the partnership's status can contribute to maintaining a healthy partnership by reinforcing that which is constructive. This can also identify problems in their incipient stage, when they are most easily corrected.

Acknowledgments

This book is an outgrowth of my previous book, *Human Relations Management in Young, Growing Companies* (Quorum Books, 2001). That work led to my desire to better understand the dynamics of partnerships. I am very appreciative of Carl Israel's willingness to share his legal experience and insights on partnerships and for his willingness to coauthor Chapter 20 in this book. I am indebted to many people for sharing their experience in partnerships. These include Herman Blumberg, Harold Butler, Paul Cole, Norman Fine, Edward Gates, Michael Glick, Rachel Grant, Robert Harrisburg, Arnold Kerzner, Kenneth Krowne, David Mofenson, Judith Nast, Martin Norman, Wilma Peebles-Wilkins, Michael Rosenfeld, Richard Rubino, Craig Snider, Stuart Steele, and Herbert Zarkin. The insight and support of Eric Valentine, formerly of Greenwood Publishing Group, played a major role in the evolution of this book; the book would not have been possible without his guidance, patience, and support. I want to thank Hilary Claggett for her guidance in the final stages of this book. The quality of writing was greatly improved with the editing help of Betty Pessagno. I am particularly indebted to my wife, Faye, for her support, encouragement, and feedback in the writing of this book.

CHAPTER 1

The Metaphor of Marriage

Partnerships function parallel to human physical functioning. Just as a person's physical survival depends on the coordinated functioning of the body's various systems—circulatory, nervous, digestive, and so forth—a partnership's survival depends on the coordinated functioning of its various components—communication, accountability, the ability to resolve differences, and more.

MARRIAGE AS A METAPHOR FOR PARTNERSHIP

Marriage provides another perspective for our understanding of business partnerships. Many insights may be gained from the parallels between a business partnership and a marital partnership, and those insights can be applied in achieving successful business partnerships. Both marital and business partners

- start with the expectation of a long-term commitment;
- are accountable for one another's behavior;
- may negotiate a formal commitment;
- make a strong emotional commitment to each other;
- share financial obligations;
- play a dominant role in each other's life;
- require a commitment to resolving differences to succeed;
- are likely to have a major impact on each other even after the partnership ends;
- require a balanced division of labor to make the partnership work;

- have to compete with other personal and extended family interests and commitments; and
- usually share a common physical space.

In many ways, though, these partnerships are very different:

- Business partnerships don't involve a physical relationship.
- Business partners don't produce children; however, investment in the partnership's product can parallel the emotional investment in a child and result in a similar struggle for control or custody when the partnership dissolves.
- Marriages have a different level of emotional commitment.
- Marriages usually involve a deeper level of commitment to one another's families.
- Marriages have more clearly defined legal guidelines for how they are dissolved.

This comparison suggests the value to be gained from considering a business partnership with the same care as you would a marriage. It also shows that you may well be able to apply what you have learned in one of these partnerships to the other.

DEFINITION OF PARTNERSHIP

Not enough has been written about the various dimensions that define how a partnership functions and about the different forms partnerships may take. In this book, I emphasize that a relationship is a partnership when it involves the constructive collaboration of two or more partners, with both of them sharing responsibility for a compatible definition of success.

In practice, there are many definitions of partnership, including the following:

The *American Heritage Talking Dictionary* (Version 4.0, 1995) defines partnership as a legal contract entered into by two or more persons in which each agrees to furnish a part of the capital and labor for a business enterprise, and by which each shares a fixed proportion of profits and losses.

One law dictionary defines partnership as an association of two or more people who agree to share in the profits and losses of a business venture. The members of a partnership are called partners.

According to Robert L. Davidson III, author of *The Small Business Partnership* (1992), a partnership is a business that is owned by two or more persons who, as co-owners, carry on a trade or business for profit.

According to authors Chip R. Bell and Heather Shea (1998), a partnership is a deliberate blending of capacities for the continuous mutual benefit of the involved parties.

All of the preceding definitions are inadequate because they are ambiguous and do not provide sufficient perspective for understanding what makes a partnership work and how one partnership is different from another. I propose a more comprehensive definition that has both a conceptual and an operational component: *a partnership is a relationship, defined formally or informally, between two or more people who share responsibility in a cooperative effort to reach a common goal for mutual benefit.* Let us consider what is meant by the major terms in the preceding definition.

Partners who are in a *relationship* agree to work toward a *common* business objective. Their relationship requires that they pool their resources and determine how to use them in pursuit of their objective. They also establish a framework for how they will relate to each other in pursuit of their common goal. To do that they must find a way to integrate personal and partnership goals.

A relationship is not considered a partnership when one person directs the behavior of another person who is not involved in determining how the job is to be conducted. The subordinate's only obligation is to perform as directed, and that deprives the relationship of the subordinate's potential creative contribution. The subordinate is comparable to the person who puts in his or her eight hours a day at a routine job and who has no say about how the job should be done.

Partners' agreement on goals doesn't necessarily translate into agreement on how to get there, either in terms of method or time frame. Different opinions about how to achieve goals will seriously affect the business unless the partners develop ways to deal constructively with their different views and engage in a *cooperative effort.* Conflict resolution involves the recognition that input is needed from both parties in a complementary manner that is personally acceptable and is necessary to accomplish the collective objective. It also requires that both parties possess the needed skills for the required performance of their respective responsibilities. (See chapters 7 and 8 for more discussion on decision making and conflict resolution.)

Partnerships in business, as in marriage, can easily result in a struggle for power and control to the detriment of the business. Working out a mutually meaningful division of labor will contribute to a healthy, collaborative relationship. The partners will avoid a major source of conflict if they can agree on their respective responsibilities and avoid micromanaging one another.

Shared responsibility is enhanced when both parties make explicit what they need from one another in order to accomplish the goal of their relationship. For that to happen requires communication that includes a commitment to effect a mutually acceptable resolution of differences. It also requires partners to accept responsibility for fulfilling commitments to their partnership. An operational definition of expectations leaves less room for error that can come from untested assumptions. Such a definition also minimizes the conflict that arises when each partner has a separate vision. Whereas two partners can easily agree that they will have to work long hours, they may have quite different ideas about what that means in practice. Difficulty in establishing a common behavioral standard can readily become a source of contention, threatening the success of the relationship.

Reaching a common goal for mutual benefit can be understood at two levels: conceptual and behavioral. The conceptual level is easily defined—to make money and provide a service or produce a good product. The potential for conflict arises when the goal is not defined in concrete terms: the partners may disagree on what constitutes adequate earnings or may differ on the service to be provided or the exact nature of the product to be made.

Partners may agree that their efforts should result in mutual benefit, but they may have trouble appreciating each other's definition of benefit. Differences may occur on both a qualitative and quantitative level. This may involve how much money is made and other gains such as desirable working conditions, exercise of power, prestige, and more. Differences regarding what benefits are desirable could create conflict if one or the other partner sees a so-called benefit as negatively affecting the business.

The goal of making money is readily accepted by all parties, but agreement on how profits will be used is more elusive. Partners who have different approaches to how profits should be used will likely be in conflict. Under the pressures of starting the business and the uncertainty of whether there will be any profits, this concern doesn't command much attention. Agreement on goals becomes critical only when the prospect of making a profit becomes a reality. Contention results when partners differ on whether to take the profits out of the business or invest the profits in building the business.

All business relationships are essentially partnerships. That is, the partners' relationships with employees, bankers, lawyers, accountants, and even their customers, as well as any other business relationship, are partnerships of a sort. The success of those relationships is materially enhanced by applying the definition of partnership I proposed earlier. When a businessperson categorically defers to a consultant because of the consultant's presumed expertise and the belief that the partner has nothing to offer, the relationship suffers. Expertise is of value only when it is applied in the context of a particular business, and that information can come only from the partners. One example is the relationship between the partners and their lawyers. It is not a partnership when they permit a lawyer to tell them how to manage their business. It *is* a partnership when the partners interact with their lawyer until both are satisfied that a given course of action addresses both the partners' and the lawyer's concerns. The same principle would apply to any other consultant.

TYPES OF PARTNERSHIPS

As indicated earlier, the most familiar form of partnership is the collaboration of two or more entrepreneurs who combine their resources in pursuit of profit. That partnership is one example of what I refer to as *active partnerships*—those that provide a service or product to the public. Also included in the active partnership category are silent partnerships, small corporations, professional partnerships, family business partnerships, and product partnerships (partnerships in which an employer or partners collaborate in producing a product or service). *Collateral partnerships* are a second category—those relationships with banks, lawyers, accountants, family, consultants, consumers, and the like. A collateral partnership provides services to an active partnership necessary to conduct its business. Each of these partnerships has its own unique characteristics. Understanding the dimensions that define a partnership will be useful in helping an entrepreneur decide if and what kind of a partnership will best suit his or her needs. These partnerships are discussed in Part III, "Types of Partnerships."

The partnership concept is also applicable to large corporations, religious and educational institutions, public agencies, and social and political organizations. In such entities, a chief executive, or other leader, has the challenge of managing partnerships on multiple levels:

- A CEO of a large company has to manage partnerships with his or her board of directors, investors, and the people who report to him or her.
- In religious institutions, the clergy have to manage partnerships with their lay leaders, congregants, professional staff, clerical hierarchy, other religions, and with the community. A clergyman or -woman has the added challenge of managing multiple relationships with the same person—for example, with a member of the lay administration who also is a congregant, who is an educator of the clergyperson's children, and who at times may seek counseling.
- The president of a university has to manage multiple partnerships with the board of directors, officers, deans, administrative staff, alumni, and others.
- Leaders of other entities such as public agencies or social and political organizations face the same kind of challenge of having to juggle various partnerships.

In all of these situations, the objective is to manage partnerships constructively and individually so that dealing with one does not cause conflict with another. For example, a CEO has to manage the partnership with one of his or her vice presidents in a manner that does not cause conflict with other vice presidents and is consistent with board policy. The task becomes easier when the partner or executive can skillfully manage the dimensions of a partnership, as discussed in Part I, "Dimensions of Partnership Dynamics."

CONSIDERATIONS IN ENTERING A PARTNERSHIP

In entering a business partnership, one is entering a relationship only slightly less complex than marriage. As noted earlier, in its dynamics, a business partnership has many similarities to marriage. The marital experience will prove an asset in a business partnership if it has been positive and if the partner is able to adapt what he or she has learned from that experience to the business partnership. Even a negative marital experience can be an asset if the learning gained from it is applied constructively. It will be a liability, however, if it colors one's ability to engage in a future business partnership.

Foremost for success in both relationships is the ability to resolve differences in a way that is acceptable to both partners. A partnership also requires one to be comfortable moving from being accountable only for oneself to also being accountable to and for another person. Business partnerships require a more concrete definition of goals than do marriages. A major challenge in both relationships is the ability to pursue individual needs and goals that are compatible with partnership goals. Partners can better meet that challenge by keeping differences focused on issues and not on personality. The following paragraphs consider the variables involved in making a partnership work.

Marriage starts with a focus on the relationship. Later, the demands of career and raising children can tax the psychic energy of both marital partners. The marital relationship will suffer unless the partners are able to maintain a balance between family responsibilities and nurturing the relationship.

The same principle applies in a business partnership. It, too, starts with a focus on the partnership. But as the demands of the business consume the partners' available psychic energy, they too often neglect the needs of the partnership. Those needs include ensuring constructive communication and acknowledging one another's concerns and contributions. As in a marriage, the quality of the partnership is enhanced by preserving the balance between the business's needs and the partners' needs.

The marital analogy reveals an important dimension that gets too little attention in business relationships: the part that managing emotions plays in a successful relationship. This involves partners showing respect for each other's constructive expression of feelings and being able to express anger without personal attack. It also involves recognizing that emotions need to be addressed before adequate attention can be paid to solving problems.

Many marriages end in divorce because of disagreements over values, money, sex, and child rearing. Business partners often overlook the importance of compatibility in values and beliefs. As a result, their ventures, too, often end up in divorce. This consideration is extremely important not only in business-related matters but also with regard to how personal values and beliefs affect the partner relationship.

Compatibility in values and beliefs does not necessarily translate into *shared priorities* in marriage as it does in business. Agreement on priorities is necessary for business partners to focus their collective resources on effectively managing their business. This is especially true in a start-up effort. Agreement on priorities is more readily achieved when both partners feel their concerns have been adequately attended to by the other.

In both marriage and business, it is tempting to take what a partner says at face value. But often we find that what one says doesn't match the way it is said or the behavior that follows. Effective communication depends on understanding the relationship between verbal and nonverbal behavior. (These concepts are elaborated on in chapter 4, "Communication.")

A common difficulty in marriage and business partnerships occurs when partners treat their assumptions as fact. Such occurrences readily give rise to unnecessary tension. Many problems can be avoided when assumptions are checked out before taking action. (Issues related to assumptions are discussed in chapter 4.)

Marital partners frequently take one another for granted; business partners also tend to give inadequate attention to affirmations. It gets too easy to take positive behavior for granted and to give it short shrift. This may happen for various reasons: competition, envy, the belief that virtue should be its own reward, and concern for how others will view the behavior. Affirmation is something we all covet. Paying as much attention to acknowledging what is positive as well as what is negative will contribute to a productive partnership.

Trust and loyalty—these qualities go together and are basic to successful partnerships in both marriage and business. They involve knowing that a person will honor his or her commitments and will invest his or her energies in maintaining the quality of the partnership. These qualities are essential ingredients in ensuring that your partner will be there through thick and thin.

Partnerships of any kind pursue activities that will yield benefits warranting the cost of getting them. When the benefits far outweigh the cost of obtaining them, the outcome will be satisfying and comfortable. But when the benefits gained become questionable relative to the cost of obtaining them, a relationship may become unstable and vulnerable to fracture. Partners should pay attention if they begin to sense that the cost-benefit ratio in their relationship is reaching a precarious point for either of them. Early identification of this condition provides a greater opportunity for correction. Allowing it to go on too long may make remedial action useless and ensure a divorce. (See the discussion in chapter 9 of benefits versus costs.)

Marital and business partnerships run into trouble when the people in them focus too much on the product and too little on the quality of the relationship. Taking the relationship for granted is likely to lead to problems as partners mature and their needs change, pushing them in different directions. As I say, this is the same in business as in marriage. Ongoing attention to nurturing the relationship is in the best interest of the partners' business objective. This is the case even though tending to the relationship may momentarily be at the business's expense. A parallel in marriage is the importance of nurturing the marital relationship separate from child rearing.

Problems in relationships are not about differences but about the inability to resolve differences to the partners' joint satisfaction. Some states recognize irreconcilable differences as a basis for granting a divorce. There is no higher priority in a relationship than to resolve differences in a mutually acceptable manner. An inability to attend to differences will unnecessarily drain psychic resources from business matters.

Injecting past resentments into current issues is a major cause of marital divorce. Carrying resentment drains psychic energy from more constructive pursuits. To avoid this mistake, partners need to take care of relationship concerns as they occur so that the issues can be resolved and do not leave a distracting residue.

Dealing with a problem by judging who is responsible takes attention away from constructive problem solving. A more productive approach is to ask how the partners can make the most out of the process of coping with a problem situation. One should look at past history only to learn from it and not to assign fault.

Conventional wisdom dictates that one learn sufficient facts about a prospective marital or business partner before entering a partnership. Embarking on a marital partnership on impulse after a brief courtship is at best questionable judgment. This same mistake occurs in business partnerships. In both cases, the prospect for a successful, long-term outcome is not good. That is the easy part. The underlying questions are what do you need to know about a prospective partner, and how long will it take you to get that information? How much is enough? How do you go about finding out what you need to know? This rational approach is complicated by the way business partnerships evolve. The start-up is often guided more by emotion than by intellect. Partnerships commonly are born when people come together fueled by a shared vision. That enthusiasm and the press for fulfillment often obscure the need to give adequate consideration to the prospective partners' compatibility. Partnerships are at risk to the degree that enthusiasm exceeds attention to the compatibility of prospective partners.

Even the most innovative ideas and the best business plan will fail if the two partners are unable to work together constructively. Partners must therefore possess compatible work ethics, value and belief systems, and goals. To be useful, the concepts of work ethics, values, belief systems, and goals have to be defined in operational terms as behaviors that can be observed and measured. Unfortunately, partners may both believe in hard work but have difficulty finding common standards. Defining a common standard such as fulfilling one's commitments and performing responsibilities in a timely manner is not easily accomplished.

Moreover, a concept is always easier to define than to implement. There is no clear answer to the question of how well one should know a prospective partner before engaging in the relationship. The general answer, in business as in marriage, is to decide on what characteristics you want in a partner for the prospective relationship. Then, only by knowing the prospective partner well enough over time can you be satisfied that he or she does indeed have the desired characteristics. On the personal side, this is best accomplished by interacting with this person under a range of circumstances that are likely to occur in business—working under pressure, managing anger, showing honesty, being able to compromise, and more.

On the business side, the partners need to agree on both the conceptual and operational definition of the business objective—that is, agree on the goal of the partnership and how to know when it is achieved. Also needed is a careful and realistic assessment of both partners' emotional and financial risk. The partners must jointly possess the needed material and emotional resources to accomplish the business objective. Lastly, the partners must realistically assess how the business partnership will affect other parts of their lives. Paying inadequate attention to how the partnership will affect families is likely to create a problem that doesn't need to be created.

A shared vision usually is what brings potential partners together. Agreeing on how and when that vision will be fulfilled becomes a more complex matter and is often difficult to do. For partners to move from concept to implementation requires achieving a work culture that combines both their value systems and personality styles. Also needed is an evaluation of how balancing the competing needs of business, personal, and family priorities might affect the pursuit of their vision.

The pressures of conducting a business give rise to many feelings. Partners enhance their ability to cope when they are able to express their feelings in a constructive way in a nonjudgmental atmosphere of trust and support. Having the opportunity to vent their feelings will help partners make business decisions that are not unduly influenced by pent-up emotions.

Vulnerability refers to the comfort level a partner experiences while sharing his or her feelings and thoughts. Can he or she share such feelings without being hostilely judged and without them being thrown back at one during an argument? Vulnerability also involves trusting that one's partner will respect a shared confidence. Sharing vulnerabilities becomes part of a working, active partnership. Lack of comfort in such sharing can result in the buildup of tension, which may ultimately undermine the partnership. (These considerations are discussed further in chapter 4, "Communication.")

A partnership is frequently defined as an *equal partnership*. This is simple in concept but more complex in implementation. Equality in terms of share of ownership is concrete and easily understood; beyond that, the path becomes less clear. How can partners be equal in personality, creativity, or knowledge? Financial equality is predicated, often tacitly, on other assumptions of equal investments of time, money, talent, commitment, and quality of contributions. A partner's perception of significant differences in these contributions will lead that partner to feel that he or she is providing more than his or her share, and that partner will want to address the equality issue and its impact on division of profits. That approach will not be received kindly by the other partner. Each partner may have his or her own idea of what combination of variables should support shared equality of profits. That lack of a shared definition of expectations along various dimensions provides the potential for future dissension.

Perceived equality is not a static dimension. Partners may start out equal in all dimensions that affect the generation of profit. Over time, however, the partners' contributions will vary. Ultimately, one partner will assume a more dominant position than the other, though the dominance may shift back and forth as each partner's unique qualities take precedence. This can result in a constructive or destructive competition. The competition may remain *constructive* when the partners are relatively equal in their periods of dominance; it can become *destructive* when one partner dominates for longer periods than the other. Such competition may not develop if partners are able to accept these differences and work with them to each other's satisfaction. Otherwise, tension will gradually grow and be reflected in destructive ways that can negatively affect their product and ultimately the success of their partnership. That outcome can be avoided if both partners periodically review their respective contributions and how their contributions should affect compensation. In this way, they can avoid developing resentment and its destructive expression.

A partnership is likely to be unstable if the partners are not equal in self-confidence and in strength of personality. In no time, the purported equality of the partners at the start of the partnership will drift into inequality. The partnership will become characterized by a dominant and a subordinate partner. For all practical purposes, the dominant partner will be managing the business. The formal partnership can survive if the subordinate partner finds a role suitable to his or her interests and abilities and is able to make a meaningful and satisfying contribution to the partnership.

ADVANTAGES OF A PARTNERSHIP

When considering a partner one should consider the advantages and disadvantages of a partnership. Oftentimes the benefits of being in a partnership are so great that one tends to pay too little attention to the downside of it. It is all to easy to avoid looking at things that get in the way of a desired experience. The following sections describe some of the benefits of partnerships. Then we will look at some of the drawbacks.

Shared Risks

Sharing the financial risk increases the available resources for the business start-up. This kind of sharing will likely help attract outside financing. There will be less to lose should the business venture not succeed.

Shared Challenges

A partnership can lessen the load of running a business by distributing certain challenges. A partner can

- share the day-to-day stresses, risks, decisions, responsibility, and workload;
- share the emotional stresses and exhilaration of turning a vision into reality;
- share the anxiety of uncertainties in managing a business;
- help one cope with fear of failure and how it might affect the future;
- share in decision making—having the affirmation of another respected person can ease the emotional strain of uncertainty in making decisions and provide a check on one's judgment.

Division of Labor

A partnership allows partners to divide the areas of expertise, enabling each partner to become more competent than would be possible if expertise were required in all aspects of the business. (See chapter 10, "Delegation.")

Shared Resources

A partnership may lead to an entrepreneurial effort that would not be possible otherwise, because singly neither partner has the resources needed to launch the desired business venture. A common combination is the pairing of one partner who has technical or creative resources with another partner who has the business experience. In this case, the lack of needed personal, financial, or business resources makes partnership a necessity.

Companionship

Engaging in a business venture can be more attractive when it is shared with another person. The shared experience becomes an added bonus to whatever success the business may have. It also permits each partner to become an emotional support for the other.

Potential for Increased Success

The combined intellect and experience of partners able to work collaboratively increases the business's chance of success.

More Time with Family

A partnership may provide a businessperson more time with his or her family than would otherwise be the case. The demands of one parent's business involvement too often deprive the family of that parent's needed involvement in family matters. The added strain on the managing parent stresses the relationship with both spouse and children. Many partners look back in regret at how their preoccupation with their business damaged their family relationships.

DISADVANTAGES OF A PARTNERSHIP

Coping with Difference

That partners have different points of view can be either an asset or a liability. It is an asset when the parties involved have the means to resolve differences in ways that are acceptable to both. An added value accrues from their combined wisdom. The different viewpoints become a liability, however, when difficulty reaching consensus leads to unresolved conflict. The result may be a shift in priorities from the joint venture to personal interests. Competition develops that results in power struggles. The more psychic energy the partners must divert to coping with polarization, the less is available for the business. It doesn't take very long before the business suffers.

Sharing of Profits

Having to share profits is not a happy prospect when one partner feels that he or she could do better without the partnership. The attitude will be quite different when profits depend on the partnership. Problems develop when profits are not shared equally, even if that is by agreement. A partner may initially agree to an unequal division of labor, but over time, the reason for agreeing to the inequality may no longer be relevant. Changing the basis for sharing profits is hard to do once established. This issue should be addressed at the time it becomes a concern; otherwise in time it will undermine the partnership. To avoid such problems, a procedure should be in place at the onset of the partnership for reviewing how profits are managed.

Potential for Limiting Creativity

Creativity is a personal experience; what one partner deems creative the other may not. The ultimate measure of creativity in business is what produces desired results. Differences between partners regarding this issue may create serious problems. The problems may result from conceptual differences about whether a particular idea is creative. This may be resolved by agreeing on a third party to act as mediator. Or it may be that differences stem from competition, envy, desire for power, or differing priorities. This can be anticipated at start-up by anticipating that these feelings may occur and having a commitment to openly address them when they occur.

Being Accountable to and for a Partner

Accountability is an integral part of being in a partnership. Since partners are legally accountable for each other's behavior, they must define a process for how they make decisions that affect the business. Second, the partnership needs to define how partners can pursue individual needs and interests that are compatible with partnership ethics and goals. Compatibility of values and beliefs makes it easier to deal with accountability.

Added Risk

Paradoxically, being in a partnership both adds risk and reduces it. Reduction of risk was covered in a previous section. Risk is added because the partners are responsible for each other's behavior. A problematic partnership increases risk by draining psychic energy from the business of the partnership to coping with conflict in the relationship.

TYPES OF PROBLEMS IN PARTNERSHIPS

A business has a better chance for success when all of the relevant partnerships are functioning smoothly, with business partners, employees, family, banker, accountant, lawyer, and customers all working in tandem.

The conceptual framework of defining various forms of partnership is useful both in building a business and in diagnosing the source of difficulty when problems arise. Understanding what is needed to make each partnership function provides a basis for determining the source of problems and thereby how to prevent conflicts in multiple partnerships. The following categories of problems most often occur in a partnership:

- *Compatibility problems.* Partners may experience personality conflicts, may hold different values and beliefs, and may have different work styles and ethics.

- *Partnership agreement problems.* Ambiguities or misunderstandings often occur with regard to what two prospective partners have agreed upon. Two partners may agree in concept to work together, but they may run into difficulty when their agreement has to be translated into behavior. This conflict may involve personality clashes, different views on division of labor, different expectations of what each partner will contribute, and different work habits.

- *Goal definition problems.* The common vision that partners have at the start of their partnership may change over time, much as happens in a marriage.

- *Methodological problems.* Partners may disagree over how to accomplish their common goal both in concept and in performing their respective responsibilities. One example is partners who have different standards for the behaviors they consider appropriate and necessary.

- *Adaptability-to-change problems.* Sometimes partners are unable to jointly adjust to changing circumstances that present themselves in the life of the partnership. Partners may initially agree on method and objective but run into trouble when they try to adjust to changing circumstances.

- *Having multiple partners.* The greater the number of partners, the more difficult the politics in managing the relationship and in making decisions. The problem becomes more manageable if the number of partners is large enough to use a manager or management committee and the partnership has an established procedure for decision making. Commonplace experience in law firms suggests this is a viable model for business.

All of the aforementioned problems afflicting two-partner businesses apply to partnerships of three or more people. An additional problem is the potential for developing destructive alliances. The most difficult of these alliances occurs in a three-way partnership, because partners so readily split into "a pair and a spare." This does not apply to differences of opinion when the threesome has a good working relationship. Serious problems occur when the split is based on an ongoing alliance between two partners who collude to control the remaining partner. Often that is a strategy for getting a partner to leave the partnership and is based on a political alliance rather than on the merits of specific issues.

REFERENCES

American Heritage Talking Dictionary (1995). Version 4.0.
Bell, C. R., & Shea, H. (1998). *Dance lessons*. San Francisco: Berrett-Koehler.
Davidson, R. L., III. (1992). *The small business partnership*. New York: Wiley.

PART I

Dimensions of Partnership Dynamics

CHAPTER 2

Values, Beliefs, and Goals

Two people work together best when they share a common language through which they define their relationship, their goals, and their means of achieving those goals. This commonality is made possible when their value and belief systems are compatible; without this commonality the partnership will fail.

What leads us to behave in one way rather than another? Values and beliefs are major determinants of behavior, and understanding behavior is a key ingredient in the partnership's success. This chapter discusses the variables that affect how we form, hold, and change our values and beliefs. Appropriate application of these concepts is essential for a successful partnership.

A number of years ago, Milton Rokeach (1968), a social psychologist, defined a number of terms important to value systems. He defined *values* as statements of what ought to be—statements of ideals. For example, a person should be honest. *Beliefs*, he said, are statements of what was, is, or is expected to be; for example, many people are dishonest when it suits their purpose. He described *attitudes,* on the other hand, as the behavioral expression of both values and beliefs—the predisposition to approach a given situation in a particular way. Whether a person behaves in that way will depend on the circumstances. A number of considerations influence how values and beliefs are defined, as described in the following section.

DIMENSIONS OF VALUES AND BELIEFS

Values and beliefs are multidimensional concepts. Understanding the defining interaction between their components will help partners effectively implement their partnership. Compatibility between values and beliefs facilitates a successful partnership.

People hold values about what is important to them, and they assign them varying priorities—that is, some value money greatly; some value religion greatly; and so forth. Each value carries a belief about the degree to which the ideal actually occurs. A person may value honesty as a goal to be achieved while recognizing that often people are honest only under certain circumstances.

Sometimes values are defined by one's experience. One may learn that being forthright results in a more satisfying relationship. Hence, being forthright becomes a value. At other times a value derives from a philosophical or idealistic consideration. Behaving ethically is an example. One values such behavior while being fully aware that it often doesn't occur. In this case, holding the value is intended as a guide to remind oneself and others to behave ethically. The hope is that eventually the value and the belief will become the same: people will value behaving ethically and behave accordingly.

Discomfort occurs when values and beliefs are in conflict—that is, when a person's experience doesn't fit his or her idea of what should be happening. He or she may attempt to resolve the discomfort; that can be accomplished in one of four ways:

- The person changes her belief to fit her value. She convinces herself that these deviations did not really violate her value.

- She changes her value to fit her belief. She decides that her value is unrealistic and redefines it. For example, she should be honest except under certain conditions.

- She denies that the discrepancy is accurate. She didn't do anything that was dishonest.

- She accepts the discrepancy. She doesn't like it when she is dishonest, but she knows that it will happen and she will do her best to avoid its occurrence.

This process becomes considerably more complicated in a partnership. Each person has to resolve for him- or herself any value-belief conflict and in addition cope with the same issues between partners.

An added consideration is whether values apply only to the person who holds them or to people in general—men, women, both, and so on. Knowing to whom a value or belief applies is useful in establishing and maintaining a relationship. It is also useful to know whether the value applies to a person or to a group. Being able to make that distinction can make a difference in how to relate to holding a particular value.

Under What Conditions Does the Value or Belief Apply?

People don't always behave in a way that is consistent with their values. Take, for example, a person who takes the public position that one should not use drugs but all the while uses them in private. When such an inconsistency becomes a problem for a partner, he or she will do well to determine the basis for it before reacting to it. Possible reasons for the inconsistency include weakly held values or beliefs, an inability to implement values in practice, a conflict with higher priorities, and difficulty in coping with anxiety or conflict. By knowing which one is responsible, the partner can respond more effectively to it.

One's commitment to a particular value or belief may range from inconsistent to intense and unwavering. The more fervently a person holds a value, the less likely the person is to accept contrary information and the more resistant he or she will be to changing his or her current position. Resolution of differences between partners is facilitated when one partner has a strong commitment to a point of view and the other's viewpoint is more weakly held. But that may not be the case if deferring to the partner with the strongly held view is perceived to change the balance in the relationship.

Experience consistently demonstrates that the more specific the subject matter of a value or belief, the greater the potential for reinforcing or changing behavior. By defining a value or belief in terms of observable behavior, partners invite greater clarity in communication and increase the likelihood that each will perform in the desired manner. To do otherwise is to invite problems resulting from different definitions of what is expected.

Knowing the source of a particular value or belief may help one better understand how to relate to it. Here are some common sources, which are not mutually exclusive:

- *Family values.*
- *Personal experience.*
- *Traumatic experience.* A traumatic experience from personal history or from the experiences of others can give expression to values and beliefs. For example, experiencing the death of a close friend as a result of drug overdose can easily lead to a resolve never to use drugs.
- *Education.*
- *Respected figure or reference group.* One may identify with the perceived value of a respected person or organization. For example, if the American Management Association is a respected source of information for the entrepreneur, he or she will be receptive to adopting the recommended value position.

Knowing the source of a value provides one a focus for adopting, reinforcing, or changing the value. That applies both to an entrepreneur's self-awareness and to his or her relationship to a partner.

The firmness with which one holds a value or belief indicates how susceptible values are to change. Firmly held values and beliefs will not be affected by information that seeks to challenge them. Change is most readily accomplished when both cognitive and emotional concerns are addressed. Of those two concerns, addressing emotional attachments to a given value or belief is more difficult. A partner may readily acknowledge holding a given value or belief but have trouble modifying it because of his or her emotional attachment to it. People are generally able to change their way of thinking when provided with new information. On the other hand, emotional attachments can be far more resistant to change, even when it makes sense to do so. This happens because one does not control what one feels. It takes time for a person to accommodate his or her feelings to what he or she thinks. Even then, the power of familiarity can lead people to live with inconsistency between what they feel and what makes sense.

One's self-doubt about one's perceived ability to accomplish a desired change is often expressed in inflexibility toward modifying an attitude or belief. The uncertainty about being able to change, coupled with the fear associated with a new situation, leads one to stay with the familiar.

Not surprisingly, partners must constantly deal with multiple demands on their time. Their success depends on their ability to set priorities regarding how to commit their energies. A consideration in setting those priorities derives from the value and belief systems that guide their behavior. A partner, for example, has a better chance of getting a proposal accepted if it fits his or her partner's priorities. Knowing a partner's underlying value and belief system provides a broader range of options for addressing that partner's needs or for persuading him or her to change his or her priorities.

Understanding the purpose of holding a value is yet another reason for continuing to hold or change it. Lawyers, clergymen and -women, and therapists belong to disparate professions, but they have one thing in common: they place value on confidentiality because it provides an atmosphere of trust for their clients. Conversely, one way to accomplish a value change is to demonstrate that the purpose for holding it is no longer valid. This is the case when a manufacturer recognizes that the reason for giving a rebate is no longer valid.

People hold values and beliefs because of the consequences that result from doing so, and they abandon them when they no longer serve their desired objective. Companies depend on employees to behave in ways that are consistent with company values. When problems develop in employee performance, the partners need to determine whether the difficulty lies in employee behavior or in the company's value system. An additional consequence of changing a value is the impact the change may have on other company values. For example, management may want to change its value system regarding the company's benefit package but does not do so because it may adversely affect employees' loyalty to the company.

GOALS

Whereas values provide the ethical context that influences how partners define and implement their vision, goals express the operational application of values and beliefs. Success in achieving goals correlates with the clarity with which the partners define specific observable outcomes. Setting dollar amounts, a specific time for project completion, the number of hours worked, the number of people hired, and so on provides the criteria for knowing when a goal is achieved.

Certain problems commonly develop in the pursuit of goals, notably the following:

- *Vague definition.* Making money, developing a better product, and being happy are not sufficient measures of whether the desired goal was achieved because partners may have different criteria for what constitutes making money or for the standard of quality for a product. The partnership becomes threatened when the differences between the partners' respective definitions of success become chronic and do not yield to resolution.

- *Goals for which the partnership has insufficient resources (time, money, energy, or knowledge) to accomplish.*

- *Goals that contradict the values or beliefs on which the partnership is based.* Frank, a manager in the production of auto parts, defined a production goal that could not be achieved without sacrificing company values of quality. The result was a conflict in priorities between meeting a production goal and adhering to company values. Management gets into trouble when it sets goals that are not consistent with the company's values.

- *Uncertain values and beliefs.* Uncertainty about what values to hold and what expectations are unrealistic makes setting goals difficult.

- *Conflicting commitments.* Compatibility among values, beliefs, and goals will not result in the desired outcome when holding them conflicts with commitments to other values, beliefs, and goals. Partners may have one set of values and beliefs with respect to making a profit. Those may conflict with the values and beliefs consistent with running a company that places a high priority on the welfare of employees. The partners will have to find a way to combine their competing commitments if they are to succeed.

- *Felt inadequacy.* Undertaking goals without having the confidence that they will be accomplished diminishes motivation and ensures failure. If one partner has that confidence, however, the impact is moderated.

- *Conditions external to the company over which it has no control.* Competition, changes in the economy, and fluctuation in the demand for the company's product interfere with achieving the desired goal.

- *Underestimation of the time needed to accomplish goals.* Frequently, partners grossly underestimate the time required to accomplish a goal and often have difficulty recognizing that as the problem. This problem may arise for a variety of reasons: lack of knowledge, interference from outside sources, underestimation of the amount of energy needed, difficulty of the task(s) involved, mistakes, and so on.

Prioritizing Goals

It is often easier to define goals than to prioritize them, especially when too many goals need to be accomplished at the same time. Problems that make prioritizing goals difficult include competition for resources, insufficient information, competition between different interests within a company, interdependence among goals, and uncertainty about how to set priorities.

The pressures of running a business, especially a start-up business, can leave little time for the partners to do more than meet the demands of the moment. Attention to the relationship between values, beliefs, and goals can provide a structure for gaining a perspective on business issues that may not be evident under the pressure of immediate demands. That framework can also provide insight into problems that might not otherwise be apparent. Periodic review of the compatibility of planned courses of action with the guiding value and belief systems helps partners grow a successful and satisfying business. The difficulty one person has in coping with prioritizing is exacerbated in a partnership when conflicting priorities and relationship struggles occur.

EVALUATION

Inherent in everyone's value system is an ongoing assessment of whether a given held value should remain the same, be modified, or be eliminated and of whether it occurs on a conscious or subconscious level. An indication of the subconscious level occurs when a person is uncomfortable holding a given value but can't identify why. That evaluation may be gradual as circumstances change, or it may be precipitated by some event that calls a given value or belief into question. Often, the values and beliefs that are relevant at start-up change as the business becomes established; that precipitates a revision of the existing value system for managing the business. The situation is more complex in a partnership because partners may develop competing views over time about whether their value system needs to change.

Values remain the same if one or more of the following conditions obtain:

- Holding a given value or belief fits the desired image for the partnership
- Ongoing experience continues to support holding the value or belief

- New information supports holding the value or belief
- Holding a particular value or belief does not interfere with holding other priority values and beliefs

Values and beliefs tend to be stable and to change only when one's needs or experiences change. Specifically, they change in response to new information, shifting priorities, undesired consequences for continuing to hold them, the inability to behave consistently with the value or belief, and the need for financial gain. Dissatisfaction with a held value or belief is not sufficient reason to change. Staying with a familiar position, even if unattractive, is appealing because dealing with the known involves less risk than dealing with the unknown.

Values and beliefs are based on a combination of emotion and logic; change is most effective, therefore, when it addresses both the logical and emotional basis for holding them. Generally, people function in their daily lives with logic as the dominant mode and through emotions as its subordinate. However, when emotions become too strong, they will short-circuit logic. At that point, a person's actions are driven primarily by emotion, and the person, though aware of his or her inappropriate behavior, may for the moment not care. Most of us have had the experience of being so angry in the moment that we don't care about what we say or do. Inevitably, regret follows once the logical mode reasserts itself. The greatest challenge that partnerships face in resolving value, belief, and goal conflicts occurs when logic gives way to dealing with emotional issues of competition, power, and control.

With regard to business goals, the partners' values (what ought to be) define the objective to be achieved, and those values are reality-tested by the partners' beliefs (the perception of what is—what happens). The end result is a business goal that the partners consider realistic.

Example: Fred and Alex agreed that the success of their partnership depended on honest, frank communication between them. They therefore agreed to hold weekly meetings to review the status of their relationship. After a year or two of relative harmony and a growing business, however, they began to develop different goals for the business. Their ability to resolve differences became secondary to each other's conviction that his view should prevail. As a result, they began to quarrel, and soon their unresolved differences reduced their communication to a minimum, which negatively affected the business. The belief that good communication was possible was replaced by tenuous coexistence. They decided to end the partnership before they destroyed the business entirely. Fred defined the buyout price, and Alex had the choice of whether to buy or sell.

Consistency among values, beliefs, and goals increases the probability of a successful business outcome. Signs of incompatibility indicate that one or more of the following conditions are present: values are unrealistic; little or no attention is being paid to experience; or goals are poorly defined or unrealistic. Evolving indications of incompatibility among values, beliefs, and goals should be treated as an early-warning indication. The point of having an early-warning system is to deal with problems when they are easiest to manage.

REFERENCE

Rokeach, M. (1968). *Beliefs, attitudes, and values: A theory of organization and change.* San Francisco: Jossey-Bass.

CHAPTER 3

Leadership

Can a ship have two captains? Each partnership needs to address that question. This should pose no problem for partnerships in which both partners agree that one of them will fill the leadership role while the other serves in a managing role. Commonly the leadership role evolves from the personalities and talents of the partners without any formal definition. Problems develop when both partners aspire to lead but do not openly address that ambition. Such cases invite competition and destructive conflict until the question is addressed.

Sometimes a problem develops when a partner finds that he or she doesn't have the needed qualities to perform in the desired leadership role. The partnership will be at risk unless he or she finds an integral role that fits his or her experience and talents.

LEADING VERSUS MANAGING

Partners must understand how the functions of leader and manager overlap. A leader inspires his or her subordinates, is guided by an envisioned goal, and can anticipate when and what will be needed. He or she helps subordinates find ways to meet their personal objectives consistent with company objectives. The ability to motivate others to perform is especially needed when the task to be achieved is demanding or unpleasant. A leader also learns to balance his or her attention between strategic planning and coping with tactical concerns.

Bennis (1989), in a five-year study of 90 of the most successful leaders in the country, describes four competencies of leaders: *meaning*—the ability

to make ideas tangible and real to others; *attention*—clarity in desired outcome, goal, or direction; *trust*—reliability that derives from being constant
and focused; and *self-knowledge* of one's skills and effective deployment of
them. Bennis views empowerment as the collective effect of leadership
that is expressed in four themes: people experience feeling significant;
learning and competence matter; people are part of a community; and
work can be exciting. Creating an environment of empowerment invites
employees to give their maximum effort in terms of time, energy, and
capability. Bennis reminds us that effective leadership sets the pace and
energy level for the work and empowers the workforce.

Shefsky (1994) provides another perspective on leader and manager
functions. He views an entrepreneur as one who seeks opportunity and
a manager as one who preserves existing resources. Shefsky, a lawyer
who specializes in cases involving entrepreneurs, believes that leaders
operate in a positive-sum game: they generate new talents, markets, and
capital resources. In contrast, managers operate in a zero-sum game:
they deal in an existing environment and attempt to increase their share,
thereby reducing someone else's share. Leaders focus on "what to do,"
whereas managers concentrate on "how to do." Leaders ask for help in
reaching a goal, whereas managers explain how to solve a problem.
Leaders create an atmosphere that converts the optional to the impera-
tive and the improbable to the likely. Leaders help to make rewards
more certain and desirable, whereas managers help to evaluate risks and
rewards.

For Kotter (1990) management involves functions such as planning and
budgeting, organizing and staffing, controlling and problem solving. In
contrast, leadership involves establishing direction: developing a vision of
the future and strategies for producing the changes needed to achieve that
vision; aligning people into teams and coalitions that understand the
vision and strategies; and motivating and inspiring others to accomplish
the vision.

PARTNERSHIP PERMITS INDIVIDUAL AREAS
OF EXPERTISE

Every partnership needs to decide on the best way to make use of leadership and managerial abilities. Accordingly, the partners need to define
what is best for their energies and talents and what they require from others. Such an allocation is not a static process; once defined, it must have
the capacity to be changed as circumstances dictate.

REQUIREMENTS OF LEADERSHIP

Here are some essential characteristics of effective leadership:

Noncompetitiveness in the management role. Leaders and managers should respect the competence of others. Those leaders and managers who give in to their competitive urges with subordinates undermine their ability to accomplish their mission and fail to provide an appropriate role model.

Awareness of how one's behavior affects others. Leaders and managers cannot simply assume that intentions will necessarily get communicated through their behavior. They must therefore be aware of how they respond verbally and nonverbally and whether their performance matches their words.

Sufficient knowledge to supervise. Leaders and managers do not always need to possess all the expertise needed to accomplish their goals. More important, they need to distinguish when to use their own resources and those of others.

Skill in conflict resolution. In the inevitable conflicts that arise when people work together in a group, the objective is to mobilize as much of the psychic energy of everyone involved and to resolve conflicts in a way that are acceptable to all concerned.

Confidence in one's own strengths and knowledge of one's limitations. Knowing one's own strengths and limitations and the best way to use them will contribute to leaders' and managers' self-confidence in performing their responsibilities. At the same time, it provides a positive role model and inspires confidence in management.

Ability to meet personal needs in the context of assigned tasks. Leaders and managers will be more successful when they help subordinates meet their personal goals in the context of their assigned tasks. This approach recognizes subordinates as individuals and not just as tools to achieving business objectives.

Good communication skills. Good listening skills are a prerequisite for the effective leader or manager. Attentive listening enhances mutual respect and motivates subordinates both to be creative and to develop a positive attitude as they perform their responsibilities. Effective speaking skills are an important part of good communication. The leader knows he or she is being heard and is speaking in a meaningful manner through certain cues: notably, comments made by subordinates and nonverbal cues that indicate attentiveness. Lecturing and lengthy discourse without interruption should be avoided. Instead, the leader should encourage interactive discussion, soliciting responses to his or her comments at various points.

Skill in giving balanced feedback. Critical feedback involves attention to both the positive and the negative. Generally, one should start by acknowledging positive acts because that makes it easier for the person to hear any negative comments that may follow. In this way, the leader conveys the message that the total person is recognized and not just the negative aspects. Positive affirmation contributes to self-confidence and motivates the person to perform his or her responsibilities. Critical feedback should focus on how to improve performance rather than be aimed at the person's competence.

REQUIREMENTS OF MANAGEMENT

A manager should have the following characteristics:

- *Organizational skills.* Effective implementation of the operations necessary to achieve one's mission requires good organizational skills. Of special importance is attention to details and to their relation to achieving operational goals, as well as coordination of the efforts of all so that all personnel can work together in a compatible manner.
- *People skills.* A manager needs the same people skills that a leader needs and in addition must have the patience and skill to manage subordinates on a daily basis.
- *Comfort in dealing with implementation.* A good manager finds satisfaction in accomplishing the day-to-day operations required to accomplish the partnership's mission.
- *Satisfaction in fulfilling objectives.* Implementing the goals of the partnership should be satisfying to a manager.

NEED FOR CONTINUING EDUCATION

The skills required to be an effective leader and manager are not static. The partnership can ensure those skills' continued effectiveness by providing its leader and managers an ongoing opportunity to keep abreast of new developments. A continuing-education program can increase their knowledge and sharpen their skills.

REFERENCES

Bennis, W. (1989). *Why leaders can't lead.* San Francisco: Jossey-Bass.
Kotter, J. P. (1990). *A force for change: How leadership differs from management.* New York: Free Press.
Shefsky, L. (1994). *Entrepreneurs are made not born.* New York: McGraw-Hill.

CHAPTER 4

Communication

Communication, a complex process that functions on multiple levels, is the lifeblood of a partnership. Problematic communication will ultimately cause the partnership to fail if not remedied.

PERSONALITY CHARACTERISTICS

Accountability to One's Own Values in the Partnership

The importance one partner places on his or her partner's approval influences the quality of their communication. When a person's values, beliefs, and behavior are excessively dependent on the partner's approval, the result will be an uncertain sense of self. Under such conditions, the person's self-approval will depend on how the partner views him or her. That dependence undermines a person's ability to attain a consistent sense of self, inhibits the pursuit of goals, and reduces the effectiveness of communication. A partner has a greater chance of success if he or she has a well-defined sense of self, which is enhanced when his or her behavior is guided by self-accountability—that is, the partner's behavior is consistent with his or her values. That provides a context for accepting feedback from others.

To get support from one another, banks, and investors or to attract high-quality employees, partners must be able to demonstrate self-confidence and inspire confidence in their vision. A person who has self-confidence and respects the views of others is more likely to succeed.

Mutuality, or Empathy

The quality of communication between partners is the responsibility of both parties involved. The best long-term outcome is achieved when both partners are satisfied with the way they communicate. Communications based on one party prevailing at the expense of the other (win-lose) are unstable and ultimately constitute a loss for both partners (lose-lose). That occurs when the unsatisfied partner (loser) seeks to recoup his or her losses or prestige. In so doing, the win-lose process continues. The "winner" ultimately loses because in the course of his or her victory, the relationship he or she had is likely to suffer.

Empathy—identifying with and understanding another's situation, feelings, and motives—contributes to the goal of mutual benefit in communication. It has nothing to do with liking or agreeing with one's partner; rather, it involves understanding the way that partner thinks or feels.

Trust

Trust is the expectation that a person will behave in a manner consistent with his or her verbal commitments and with whatever established norms exist within the context of a relationship. It also involves reliance on a person's integrity, ability, and character. Words are promissory statements that appropriate action will follow. When trust is violated, we lose confidence in the violator's word and are on the lookout for further disappointment. Trust takes time to build, but it is quickly lost when it is violated; rebuilding it can take a long time, primarily because of the concern that violations will recur. The length of time it takes to regain trust depends on how important its violation is to either partner.

Respect for Difference

A partnership cannot survive unless the partners respect each other's differences. In the absence of confidence that they can resolve their differences in an acceptable manner, those differences may well threaten the survival of the relationship. The psychic energy the partners expend on such concerns is at the expense of attention to the business.

Expression of Feelings

Reluctance to express negative feelings concerning the partnership relationship breeds tension and will ultimately erupt in conflict. Inadequate discussion of the true source of the conflict will make the conflict more difficult to resolve. Reluctance to express positive feelings deprives the other partner of affirmation that nurtures the relationship. That reluctance is at least in part blocked by the presence of negative feelings. It is harder to give affirmation if you are angry with your partner. A partnership, like a marriage, benefits from the partners being able to express their feelings, positive or negative, without fear of judgment or attack. This occurs when this expression is not judgmental or hostile towards the other partner, but a statement of the expressing partner's feelings.

Risk

Not knowing the consequences of a behavior entails risk. In practical terms, no behavior is without risk. The question is not whether one takes risks but on what basis they are taken. *Considered* risks are those taken after giving careful thought to their possible consequences, whereas *careless* risks are taken impulsively and without due consideration of consequences. Inherent in a partnership is the risk that comes with partners being responsible for one another's behavior. In making decisions, therefore, it is important that one take into account a potential partner's approach to risk taking. Accordingly, knowledge of a potential partner's personality and previous history is very helpful.

Self-Confidence

Every partnership involves making decisions, sometimes with less than adequate information. Decision making requires confidence in one's judgment and the ability to cope with any potential outcome. The potential advantage of the partnership is that decisions are based on the collective wisdom of two people. The downside occurs when differences in self-confidence are expressed in conflict rather than in consensus.

Values, Beliefs, and Goals

Understanding a person's values, beliefs, and goals enhances one's skill in communicating. As suggested in chapter 2, values, beliefs, and goals act as a compass guiding us to a person's thinking and behavior. An example of a value statement is "A partner should have integrity." In contrast, a belief statement concerns what a person understands has actually occurred—for example, "Not all partners have integrity." The goal is to relate to people whose behavior is consistent with the value of integrity.

An inner state of tension results when a contradiction arises between a value (the way things ought to be) and a belief (the way things are). The extent of the tension one feels will depend on the importance and size of the difference. A person can decide that his or her long-held value is unrealistic or is no longer relevant and change it to coincide with his or her beliefs. Another person may try to change the belief so that it coincides with the value. For example, to attract new clients, an accounting firm's policy may be that its accountants should on occasion engage in pro bono work. If this policy does not have the desired effect, the firm must then decide whether the value needs to be changed. Corrective efforts will result in changing either the value or the way it is implemented.

Often one partner erroneously assumes that the other partner shares his or her values, beliefs, and goals on a particular subject. A problem arises when the discrepancy between each partner's value and behavior causes tensions that cannot easily be overlooked. Ultimately, the partners must learn how to live with disparity if their efforts to find consensus are less than successful.

MANAGING ASSUMPTIONS

A partner often makes assumptions about a copartner's thoughts, feelings, or behavior, thereby causing many a communication problem. For example, two partners develop a partnership agreement and both agree that they will work full time, and both assume that they mean the same thing by full time. Later, when one of the partners becomes upset that the other one is not devoting enough time to the partnership, they discover that they have different standards. The partner who is upset is a workaholic bachelor who works seven days a week. The other partner, whose idea of full time is 40 to 50 hours a week, is married with three children. Once they realize the error of their assumptions, they are able to agree on an appropriate time commitment.

The Consequences of Assumptions

People make assumptions because they are not sure their perceptions are correct, because they are not interested in whether they are correct, because they don't feel the need to check them out, because there are no consequences to being wrong, or simply because they aren't aware they are making assumptions in the first place. Some people hope that an assumption will be treated as a fact by one's partner or by anyone else involved, especially in ambiguous cases. For some partnerships, making assumptions is a tactical maneuver expressing the hope that they will be received as fact by the other partner. To check out the assumption would invite question.

A company that functions with untested assumptions is engaging in risky behavior, because being wrong, even just once, can have disastrous results. The more a partnership is willing to risk being in error, the more vulnerable it will be to making major mistakes. Frequently, however, partners have no other choice but to operate on assumptions. Their skill comes into play in deciding how far they can proceed on the basis of untested assumptions until they are able to obtain adequate information.

Checking Out Assumptions

Don't take for granted that a partner knows he or she is behaving on the basis of assumptions. Often a person becomes so deeply committed to a particular viewpoint that he or she discounts the possibility of any other perspective. A handy rule of thumb is as follows: never assume that a given perspective is the only one without checking it out, even when it may seem obvious. The possibility of other perceptions should always be considered until determined otherwise.

Checking out the obvious sometimes appears redundant. Although it might make a partner feel foolish, it is the safest option. Doing so tells one's partner that his or her point of view is respected and that it was heard correctly or was accurately inferred from his or her behavior. The least effective way of checking out the obvious is to ask, "What do you mean by... ?" A better way is to ask, "Do I correctly understand what you mean by... ?"

The second approach puts the burden on the listener, whereas the first may come across as a challenge. The effort to achieve a common understanding will likely result in constructive communication. Failure to clarify an understanding increases the possibility of conflict based on a misunderstanding rather than a true difference of opinion. Conflicts based on misunderstanding are far more frequent than those based on real differences.

Productive communication starts with the assumption that one's partner will operate with openness and honesty. Behaving this way will tend to elicit the same behavior in return. At the same time, it is prudent to be alert to signs that one's partner is less than honest. A useful guideline in this context is to determine whether a partner's statements are consistent with his or her speech and conduct. A partner's good faith in communicating should be questioned when the following occurs:

- Your partner gives you a compliment in a tone of voice that sounds insincere or patronizing.
- Your partner tells you he or she is not angry, when his or her tone of voice and facial expression tell you otherwise.
- Your partner does not honor his or her commitment.

What appropriate responses should be made when such questions arise? Feedback should be given in a way that will invite a constructive response, as follows:

- "I'm confused: you said you weren't angry, yet you look and sound angry."
- "I'm confused: I thought you were committed to doing X, and I'm wondering if I misunderstood you since it didn't happen."
- "Thank you for the compliment, but I'm not sure how to take it."

If a partner responds defensively to any of these comments and denies his or her anger, there is no point in pressing any further. It may be sufficient to acknowledge the partner's feelings and conclude that he or she is either unable or unwilling to reconcile the contradiction between his or her words and demeanor. The listener should be alert to whether this kind of response is a one-time occurrence or a general characteristic of this person's communicating style.

Problems Associated with Assumptions

One's behavior should never be based on assumptions about what one's partner thinks, feels, or intends by his or her action or behavior. People are very protective of their privacy and do not like to find that their thoughts are transparent. It should be their choice as to whether they will share their thoughts or feelings, especially when perceptions about their thoughts or intentions are correct. When it is not their choice, they may experience the emotional equivalent of being stripped naked.

When speaking, a partner should never assume that the other partner can read his or her mind. That is, a partner may be so preoccupied with his own thoughts that he doesn't track whether the listener is with him and assumes that the listener can read his mind. He may even be irritated if the listener asks for clarification. One way to guard against that presumption is to watch for nonverbal cues that the listener is confused or bored. Among those cues is a look of discomfort or a glance out the window or at the ceiling. Noticing such cues should be followed by an inquiry about whether what is being said seems clear or presents a problem. Another indication of confusion is the partner's inappropriate response to what has been said.

When people work together, they naturally assume that everyone knows what is meant or needed. Often that is indeed the case, as when a secretary has learned to read subtle cues and can anticipate the boss's needs or thoughts. It can backfire, though, when two partners who work together presume that each other knows what is needed or intended based on past experience. Tensions created by such misperceptions can be minimized by checking out assumptions.

Assumption of Topic under Discussion

Partners engaged in conversation may believe they are talking about the same subject when they are actually talking about two different things. Some people react by taking offense, getting angry, or becoming defensive. A better approach is to verify the assumption early in the conversation that both people are talking about the same thing.

When the difference between subjects isn't very clear, the underlying confusion about the topic under discussion is likely to be expressed in a power struggle. As long as the partners focus on the power struggle, they won't address the original issue, resulting in heightened conflict and a blurring of the issues. The relationship will be strained until the issue underlying their conflict is resolved.

MANAGING FEELINGS

Telling a partner what he or she thinks or feels is an invitation to troubled communication. It is intrusive and carries the message that the speaker knows what is in the listener's mind. A more productive approach is for the speaker to ask whether his or her impressions are correct. That shows respect for the listener's integrity and provides an opportunity for the speaker to be sure he or she correctly understands the listener. It also helps prevent embarrassing mistakes and encourages the listener to be more receptive. Sometimes entrepreneurs, despite the best of intentions, get into trouble when they tell their colleagues or customers how they should feel or think about their concerns.

The process of providing feedback can be a problem depending on the way it is done. Rather than saying something like, "What you mean is... ," "You're angry," or "You're trying to confuse me," it is better to ask, "Is this what you mean [feel] [intend]?" Telling someone what he or she thinks, feels, or intends creates an adversarial climate in the course of a contract negotiation. This approach is sometimes deliberately used as a tactical maneuver to distract or take advantage of perceived uncertainty in the other person. The tactic works well when one wants to arouse a negative reaction as a way of shifting attention from a discussion that is not moving in the desired direction.

Relationship between Feelings and Action

Reacting to a partner's feelings should not be considered until the parties to the conversation understand the feelings relating to the behavior. At times feelings run so high that they will short-circuit intellect. Attempting to get an upset partner to respond to logic is an exercise in futility. A more appropriate approach is to address the partner's feelings before any attempt is made to communicate on a logical basis. Results will also be more productive when feelings about an issue are addressed before anything is done about the substance of the issues. Attending to feelings usually involves acknowledging what the partner is expressing and responding sympathetically.

A speaker does not always know what response he or she is seeking when that speaker is expressing his or her feelings. Accordingly, it is important to recognize that all communication has two components: a *cognitive mode* and a *feeling mode*. The cognitive mode refers to statements of logic, analysis, or intellect, whereas the feeling mode refers to an expression of emotion without concern about making any sense. The cognitive mode is usually dominant and may be tempered by the feeling mode, as happens in rational discussions. The situation is quite different when the feeling mode becomes dominant, as occurs when people are more concerned about expressing their feelings than about what they think. All of us have run across a person who gets so angry he says, "I don't care whether or not it makes sense—this is the way I want it." That statement is an expression of frustration without any regard for logic, and it should not be presumed that an action is necessarily expected in response. Such statements require acknowledgment of the speaker's feelings before any attempt is made to address the source of the listener's frustration. Frequently, that is all that is needed.

A listener who misinterprets a speaker's words can form a negative attitude. The speaker should let the listener know what he or she expects in return when that speaker expresses his or her feelings. The listener also bears responsibility in this and may ask the speaker what form of response is desired: whether he or she is expected to act as a sounding board, acknowledge or validate the speaker's feelings, offer suggestions, or give critical feedback.

Confusion about whether one should give more attention to feelings than to substance can complicate the settling of disputes. Communication is more productive when feelings about a given issue are considered separately from any necessary action. The problem one faces when dealing with them together is that failure to attend to feelings can bias consideration of an appropriate response and make it difficult to know whether the outcome was based on substance or emotion.

The situation is simpler when the expression of feelings doesn't require any action by the listener. In this situation, it becomes easier for the listener to understand the speaker's feelings without having to be concerned about the expectation of a particular behavior. The listener who jumps to inaccurate assumptions and conclusions and takes action without sufficient clarification will be behaving inappropriately. The speaker will likely think the listener is not listening, and is being presumptive and impulsive.

Being Responsible for Actions, Not Feelings

People often struggle needlessly against their feelings, making comments such as "I shouldn't be angry," "I should respect ... ," or "I shouldn't feel guilty."

Trying to forcibly change one's feelings is futile. The primary concern should be with what one does as a result of one's feelings, and not with whether one should have the feelings in the first place. The challenge in coping with anger is to communicate feelings in a way that will elicit a constructive response from the targeted listener. The listener cannot be expected to respond constructively unless he or she understands what the speaker finds troublesome. If the listener wants to maintain the relationship, he or she will respond in a manner that is respectful to all parties.

Sometimes one person holds another responsible for his or her anger. "You made me angry" is a commonly heard remark. All too often the accused accepts that responsibility at face value. But doing so may be an injustice to both, as happens when a person allows his or her behavior to be defined solely by that of another person. A more desirable approach is to recognize that a person is responsible only for speaking in a respectful manner. If a listener takes umbrage, the speaker can be sympathetic but is not responsible for the other person's anger. To do otherwise gives the listener unwarranted power at the expense of the speaker. There may be reasons for the person's anger other than the issue at hand: leftover anger from an earlier unpleasant situation involving the speaker, the listener's refusal to accept responsibility for his or her behavior, or illness. Not knowing what combination of reasons has made the other person angry, one should simply be accountable for one's own behavior.

Outlet for Feelings Not Expressed

People commonly believe that they can divorce feelings from behavior. Although a person can avoid vocalizing his or her feelings, he or she may then express them indirectly (expressing anger at someone other than the source that stimulated it) or nonverbally. Feelings are reflected in facial expression, body language, and especially tone of voice. Research data and personal experience demonstrate that when verbal and nonverbal behavior conflict, nonverbal behavior will carry the message. Who has not experienced hearing a person claim not to be angry when his flushed face and angry look give the opposite message? One's feelings may well be suppressed when they aren't too strong, but the effort becomes more problematic when the feelings are strong and chronically held. Under those conditions, feelings that are intentionally suppressed will ultimately be expressed in behavior. Some forms of expression include physical symptoms, diminished performance, and lack of interest in the subject of concern.

Comfort with Feelings and Intellect

Our culture places a high priority on developing cognitive competence. We spend heavily on education from nursery school all the way through college and graduate school. For a large segment of Americans, going to college is a given. But we make no comparable systematic effort to develop emotional competence, which is mainly the parents' province. School systems and the health community pay greater attention only when undesirable social behavior is in evidence. Constructive communication depends on balanced guidance by one's emotions and one's intellect. At times one's behavior is ruled primarily by feelings, with intellectual considerations playing a lesser role, as noted earlier. More often, the reverse is the case. Ideally, people should be as comfortable in expressing their feelings as they are in developing their intellects.

Communication improves when partners use their feelings and cognitive abilities in concert. Earlier we spoke about the importance of developing the ability to be as aware of a person's feelings as of the person's thinking. A good illustration is the lecturer whose message is lost because he presents his material in a dry, steady monotone rather than in a stimulating and dynamic manner.

Directing Anger at the Wrong Target

A partner who feels offended can direct his or her anger at the counterpart's character or at the behavior or issue that stimulated the anger, or the partner can throw something or hit a wall. Attacking one's partner's character involves generalizing from a particular statement or behavior to that partner's personhood. For example: "How could you say such a stupid thing"; "I can't believe you would say such a thing"; and "You are stupid." When such statements are made, the focus shifts from the immediate issue to a personal attack. The result is a conflict of two wills seeking to preserve self-esteem instead of dealing with a particular issue or behavior. This establishes a context for future conversations, which are then conducted in the same manner unless someone makes a conscious effort to interrupt the process.

When anger is confined to the situation that gave rise to it, the parties stand a better chance of reaching a mutually acceptable resolution. Both parties are left with the positive experience of resolving a difficulty, heightened self-confidence, and a positive attitude toward future communications.

Acknowledging the Thoughts and Feelings of Others

A partner whose thoughts and feelings are considered will become a more constructive listener and a more productive businessperson than one whose thoughts are given little consideration. People assuredly need to know that they are acknowledged.

BEHAVIORS THAT FACILITATE COMMUNICATION

A person must speak in a language that is comfortable and that the intended listener understands. It is difficult to listen to a message when the language is crude, offensive, ambiguous, erudite, full of jargon, alien, or on a subject of no interest to the listener.

To communicate in a given situation, a partner should speak in simple, clear language and in a way that is warm, respectful, and nonjudgmental. In this way, he or she has the best chance of being heard. It is a turnoff when a partner speaks and doesn't make the effort to find out if she or he is understood. She talks at her partner, not to him or her. This communicates lack of empathy and forces her partner to acknowledge her lack of understanding. Such an approach only shows one partner's insensitivity to the other.

Another facet of language concerns how a partner speaks. Speaking in a manner that invites listening will elicit a more positive response than if the manner is offensive, superior, demeaning, critical, or hostile. The speaker should examine whether he or she has said anything offensive. If in doubt, soliciting some feedback will remove any ambiguity, providing a clearer message and communicating an interest and respect for the listener. Some entrepreneurs actually believe that jargon enhances the client's confidence in their business dealings, but it's more likely to be a burden than an asset.

Thinking before Speaking

Thinking before speaking ensures that what is said and the way it is said will gain the desired response. This is minimally necessary in a partnership. However, what generally works will not apply in the context of a conflict. The latitude that partners may give one another under normal circumstances can be expected to be much narrower when they are in the throes of resolving a conflict.

Avoiding "You Are" Statements

One of the more common problems in communication is to hold another person responsible for one's experience. Such statements usually provoke defensive and reactive statements in kind. A far more constructive hearing is likely when the same message is stated differently: "I disagree"; "I got angry at what you said"; or "I think you made a mistake." Every partner must take responsibility for his or her own experience. No one likes to be made accountable for another person's thoughts, feelings, or behavior.

Responsibility for How One Speaks

A partner is responsible for what he or she says and how it is said; that speaker is not responsible for how someone hears him or her. "What you said hurt me"—when confronted with that accusation, a partner takes responsibility. After all, the presumption is that the other partner would not have gotten angry if the speaker hadn't said what he or she did. Wrong! Not necessarily. When faced with that accusation, a partner's first reaction should be to decide if his or her manner of speaking could reasonably be construed as offensive. Only if he or she decides that that is not the case should the speaker consider that the basis for his or her listener's anger lies elsewhere.

The way a person responds to what he or she hears is determined by more than merely what is said to him or her. Here are some other reasons for a particular response:

- The speaker's comments trigger an unpleasant association or memory.
- The listener doesn't like the content of what was said.
- The listener doesn't understand what was said and is too embarrassed to let that be known.
- The listener is not feeling well.
- The listener has a low tolerance for frustration.
- Anger at another situation spills over into the current conversation.

Lawyers frequently serve as the messenger of bad news to entrepreneurs, such as when they report that a contract has been rejected or that the bank has refused a loan application. Not surprisingly, the entrepreneurs then vent their anger at their attorney. When that happens, the attorney must decide whether he or she has any responsibility for the client's feelings—specifically, the attorney should separate out the times he or she merited the client's anger from those times when the attorney was a convenient target for the client's anger.

Vulnerability in Communication

Sharing thoughts and feelings, as well as the experiences that give rise to them, is basic in meaningful collaborative relationships among partners, lawyers, and some subordinates. Such sharing may not be understood or appreciated, and it may even be abused; indeed, there are no guaranteed outcomes in communication. People take the risk of exposing their vulnerability knowing that a meaningful relationship can be had only when people can be forthright in expressing their thoughts and feelings. They will take the risk when they feel there is reasonable likelihood of a sympathetic response to warrant the risk of vulnerability.

The same principle applies when partners communicate with banks, colleagues, customers, and competitors. Partners need to risk communicating their needs, concerns, and feelings in a forthright manner that takes into account the political realities of what is and isn't possible. Making clear relevant information to banks or suppliers or in negotiations provides the best chance for a desired outcome. To do otherwise breeds ambiguity and mistrust and can mean no deals!

Starting a partnership is a stressful exercise for most people. The tension it entails can be minimized by the approach used to negotiate with a prospective partner. Getting to know the other person usually starts with modest explorations of surface interests and goals. In the absence of positive attraction, the effort is quickly terminated, with minimal negative impact. If the overtures are successful, then one takes the greater risk of sharing more about oneself and of furthering the relationship. The relationship may deepen with an increased ability to share more of one's personality. Finally, a partnership evolves when sufficient compatibility is discovered on both a personal and business level.

Being able to reveal one's vulnerabilities is an important ingredient in a partnership's success; it enables the partners to use each other as a sounding board, to get help when needed, and to be supportive in times of difficulty. Such sharing is possible only when the partners trust that in sharing their vulnerability they will not be violated. Partners need to remember that violating the trust of shared vulnerabilities will compromise the relationship.

Behavior as a Carrier of the Message

Sometimes partners erroneously expect to be treated in accordance with their intentions rather than on the basis of how they act. This happens when they presume their intentions are obvious in a longstanding relationship. When challenged about a bothersome behavior, the person typically responds, "That wasn't my intention"; but that response does not address the concern about the objectionable behavior. Defending the behavior on the basis of intention only compounds the problem. Communication improves when a person remembers that other people judge him or her on the basis of behavior, not intention. The added complication is that the listener cannot know the speaker's intention unless it is explicitly stated.

Conflict of Words and Behavior

Partners do not always get the response they expect to their communication. As discussed earlier, nonverbal behavior conveys the meaning when the words in a message and how the message is said conflict. In his study, Birdwhistle (1988) showed that nonverbal behavior—facial expression, eye contact, and body language—accounted for 55 percent of the message. A speaker can quickly become unnerved when the listener begins looking out the window, looks bored, becomes angry, grows fidgety, or shows other behavior that reflects lack of interest in what the speaker is saying. Another 38 percent of the message was accounted for by tone of voice. Different meanings can be attached to the same word simply by tone of voice. A simple example involves the word *dear*. That word may be heard as an expression of affection or anger depending on the tone of voice. In addition, someone may offer a seeming compliment but in a tone of voice conveying that the message is insincere. The remaining 7 percent of the message in the study sample was attributed to the content of what was said. A message will have the greatest impact when the tone of voice carries the same message as the content.

Communication of Respect

Giving compliments, though a well-known means of showing interest and appreciation, is not one of the more effective ways to communicate appreciation. Too often, compliments come across as superficial, perfunctory, too readily given, or self-serving. A more effective way of communicating respect for another person is to show genuine interest in that person's thoughts and feelings. This spans differences in power, economic and social status, intelligence, and experience. This is the case whether it involves subordinate-to-superior, superior-to-subordinate, or peer-to-peer relationships. Asking for opinions provides the opportunity for extended conversation, whereas compliments are more likely to lead to dead-end conversations. And when compliments are perceived as insincere or manipulative, a double problem results. The compliment is not believed, and trust in the speaker's sincerity is compromised. The speaker's point of view should be acknowledged by the listener whether he or she agrees with it or not. Such acknowledgment carries a message of respect between speaker and listener. Partners will more readily accept critical feedback when they also receive appropriate positive feedback from one another, thereby indicating a commitment to a balanced assessment.

The Two-Time Rule

Repeated efforts to end objectionable behavior are not always successful. The more the unsuccessful efforts continue, the greater the problem becomes. In time the person who is feeling offended is viewed as a nagger, and the offending person gets tacit permission to continue the behavior.

The *two-time rule* can be used to avoid this problem. That rule states that if an effort to correct an offending partner's behavior fails after two attempts, the offended partner should not repeat the same behavior a third time. The third attempt should consist of something qualitatively different. One example of a third attempt would be to ask for clarification as to whether there was some reason why the offending partner was unable or unwilling to respond to the original requests for a modification of behavior.

Active Listening

To make communication as productive as possible, the speaking partner should speak in a clear, interesting manner and use language that his or her audience will readily understand. The listening partner should listen actively, giving the speaker ongoing feedback. Such attention is communicated through regular eye contact, sympathetic facial expressions, body language, periodic vocal affirmation, and requests for clarification.

Regular Eye Contact

The way a partner looks can communicate warmth, interest, or boredom. A glazed look, for example, signals boredom and states, "I'm somewhere else." In addition, attention focused on objects other than the speaker is distracting and is likely to suggest disinterest.

Sympathetic Facial Expression

A pleasant facial expression accompanied by a smile, as appropriate, communicates interest. The interest must be genuinely felt, however; a smile, for example, can be offensive when the speaking partner hasn't said anything to warrant a smile. A fixed frozen smile also conveys a negative message. The attentive listener will know that he or she is doing something wrong when the speaker gives cues of discontent, such as irritation in his or her voice or facial expression.

Body Language

Periodically nodding the head in affirmation; sitting in an upright, alert position; or leaning slightly in the direction of the speaker are also positive signs for the speaker. To be avoided are distracting audience behaviors such as doodling, foot rocking, finger tapping, picking at finger nails, and toying with objects.

Periodic Vocal Affirmation

Periodic statements such as "Uh-huh," "Yes," or "Good point!" are welcomed, but they should not be made so often that they become meaningless.

Request for Information or Clarification

Asking for clarification carries a message of interest, though it can become distracting to the speaker if done too frequently. However, if the listener anticipates that frequent interruptions may be necessary, he or she should negotiate with the speaker the best way to address that concern. This is respectful to the speaker and helps to preserve a positive relationship.

There is no established, "correct" formula for constructive listening. One objective is simply to be aware of the many ways that listening contributes to satisfying communication. One's communication skills will improve when as much attention is paid to listening skills as to speaking skills.

Active Speaking

A speaker can encourage a positive response by making eye contact, speaking in a comfortable manner, periodically asking for feedback, balancing the conversation, validating the listener, and using stories.

Eye Contact

Eye contact is just as important for the speaker as it is for the listener. A partner who speaks while glancing around the room or who talks to the walls or ceiling is likely simply to irritate his or her partner, especially when discussing critical issues or when conflict arises over an issue.

Manner of Speaking

Speaking at a pace that is comfortable to follow with appropriate expression of affect and emphasis encourages the listener's attention. Periodic pauses should be included to give the listener time to absorb the significance of what is said. Also helpful is repetition for emphasis. Speaking too fast, too slowly, or in a monotone will lose the listening partner's interest.

Periodic Feedback

The speaking partner should periodically ask for feedback unless the listening partner volunteers comments along the way. The feedback gives the speaker some indication about how his or her comments are being received. This is especially important in one-on-one conversations. When one partner dominates the communication, it becomes a lecture.

Balancing the Conversation

Communication is mutually beneficial when views are exchanged. The speaking partner should present his or her views in a manner that acknowledges the listening partner's interests and perspectives.

Validation of Listener

Validation of the listening partner's comments will communicate the speaker's interest in what his or her partner thinks. This is likely to invite continued attention to the speaking partner. When the listening partner's comments become disruptive, however, the speaking partner should request that comments be postponed until that partner has completed his or her thought. Then, the listening partner should be given time to be heard.

Use of Stories

The presentation of even the most boring material can be made interesting when laced with anecdotes. This taps into people's natural love of stories, which is fostered by the books they read and their theater and movie experiences.

BEHAVIORS THAT CONTRIBUTE TO FLAWED COMMUNICATION

Interrupting the partner who is speaking distracts him or her from his or her train of thought; it may also convey criticism or imply that the interrupting partner's comments are more important than the commenting partner's words. As a result, the pattern of communication can transform an exchange of information into a struggle for control and superiority.

The Power of Silence

Silence is a powerful way to undermine the quality of communication. It resolves nothing, and it leaves the door open for too many conclusions. Silence can mean any or all of the following:

- Anger
- Disinterest
- Fear of giving a response
- Lack of knowledge about what to say
- Failure to understand what was said and reluctance to ask for clarification

Each of these possibilities has quite different implications. The recipient of the silence is left to draw his or her own conclusions, which often are wrong and can simply make matters worse.

When a partner is not prepared to respond in a conversation, he or she would do well to inform the other partner of that fact and indicate when a response could be expected. It is also helpful to say why a response is not possible at the time. This is respectful to both parties and encourages trust in the relationship.

Killing the Messenger

Bad news is never welcome, but becoming angry with the partner or other person delivering the news only adds a new problem. The partner may air his or her reaction to the bad news but should clearly state that that response is not directed at the messenger. Sometimes anger at the messenger is a criticism of the timing of the delivery, of the way in which the message was delivered, or of the identity of the messenger (i.e., in the recipient's opinion, someone else should have delivered the message). Such expressions of anger are a disservice to the messenger and are a distraction from attending to the presented message.

The Obstacle of Past History

Communication is most productive when it deals with current issues. Partners who invoke past history in a conversation create a problem, especially when they are presuming that another partner's past behavior will necessarily be repeated in the present. This is frustrating because it doesn't give the other partner the opportunity to behave differently. In responding to objectionable behavior, a partner should therefore refer only to current behavior. A reference to past history is allowable only when it is helpful in the current situation. Reminders of past errant behavior sometimes are used to divert attention from one's own behavior. Such tactics impede attending to current concerns.

Breach of Confidence

Partners communicate on many levels. The better the partners know each other, the more likely they are to exchange confidences, including those touching on personal vulnerabilities. One sure way to violate a relationship is to express your anger by reminding the other partner of his or her past vulnerabilities. Such behavior can severely inhibit trust in future communications, and it limits discussion to superficial or safe content. It also hampers constructive attention to the issues at hand.

Teasing and Sarcasm

Generally, the person who teases does so in a friendly spirit, and sometimes the recipient experiences it as it was intended. More often than not, however, teasing comes off as derogatory and demeaning. When the recipient makes his or her feelings known, the evolving damage to the quality of communication can be averted, as long as the perpetrator accepts the feedback in a respectful manner. When that doesn't happen, the perpetrator responds with denial and judgment: "You are too sensitive"; or "You can't take a joke." The result will be guarded communication or interruption of the relationship. The result is also negative when the recipient of teasing does not feel safe enough to give the feedback. This happens when the perpetrator is in a superior position or when the recipient fears showing his or her vulnerability. Such reluctance hampers the quality of future communication, for the perpetrator may continue teasing, thinking it was received in the intended manner.

Sarcasm is generally hostile or critical. It may sometimes be expressed in a jocular tone. However, if all of the participants can tolerate this kind of communication, no problem will ensue. But when the recipient of sarcasm experiences it as hostile, judgmental, or demeaning, the outcome is the same as that of teasing.

Joking

A joke is a joke only when it is funny to everyone who hears it. When it is expressed for the speaker's amusement at the other partner's expense, it can become abusive. When the offended partner can offer immediate, constructive feedback and get a satisfactory response from the jokester, the problem is resolved. Otherwise, a negative climate for future communication develops.

Making Decisions for Others

One partner should not make significant decisions without considering their impact on the other partner. By agreeing on what kind of decisions they consider significant, the partners can lessen the chance of problems in this area. Reluctance to do so invites conflicts that don't have to occur and can convey various messages:

- The partner is taking another for granted.
- The partner doesn't care what the other partner thinks.
- The partner isn't aware his or her decision will affect another person.
- The partner is self-absorbed.
- The partner fears the response he or she will get when consulting.

When partners consult one another, they have a better chance of making prudent decisions while enhancing confidence in the partnership. In addition, their consultation provides an opportunity for more effective implementation. When one partner avoids such consultation in order to avoid receiving an undesired response from the other partner, conflict and retaliation are inevitable.

Judging Rather Than Managing Problems

A common reaction to a problem is to judge it—that is, to blame oneself, one's partner, or something else. The net result is that the problem isn't solved, and there is the added problem of dealing with the frustration that results from judging. Managing a problem, on the other hand, involves the following attitude: "Something is wrong. How can I fix it? How can I make the most of what is possible?" Such an approach focuses energy on constructive resolution, minimizes getting into the dark hole of blaming, and invites constructive communication.

The distinction between judging and evaluating is pertinent here. *Judging* involves blaming and helps one avoid one's own accountability for a given situation. *Evaluating* is the gathering of data for the purpose of understanding what went wrong as a basis for correction. A convenient phrase to keep in mind when confronted with difficulty is "Manage, don't judge."

COMMUNICATION AND CHANGE

Communication skills play a major role in effecting change in a relationship. Such change can be accomplished by various considerations:

- *What impact the desired change will have on the needs of the communicatee—the recipient of a communication.* Strongly held views or behaviors will be very resistant to change unless the change can be made compatible with those views and behaviors.

- *Goals to be achieved.* Knowing what goal you want to attain facilitates change. Common goals include asking for information, giving information, expressing feelings, negotiating differences, negotiating a contract, sharing a confidence, and giving direction as an entrepreneur to an employee.

- *Comfort level in speaking.* People's ease in speaking, especially public speaking, varies.

- *Needed skills and information to convey the desired message.* One needs to have appropriate information and the ability to effectively communicate it.

- *Past experience.* Past experience sets the context for future efforts.

- *Nature of one's relationship with the communicatee.* Formal and informal relationships greatly affect the nature of communication.

- *Concern about and priority attached to the outcome.* The priority attached to the outcome of a conversation will influence what is communicated. The outcome of anticipating how to manage a conflict with one's partner will receive anticipatory attention, whereas a casual conversation between partners will be spontaneous.

- *Anticipated response of the recipient and felt ability to relate to it.* Anticipating a partner's response to one's message will affect what one says and how one says it, especially when there is concern about how one's message will be heard. A partner may give considerable thought to how to offer feedback to his or her counterpart on a sensitive issue and the counterpart's ability to respond in a desired manner.

- *Communicator's state of mind.* A partner who is very upset will communicate in a different fashion than one who is not.

- *Impact of communication on other people privy to information or affected by it.* Partners will temper what they say, and alter how they say it, when they suspect that their words might be repeated to other people whose reaction would matter unless the partners trust each other to maintain confidentiality when requested. An example would be the comments one partner makes about one of the partnership's employees in confidence.

The preceding variables together give rise to established patterns of behavior that become automatic. However, partners frequently find that they need to change one or more aspects of their communication style to meet different situations. Frequently, for example, people are too passive, too aggressive, too sarcastic, or too insensitive. Changing one's established patterns is difficult because the behaviors have become automatic and are not consciously monitored. The key to bringing about desired changes in oneself is to interrupt an established pattern and replace it with a more desired one. That is usually more easily said than done. The process becomes more readily manageable if the following five steps are followed.

Step 1: Determine an Observable Definition of What Is to Be Changed

The first requirement is a clear operational definition of what needs to be changed. Often one needs to set out discrete goals in order to develop a strategy for change for each goal. The process, though tedious, is necessary if change is to take place.

Suppose the goal is "I want to get along better with my partner." Since that goal doesn't define observable behavior, an evaluation would pinpoint the behaviors necessary to accomplish the objective. One such behavior might be to pay more attention to one's partner's ideas. Another could be to accept critical feedback respectfully.

Step 2: Define What Kind of Change Is Desired

Defining the kind of change one desires requires the same level of specificity as was necessary in step 1. One possibility for achieving these revised goals is to be a better listener and to give constructive feedback.

Step 3: Define How to Go from Step 1 to Step 2

Next, one must define what steps need to be taken to achieve the state defined in step 2. For example, a person who decides he or she wants to be more assertive will need to define the behaviors necessary to achieve that. This might involve defining situations where greater assertiveness is desired; visualizing behaving differently in those situations; rehearsing these new behaviors prior to the forthcoming event; or reviewing progress and areas that need more attention.

Step 4: Determine the Degree of Motivation for Change

Even the best strategy for accomplishing change will not succeed without sufficient motivation to overcome potential difficulties. The energy and commitment it takes to pay mindful attention to interrupting established automatic behavior are often more than a person is willing to give. As a result, people hold on to familiar behavior even when it is undesirable. A test of a partner's motivation is indicated by the degree of discomfort and inconvenience he or she is willing to endure to accomplish the change.

Step 5: Monitor to Ensure That Change Is Implemented

This step, monitoring, is often the most critical one in the change process. Good ideas and good intentions go to waste unless a defined process is established for ensuring that the professed changes are implemented. Suppose a partner is committed to treating her partner in a more respectful manner. She might feel comfortable with steps 1 through 4, but under the press of business her good intentions may get sidetracked. This difficulty can be avoided if she makes a commitment to end each business day with a review of how well she progressed that day. The times she feels she has done well will reinforce her satisfaction and commitment to proceed further. The times she has slipped back into old habits can be addressed by understanding why it happened and what she might do the next time to improve her behavior. When the monitoring process is maintained consistently, the targeted behavior is incorporated into behavior that requires less and less conscious attention. The length of time it takes for a new behavior to become established depends on the complexity involved and the discipline of the person in following the defined process. Oftentimes, consistent daily monitoring will yield meaningful results in a few weeks.

The Power of Familiarity

Why do people continue in relationships or behavior that they find unpleasant and sometimes even odious? The simple fact is that some people prefer to deal with the known than to face the struggle it takes to change or the fear of dealing with the unknown. The effort to change may be too great, or they may fear failure. Giving up a negative behavior may also entail giving up the positive experiences that go with it. Thus, the cost of change can be too formidable for them. Attachment to familiarity does not bode well in a partnership.

REFERENCE

Birdwhistle, R.L. (1968). An Approach to Communication. *Family Process* 1(2), 194–201.

CHAPTER 5

Use of Power

Power, the ability to influence the thinking and behavior of another, either directly or indirectly, is basic to any business. In a business, power applies between partners, between management and employees, and between management and the outside world—banks, lawyers, customers, government agencies, and more.

POWER BETWEEN PARTNERS

We can categorize attempts to exert influence within a partnership as competitive, collaborative, or dominant-subordinate.

Competitive

In a competitive partnership, the partners are always seeking to outdo or upstage each other. This can be an asset when the partners are equal in competence and self-confidence and when they regularly prevail over one another. They enjoy their competitiveness and appreciate the benefits that can be derived from it. The competitive relationship becomes a problem when one partner upsets the parity and becomes more influential over time. The inability to maintain a balance in the relationship ultimately threatens the viability of the partnership.

Collaborative

In the collaborative partnership, the emphasis is on how well the partners work together and what they jointly are able to achieve. Such an arrangement works well as long as both partners feel they are carrying their own weight.

Problems develop in this relationship if one of the partners feels that he or she is carrying too much of the load and both partners cannot come to an acceptable resolution. Added difficulty will occur if one feels the other needs excessive personal recognition over time. That is likely to shift the partnership to a competitive mode, which is likely to be unsuitable for either partner.

Dominant-Subordinate

In the dominant-subordinate partnership, the partners recognize the complementarity of their contributions and are comfortable with one partner being the more dominant one. Such an arrangement works when it takes advantage of the partners' personalities and the partners are comfortable in having reached parity in dealing with one another.

The partnership runs into trouble when the dominant partner takes advantage of his or her position and uses it to the disadvantage of the other partner. Again, that shifts the partnership into a competitive mode, which is likely to become adversarial and to threaten the union's viability if the partners cannot redefine the nature of their work relationship.

POWER BETWEEN MANAGEMENT AND EMPLOYEES

The partners focus much of their attention on influencing their employees in how to think and behave. They use a range of incentives and discipline to accomplish their goals, including bonuses, perks, benefits, promotions, and flattery. Partners get into trouble when they lose touch with how their efforts to influence are received. This occurs when promises are not kept or when employees feel mistreated. The result is mistrust and diminished ability to influence in a constructive way.

The employees' major source of influence is the contribution they make to the company. They expect their contributions to be duly rewarded—both financially and through promotion—and when no rewards materialize, the seeds of discontent are sown. When dissatisfaction spreads among employees, they are able to exercise the ultimate option of striking to get the needed consideration of their employers.

POWER BETWEEN MANAGEMENT AND THE OUTSIDE WORLD

Success in business depends largely on the company's ability to convince the outside world of the merit of its product or service. It accomplishes that initially through marketing, which is supported by the company's product or service delivering what is promised. Banks make loans when a business is able to promote its viability. That influence is quickly lost if the business fails to follow through on its obligations in a timely way. A key ingredient of an executive's success is his or her understanding of the use of power.

Power is a statement about one aspect of a relationship between two people or entities. No one can take power; rather, it is given when one person or entity *accepts* influence from another one. The exception is physical or emotional coercion. Physical coercion is the threat of physical harm with no available alternative, whereas emotional coercion occurs when someone tolerates negative treatment to avoid negative consequences— for example, being fired.

A case in point is sexual harassment. When a man or woman seeks sexual favors from a subordinate, the subordinate can either succumb or face the risk of losing his or her job, or at least face the prospect of demotion, an unfavorable performance review, undesirable assignments, and the like. The alternative of becoming a whistle-blower, as a means of self-protection, is also unsatisfactory because doing so may well lead to losing one's job. The ultimate option is legal recourse, which is emotionally draining, potentially very expensive, and time consuming. Moreover, it may also affect future job opportunities. Prospective employers may be reluctant to employ someone involved in a sexual harassment suit.

The exercise of power in business is a two-way street, with the partners and their employees exerting influence over each other. For their part, partners exercise power through various direct means: by common agreement, through expertise, through expectations, through their reward-granting capacity, and by virtue of possessing needed resources.

DIRECT WAYS OF EXERTING INFLUENCE

The partners' power to influence is recognized and accepted by *common agreement*. Employees accept the influence of their supervisors and managers on their behavior in return for having a job. The same is true of the community, which cedes certain areas of control to elected officials for leadership and to the police for their protection. People delegate power to authority figures in return for safety, economic gain, or other services they need but cannot provide on their own.

Possession of needed expertise provides people (e.g., doctors, lawyers, plumbers, auto mechanics) the potential to gain power, though by itself it is not sufficient to achieve power. Also needed is the ability to communicate the expertise in a manner that invites a constructive response. A doctor who is arrogant, insensitive, or unable to relate to his patients will not be able to hold on to patients. The entrepreneur who despite her great expertise is combative and insensitive will be unable to recruit the people she needs to accomplish her goals.

Expectations influence behavior when the recipients respect the person defining the expectations or when they are dependent on the definer. Employees are motivated to meet deadlines when they respect their boss and that boss's vision but not when they are unhappy in their work. They inevitably express their dissatisfaction, intentionally or unintentionally, in average or diminished performance.

A person or entity can be rewarded in many ways, such as through approval, money, perks, promotions, favorable reviews, or recommendations. The degree of power one gains from *granting rewards* depends on the size of the reward, how clearly defined the conditions are that warrant a reward, the time at which the reward is given, whether the reward is related to a single event or given over a period of time, and the status attached to the reward.

A reward is a motivation when it is commensurate with the effort it requires. A salesperson, for example, will work hard to meet his or her quota when the attached bonus is sufficiently attractive. A reward deemed as too little recompense for the required performance will have little or even a negative impact. The greater the ambiguity in the reward, the less influence the reward will have.

Employees' desire to turn in a stellar performance is also enhanced when the elapsed time between the effort and the actual receipt of the bonus is short. Rewards based on combinations of events or a frequent repetition of the same event begin to lose their attraction when employees begin to doubt that they can sustain the desired performance. The length of time over which a required behavior is expected needs to be commensurate with the reward to have an influence on behavior. And finally, a reward is influential to the degree that earning it has a valued status. It is difficult to generate enthusiasm for a prospective pay raise when there is uncertainty as to whether the required performance will indeed result in a raise.

Inflicting pain through rejection, deprivation, humiliation, guilt, loss of status, or withholding benefits for failure to perform as required is a compelling source of influence. A distinction should be made here between punishment and discipline, which are often mistakenly said to be synonymous. *Punishment* stems from the need to retaliate for a perceived injury or injustice, whereas *discipline* educates one in a desirable behavior. The question of whether a given behavior is seen as discipline or as punishment has to be considered first from the point of view of the person imposing the behavior and second, from the point of view of its recipient. The person who imposes the behavior may intend it as discipline, but it may be experienced as punishment. The same is possible in reverse. The person who imposes the behavior may intend it as punishment, but it is experienced as discipline. A speaker cannot ensure that his or her intent will be taken in the desired manner.

A partner who wants to discipline an employee should understand that he or she doesn't control how the other person will experience his or her action. If the partner doesn't get an appropriate response to what he or she considers discipline, the partner should first review whether someone could consider his or her method of expression as punishment. Second, the partner should examine how the message was perceived and use that feedback to correct any misperception. He or she should also consider whether the recipient of the disciplinary effort, for whatever reason, can experience what he or she is told only as punishment. An example is the person who feels guilty about his or her behavior and accepts the correction as deserved punishment rather than as a disciplinary action.

Discipline involves corrective action, and changing one's behavior depends on the ability to learn from experience. Consider the employee who makes a mistake. A disciplinary action would show the employee the error of his or her ways and how he or she could avoid repeating the mistake in the future. A punitive action would be to insult the employee's lack of intelligence or fine him or her for the error. That punishment would be magnified if carried out in front of other people. Punitive behavior simply invites negative learning and retaliation.

Example: Jack, a partner in a bio-tech company, was furious when he discovered the costly mistake made by his subordinate, Matt. His fury exploded into a demeaning tirade that he delivered in front of other employees. Once his fury was spent, he realized that he had handled the situation badly and that the mistake was based simply on Matt's lack of experience rather than incompetence. After apologizing for his outburst, he guided Matt in understanding why he made the mistake and showed him how the work matter should have been managed.

Possessing or having access to resources is another source of power. When an employee has or can access resources that an employer needs and cannot reasonably obtain on his or her own, the employee will be in a position to make demands he or she could otherwise not make.

Example: Janet and Rita, partners with a long and successful history in business, were intrigued by a new concept for restaurants. Because they had no experience running a restaurant, they hired a manager, Felicia, who possessed all the needed qualifications. Although Felicia asked for more salary and equity than they wanted to give her, they finally acceded because she had the expertise they lacked.

Even tears and anger can be effective in gaining power. The same can be said for other *emotions*, especially love, anxiety, and depression. Intensity of love has caused people to lose fortunes, betray their country, commit murder—or even give up a throne.

Influence through the *expression of affect* is gained when the people experiencing the affect are uncomfortable coping with it. Some deal with this discomfort by doing whatever is necessary to reduce it. That makes them vulnerable to being manipulated by the unpleasant expression of affect. For example, an employer may behave in an uncustomary way to avoid a valued subordinate's temper tantrums or tears.

When reasoning and pleading fail, *guilt* is sometimes used to get the other person to feel obligated to behave as desired.

Example: Two partners in a manufacturing business, Sam and Dennis, were discussing what year-end bonus to take for themselves. Sam felt they should take the usual 50/50 split, but Dennis felt the split should be 60/40 in his favor since he had worked substantially more hours than had Sam. To buttress his argument he accused Sam of being greedy. Sam disagreed but eventually went along because he felt guilty that he hadn't put in more time.

Shame becomes an issue when criticism about a particular behavior is generalized to a judgment about the person. Shame develops from within one or is accepted from another person's judgment that one deserves the reprimand. In the preceding example, Dennis imposed shame on Sam, who accepted his judgment, which led to Sam's berating himself for his excessive demands. Had he been more sure of himself, Sam would have been angry at Dennis for mounting an implied personal attack on Sam instead of confining his remarks to the inappropriate behavior.

An *obligation* is a moral requirement (duty, contract, or promise) that formally compels one to follow or avoid a particular course of action. Specifically, it is something owed as payment or in return for a special service or favor. Informally, it involves feeling indebted to another for a special service or a favor received. It may also involve the attempt by one person to impose a duty on another. A favor done carries the presumption of reciprocity. This concept is a commonly used tool in politics. The same idea operates in the work situation.

Example: Angie and Lori were partners in a service business. Angie had covered for Lori on a number of occasions, but one day when Angie finally asked Lori to cover for her, Lori was unable to do so because of other commitments. Angie felt betrayed and she couldn't understand why Lori would let her down. She felt rightly that Lori "owed" her, but she wrongly presumed that her priorities should prevail. She viewed the rejection as evidence of an uncaring attitude and was unable to separate willingness to reciprocate from conflicting commitments.

Blaming occurs when one person holds another person responsible for an action or lack of it. Blaming enables the accuser to avoid responsibility. It becomes a powerful tool when it triggers insecurity and guilt in the recipient of the blame; it fails when it arouses a hostile response.

INDIRECT WAYS OF EXERTING INFLUENCE

Partners also have indirect methods of exerting influence. Such methods are more subtle than direct means and can be expressed in both constructive and destructive ways.

Among the constructive ways is *not providing answers.* Some employees find it is easier to ask for help than to trust their own creative process. Entrepreneurs thrive through their own creativity, and they encourage and seek to stimulate it in their employees by educating them in how to balance finding their own solutions with asking for help. A useful rule of thumb for the employee is to ask for help only after he or she has exhausted his or her own resources. By asking for answers too quickly, the employee makes him- or herself dependent and diminishes self-confidence. The entrepreneur guides the thought process of employees by employing leading questions instead of providing answers, thereby stimulating their original thinking and enhancing self-confidence.

Another constructive method is *admiration of behavior in others.* This method involves the partner using the behavior of others as a model. It can be a double-edged sword, however. It is very constructive when the audience hears it as an example of what is desired; it becomes a problem when the audience takes it as veiled criticism.

Yet another method involves bringing in a third party for consultation. His or her comments are usually conveyed through formal recommendations, but they can be equally powerful when delivered informally. The value of a third-party commentary depends on the credibility of that party.

Example: Stuart and John, partners in a software business, disagreed on whether to acquire a related company. John thought it would be a good move, but Stuart felt the new acquisition would eat up all their cash resources and put them in a precarious position in the event of an unexpected crisis. Adding to his anxiety was his uncertainty that the gain would be worth the risk. After repeated discussion, Stuart realized he wasn't going to be able to change John's position. To verify his concerns, Stuart consulted their accountant, who readily agreed with him after reviewing the facts. Later in a joint meeting with the accountant, John finally saw Stuart's point. Though very relieved, Stuart was angry that John couldn't accept the information from him.

Influence can be exerted in a number of destructive ways as well: namely, through silence, indifference, incompetence, obstruction, and distraction.

One of those methods, *silence,* may have profound effects on the quality of the partners' relationship. The communicator can interpret silence in response to his or her message in several ways: the recipient didn't hear the message, is angry and is not responding, doesn't understand the message, needs time to think about it, or isn't interested in responding. Being able to determine which possibility applies in a given situation will improve the quality of communication.

Silence complicates the communication process when the anger it produces leaves the recipient of the silent treatment feeling invisible, demeaned, or frustrated. The fact that one gets no response will overshadow the original message. This is the case when the employee ignores his or her boss's request, the boss ignores the employee's request for a raise, the letter doesn't get answered, and so on. Sometimes people resolve conflict by resorting to an emotional cutoff—they simply stop talking to one another.

Example: Two partners, Camille and Elaine, had a major argument and stopped speaking to each other, communicating solely through their secretary and bookkeeper. It took a business crisis to break the impasse. When the awkward communication almost lost them a major contract, they finally settled their differences.

Indifference protects against showing true feelings or interests. One strategy an entrepreneur can use in a business negotiation to keep the opposition from knowing his or her priorities is to show little interest or even indifference to proposals that might later be fully acceptable.

Indifference is also a way to deal with vulnerability. People often tease one another whether in the office or on the golf course. That inclination to tease is reinforced when the recipient reacts with embarrassment or mild annoyance. Indifference is one way to discourage teasing. Indifference can also indicate hostility if one does not value what somebody else cares about.

Example: Two partners, Evan and Shane, met to decide how to resolve a problem with a supplier. Even though Shane became angry at Evan's superior manner in the discussion, he didn't deal with his feelings directly. Instead, Shane reacted with indifference to Evan's suggestions even when they made sense. He was fearful that if he spoke up at the time he would respond in an inappropriate manner that would distract from what he had to say. Later, after calming down, Shane was finally able to express his anger to Evan in such a way that his concerns would be heard.

Showing *incompetence* in a job that is important to another person is another indirect way to express hostility toward a coworker. This approach enables one to avoid undesirable tasks, particularly when the pressure for time and quality work is critical.

Obstruction is accomplished by withholding needed approval of resources, introducing distractions, negatively influencing others, and undoing what has been done. In the realm of politics, the president of the United States can prevent a congressional bill from being passed by refusing to sign it while Congress is not in session. This is called a pocket veto and is an example of obstruction.

Distraction becomes a convenient method of influence when one wants to postpone or avoid dealing with an issue. It involves shifting the focus from the subject at hand to another one that is less problematic. That becomes possible if one is able to make the new focus a higher priority than the issue one wishes to avoid.

Achieving influence over the behavior of others depends on the ability to apply one or more of the preceding methods. Each one varies in its effectiveness, depending on individual circumstances. Added impact is gained when they are used in combination. Direct forms of exerting power are usually more potent, although indirect forms are more likely to be useful when a problem arises in implementing direct forms.

THE POWER OF EMPLOYEES

Employees gain power through initiative. In that way they contribute to the growth of the business and invite favorable reviews from their superiors. Their impact will be enhanced to the degree that they become valued employees.

Employees also exert influence in the way they represent the company. Today, employee-customer relations are at a low point: witness the too frequent instances of the surly waiter and the rude customer service representative. Employees can contribute to the company's reputation by showing interest and enthusiasm for the company's product and giving attention to customer concerns. But employees will develop that attitude only when they feel valued in the same way that the company expects them to value customers.

Employees represent their companies even when they are off the job—in their neighborhood, church, mosque, synagogue, or club. Informal conversations provide just one opportunity to present one's employer in a positive or negative light; they are particularly important when a business depends on referrals by word of mouth. Employees have a unique opportunity to advance their company when they serve as representatives in chambers of commerce, trade organizations, and charity fund-raising groups.

Employees can also gain influence and power during times of crises and deadlines. At such times employees may be asked or even be expected to work longer hours or to travel. In short, they will be called upon to interrupt their private lives, even missing an important family occasion. The employee who develops a reputation as a person the company can count on in a crisis soon gains influence with his or her employer. Indeed, an employee who demonstrates commitment to a company by being willing to undertake any task asked of her or him—whether it be travel, overtime, or a new or difficult job—becomes a valued asset to the company. The wise entrepreneur will create an environment that fosters this commitment and will recognize that it needs to be reciprocal.

CHAPTER 6

Resources

Imagination is all one needs to have a vision, but implementing that vision requires intellectual, physical, and emotional resources as well as the efforts of many people. This chapter's discussion focuses on the resources partners need to accomplish their vision. One of the more important means of fulfilling the mission is the effective management of psychic energy.

MANAGING PSYCHIC ENERGY

A prospective partner brings to a new business venture a personal history of managing his or her psychic energy with regard to work, family, and personal needs. Engaging in a new business venture will make additional demands on a partner's psychic energy. Since engaging in a new venture tends to become an all-consuming activity, it will of course upset whatever existing balance the prospective partner may have already achieved. The entrepreneur must therefore devote some attention to reallocating his or her psychic energies and would be well advised to involve his or her family in that effort. Doing so will minimize the partner's family's felt deprivation and will therefore avert personal problems that would surely distract him or her from attending to the business vision.

The prospective partner's business and personal life presage his or her degree of success in this management. That history provides a foundation for how the person approaches the new business venture. The chance of success increases if he or she has been successful in balancing his or her psychic energy in all three areas—personal, business, and family. If he or she has been unsuccessful in that arena, the partner brings a handicap to the new endeavor. The partner will be at a further disadvantage if in the past his or her family has been upset by his or her inability to balance business and family priorities.

Every person enters a partnership with certain personal needs and interests, relationships, and a job, each of which requires some psychic expenditure. A start-up partnership has to make a decision to invest not only its time but probably a good deal of money as well. The choice partners face in becoming entrepreneurs involves the consequences that will follow from having to reorder their priorities as they allocate their psychic energies. This means giving up many things they like to do and spending less time with friends and family. Instead they must invest most of their psychic energy in pursuit of a vision that in the end may or may not materialize. They therefore must be willing to risk financial resources, relationships, and even physical and emotional health.

Effective management of psychic energy depends on recognizing that tasks require varying amounts of energy to accomplish. Generally, new situations demand more energy than familiar ones. Therefore, anticipating coming events, having to cope with new situations, or dealing with terminating unproductive projects will call for the expenditure of more psychic energy. Prudent partners will take this into consideration when they are allocating their energies to their new ventures or to their plans to terminate ventures. Elective projects and especially new ventures need to be evaluated in terms of what is available after the normal needs of daily operation are met. To be avoided are excessive combinations of efforts in planning for new ventures or in terminating existing ones. Some slack should be provided for unexpected crises, which always supercede other priorities in use of psychic resources.

Example: Todd and Mary were partners in a public relations firm. Todd had a tendency to start new projects before he completed his existing responsibilities. Their business would have failed were it not for Mary's ability to manage their psychic energies and keep Todd focused on finishing projects before he launched new efforts. She had not been able to get him to be more mindful about how he allocated his energies. The message finally got through to Todd when he had a crisis on an existing project while he was focusing on developing a new one. The anxiety he experienced in coping with the crisis got through to him in a way Mary could not do.

A partnership starts simply with a vision, but the vision rapidly begins to become more complex. The evolving business plan defines the multiple variables (finances, marketing, personnel, and production) that need to be addressed both serially and in parallel. The ongoing challenge is how to judiciously allocate a limited amount of psychic energy on a day-to-day basis. Complicating the process is the fact that priorities change with varying needs and external circumstances (e.g., the economy, competition, and even government regulations). That consideration makes the allocation of psychic energy all the more challenging and often quite frustrating. Frequently, the result is burnout, leaving the partners overworked and overwhelmed.

DEFINITION OF RESOURCES

A company's ability to thrive is a function of available resources and its ability to mobilize outside resources. A resource is any material, psychological, personal, or business aid that can help the partners fulfill their mission. Two processes facilitate the management of resources: one, maintaining a balance between coping with change and pursuing stability, and two, assessing the company's use of resources.

Balancing Stability and Change

People hold various combinations of coexisting attitudes toward change and stability. People are open to change in some areas and want to maintain the status quo in other areas. Preferences for stability or change also vary with time and circumstance, so that what is desirable at one time may not be at another. Difficulties may arise when a person embraces change on an intellectual level but resists it on an emotional level. In business, this conflict commonly occurs when an entrepreneur expresses a desire to change certain aspects of the company but behaves in ways that will only preserve the status quo.

Coping with change is not always an option, especially when changes occur in the economy, demand for the company's product declines, or key personnel are lost. Adapting to change in the workplace must often be done quickly to avoid disaster. Many a business fails when it cannot adapt to changes quickly. Such inertia may be the product of the entrepreneur's fear of consequences or lack of knowledge about what to do. In times of economic downturn, for example, the discomfort involved in laying off valued employees may become expressed in procrastination, which will only magnify the problem and invite bankruptcy.

Whereas some people have difficulty coping with change, others cannot maintain stability when it is needed. That is the case with people who get bored and need the stimulation that comes with change. Dealing with a business that has an established routine frustrates them. That leads them to seek change even when maintaining a stable situation results in a profitable business.

Example: Eric and John were partners in a high-tech software business. While working on a program for operating a robotic machine in a machine tool plant, Eric ran into a difficult problem. Characteristically, Eric spent too little time on difficult problems and would "solve" them by switching to something else. Because they had a deadline to meet, with John's support, Eric was able to work through his frustration and stay focused on the elusive problem.

Adaptability is the ability to modify one's behavior as required by changes in a given situation. Therefore, a person can be very open to change in some areas and very resistant in others. Self-confidence and past experience play major roles in developing this trait. In contrast, undesired consequences have an inhibiting effect on adaptability unless such consequences are seen as specific to particular situations and not a reflection of the value of adaptability.

Managing Self-Assessment

The major consideration in the stability–change balance is the ability to shift from one to the other as circumstances warrant rather than to pursue stability or change for its own sake. Basic to the survival of any company is its capacity to evaluate itself either through self-assessment or through information provided from outside its system. That is true of all levels of business—individual, team, department, and the company as a whole. Self-evaluation enables the entrepreneur to take corrective action. The first step in self-evaluation is to ensure that the availability of information on finances, marketing, personnel, and more is followed by an adequate process for making an assessment of their adequacy, as well as a procedure for implementing needed changes.

People's ability to absorb input depends on the source of the input and the value attached to it. The credibility of the source of input will influence how it is heard. The same information from a less credible source will receive a different hearing. One partner may question the merit of a proposal from the other partner. Hearing the same thing from a respected consultant is warmly received.

EXAMPLE: This was the case with Ann and Margaret who were partners in a dress shop. Ann was proposing that they develop a new line of sportswear. Margaret didn't think this was a very good idea until it was recommended by their buyer.

Too high a rate of feedback can be threatening and will overload one's capacity to process information constructively. In addition, too much feedback regarding too many items at the same time can overload and undermine the person's concept of self. With overload, the defensive system kicks in, which leads to denial, which takes the following forms— attacking the source of information, defending oneself, or distracting attention to other subjects.

People also vary in their ability to accept feedback. Some people need a lot of recognition for what they accomplish before they will accept a little

criticism. In contrast, those who have a strong sense of their own competence prefer to focus on the critical feedback, although it is always helpful
to get some positive feedback. For the most part, the person who is giving
feedback needs to show sensitivity to what is an appropriate balance in
each situation.

Another important consideration involved in giving feedback has to do
with whether it is requested or whether it is volunteered. A person who
requests feedback is open to receiving information, whereas volunteered
feedback may or may not be welcomed, depending on the recipient's state
of mind and the nature of the relationship with the person who is providing the information.

Some people accept feedback more readily when it is written than when
they hear it directly from the source. Written feedback, unlike verbal feedback, does not require an immediate response. Time to digest the feedback
both cognitively and emotionally permits a response, which is not always
possible when one has to react immediately to verbal information.

Resources occur in three categories: cognitive, emotional, and organizational.

COGNITIVE RESOURCES

Cognitive resources include creativity, communication and cultural
skills, past experiences, and talents.

Creativity

A company's success depends largely on whether it is more creative
than its competition. The partners set that creativity in motion when they
hire creative people and provide an atmosphere that allows their talents to
flourish. The physical and intellectual environment and the tools the partners provide should facilitate accomplishing the company's mission and
encourage ideas and the constructive resolution of differences.

Communication Skills

Accomplishing the company's mission requires that people communicate with one another. The way an entrepreneur communicates his or her
needs has an important impact on whether the company succeeds or fails,
as does the entrepreneur's ability to respectfully encourage and accept
feedback from employees.

Personnel policies provide a blueprint for the entrepreneur's relationship to his or her employees, defining the benefits and ground rules for
that relationship. (See chapter 15 for further discussion of this topic.) An
atmosphere that reflects flexibility, sensitivity to employee needs, and

openness to feedback will be strong motivation for the workforce. Areas of flexibility might be hours worked and the time vacations are taken. Sensitivity to employees means that allowance will be made for family crises and personal days and that the physical work environment will be comfortable in terms of things such as good air quality and lighting, pleasant furnishings, and a suitable place for coffee breaks and lunch. Openness to feedback means allowing workers to offer constructive responses and criticisms.

The company's authority may be unidirectional—"Now hear this! This is the way things are to be done!"—or collaborative—"Here is what needs to get done. Let's consider the best way to do it." The first method stifles communication; the second invites it. Authority, like any tool, can be used to advantage or can become a source of problems. The wise entrepreneur learns how and when to use it to advantage.

Management practices that show respect for employees' intelligence, contributions, and feelings in turn yield respect for the employer. Critical feedback is best when given in a private setting. Contributions such as exceptional effort, creative contributions, and willingness to work extra hours or travel should be given as much attention as problematic behavior.

Some entrepreneurs believe that an effective way to create a productive environment is to foster a cooperative atmosphere, whereas others believe that such an arrangement is best achieved through competition. The cooperative approach encourages and depends on open communication; whereas the competitive one discourages open communication in service of gaining advantage over others. These approaches are not mutually exclusive. Each work situation should be evaluated as to what combination best suits the needs of the business.

An entrepreneur does not always know the best way to foster desired communication for accomplishing his or her objectives. Insight into how to approach the desired communication can be gained by observing the natural communication patterns that evolve between employees. Organizational structure defines communication channels through position and responsibility. What it does not take into account, however, is how individual personalities enhance, impede, or circumvent that structure. A person gains power in an organization through his or her personality and knowledge independent of his or her formal position. Executives will benefit from taking advantage of the unique relational resources of their employees. They should also remember that changes in staff will alter communication patterns.

The advantages of oral communication are its immediacy and convenience. On the other hand, oral communication sometimes leads to speaking without adequate thought or using words that may produce undesirable consequences. Oral communication may also be distorted in the retelling. Indeed, attempts to resolve differences in recollection often lead to arguments and fractured relationships.

Written communication may be less convenient than oral communication, but it allows one to carefully think about what is said. It also eliminates the recall problem since it provides a permanent record. The downside is the time it takes to prepare, and it of course lacks the powerful nonverbal cues that are present in oral communication: facial expression, tone of voice, and body language.

Companies vary on the extent to which they restrict informal communication regarding business matters. Companies with restrictive policies require communication to go through channels. For example, an employee would have to go through his or her supervisor in order to talk to someone higher up in the organizational hierarchy. An employee could put him- or herself at great risk by attempting to communicate outside of prescribed channels. The way a partnership defines acceptable channels of communication should take into account how limiting those channels will affect the quality of the environment and work product.

The physical layout of the work environment affects communication patterns, especially informal communication. Close physical proximity of workspaces enhances easy and quick communication. It also creates opportunities for casual conversation that enables people to get to know each other on an informal basis, which affects their work relationship. Workspaces that are far apart inhibit communication. Open workspaces invite visual and oral communication; at the same time they are very distracting. Partitioned workspaces may interrupt visual communication, but they do not screen out auditory distractions. Offices with doors provide privacy and give freedom from sound and visual distraction, but separate offices also create communication barriers, cementing status and power differentials. Such barriers do not in and of themselves create problems, but they do reflect the larger work culture that defines them.

Meetings held in the workplace provide opportunities for exchanging information or points of view, making decisions, or resolving conflicts. It is a waste of resources to hold them solely to give information. When they foster open, nonjudgmental discussion, they encourage communication; they have the reverse effect when they do not. They are a major vehicle through which management defines company values. (Chapter 15 contains a more detailed discussion of this topic.)

A company that encourages employee feedback benefits from the unique perspective employees gain from the experience of doing their jobs. Feedback also helps increase performance, as well as motivation and satisfaction. A company that fails to take advantage of this resource not only loses part of its investment but also finds it difficult to retain employees, thereby incurring the added cost of having to train new employees.

The way affirmation and disciplinary actions are managed also affects the quality of communication. Attention to affirming constructive contributions in an even-handed way invites a positive response from employees and establishes a model for employee relationships. In contrast, disciplinary action exercised in a disrespectful or biased manner has a deleterious impact on communication and company morale.

Performance reviews, when conducted constructively, serve a useful purpose for both management and employees. Although firms commonly combine performance reviews with salary reviews, there is some benefit in separating the two. Dealing with them separately permits full concentration on performance issues, without considering salary evaluation, which warrants full attention in its own right. Performance reviews are generally one-sided, with management reviewing the employee. But it makes just as much sense for employees to review management. Not only will that give management some constructive feedback, but it will also create an environment that fosters bilateral, constructive communication.

Businesses that operate around-the-clock, especially hotels, hospitals, restaurants, and factories, are vulnerable to communication problems between workers in different shifts unless adequate provision is made for communication. This problem is most often managed by providing sufficient overlap between shifts to handle transition issues. Also needed is a procedure for managing communication between shifts when questions or crises that require immediate attention arise.

E-mail has greatly aided communication, making communication both within and outside the company almost instantaneous. It should not be used, however, to avoid face-to-face meetings in uncomfortable situations; nor should it be subject to improper use. Many companies find it necessary to monitor e-mail usage, which for the employee raises the specter of being watched by Big Brother. A policy for dealing with concerns about e-mail need not be set unilaterally by management; everyone who will be affected by it should be heard. This approach to the e-mail problem will increase the chances of employee compliance and encourage mutual respect between management and employee.

Both management and employees will benefit from a policy that outlines how employees should communicate while performing their job responsibilities outside the company. Employees who perform their duties in a knowledgeable and professional manner invite confidence in the company and its product. Management should also recognize that employees, when off duty, are informal public relations representatives of their company. The way in which an employee informally discusses his or her company or its product in the community can contribute to a company's goodwill. The company can make the best use of this resource by treating all employees respectfully, encouraging and acknowledging their knowledge of the company's philosophy and product.

Cultural Skills

As part of an increasingly multicultural society, U.S. firms must be ever sensitive to the way cultural backgrounds affect the work environment. Today, the workplace encompasses people from many different cultures, especially Hispanics and Asians. Every entrepreneur should attempt to understand the different cultural backgrounds along with their attendant value systems and learn how to be respectful of them in order to achieve positive work relationships. The challenge in managing diversity is to create a value system in the workplace that is compatible with company and employee value systems. That challenge can be met in various ways: providing opportunities for employees to know about one another's culture, being respectful of religious and cultural events and practices other than one's own, helping those employees who do not have adequate knowledge of English or colloquial expressions, and actively enforcing antidiscriminatory policies.

The executive's ability to establish rapport is determined largely by his or her ability to use language that makes employees feel comfortable and energized. Executives should also be familiar with current language styles within a particular culture, especially when ethnic groups live in a homogeneous enclave or have recently emigrated to this country. For example, cultures differ in the acceptability of asking questions about one's personal life. Negotiating appropriate standards in the workplace will contribute to a congenial work environment for all.

A person's unique value system or ethnic background often influences how comfortable he or she is with certain topics. Executives should therefore determine appropriate boundaries for discussion as they affect the work product. Executives should be sensitive to both verbal and nonverbal signals regarding topics that may disturb or confuse some employees. Verbal clues of impropriety include employees who ignore other employees' complaints about use of profanity, who tell off-color jokes, who tease inappropriately, and who scapegoat in topics under discussion. Nonverbal clues that people may be insulted or offended include employees' facial expressions that show disapproval or discomfort, employees becoming fidgety, their increased need to go for a beverage or to the restroom, and apparent distraction from work. Tolerance of offensive behavior implies acceptance and will negatively affect productivity and morale.

Executives should understand yet another form of language: the use of gestures different from their own. For example, most businesspeople with a Mediterranean background make liberal use of gestures and emotions and so will likely experience some difficulty when working with a staid New Englander who typically avoids the use of gesture and emotion in speaking.

Another area that presents difficulty is physical contact. In some cultures, touching and hugging are an accepted way to show support or caring, but in the American workplace they are generally considered inappropriate. Indeed, in the United States such behavior can lead to serious legal difficulty because in some cases it is viewed as sexual harassment. Developing a policy that includes contributions from employees will likely eliminate this problem.

Another factor in communicating comfortably is physical distance between people. Here a group exercise can be revealing. In the exercise, two people stand at opposite ends of a room and are asked to approach each other and to stop at the point where they begin to feel uncomfortable. The results can vary greatly. Some people may stop at six or seven feet; others may come within a foot of each other. People of Mediterranean extraction can even be comfortable "nose-to-nose," but the more common distance is three or four feet.

Modeling is a mechanism for self-assessment whereby one person seeks to incorporate the attractive aspects of another person's behavior into his or her own. People use it when they need information about how to behave in a new situation. Learning from modeling starts in childhood and continues throughout adulthood. An employee's adjustment to a new work situation is facilitated by his or her review of models he or she has experienced in previous work situations. With regard to negative models, permitting an employee to get away with inappropriate behavior will implicitly condone it and invite the same behavior from others.

The world of advertising makes great use of modeling, as witnessed by the virtual bombardment of the airwaves with sales pitches by successful people, especially from Hollywood and the sports world. Modeling issues can be a potent force in both positive and negative ways. In other situations, they become more complicated. The entrepreneur who models one pattern of behavior—with regard to work habits, respect for others, or decisiveness—and demands a different pattern of behavior from employees is inviting problems for him- or herself.

Modeling may be at a conscious or unconscious level. It is at an unconscious level when a person modifies his or her behavior to conform to that around him or her without conscious awareness of what he or she is doing. This often occurs when a new person comes aboard. The commonly used expression "Getting the lay of the land" in part has to do with looking for what models to follow without consciously thinking about it. Conscious modeling, on the other hand, occurs when a person in an unfamiliar situation models the behavior of those around him or her. This is often the case when one is in a foreign country, starts a new job, or joins a new organization. Conscious modeling is also a way to manipulate a situation, as when an employee being chastised for inappropriate behavior, such as violating company policy, defends him- or herself by saying, "The boss does it, so why can't I?"

Past Experiences

Partners seek to make their vision a reality by drawing from familiar resources such as finances, staffing, and marketing. One resource they often overlook is the learning that comes from past successes and failures. By doing a systematic review of their collective past experience, partners can uncover useful clues to information and skills that often are lost under the pressure of new events. One should not presume that the learning from past experience will naturally rise to the surface when needed.

Talents

Partners may discover another hidden resource in their and their employees' talents, skills, and interests that on the surface seem totally unrelated to their work: academic interests, sports, arts, leadership ability, organizational activities, music, hobbies, and politics.

EMOTIONAL RESOURCES

Emotional resources include empathic ability, access to feelings as well as their expression in appropriate ways, and the capacity to deal with the stress associated with today's business world. One's capacity for empathy—the ability to appreciate how another person thinks, feels, or behaves—is an important ingredient in a good relationship. To have empathy does not imply agreement; nor is it synonymous with sympathy, whereby one feels sorry for the plight of another person but may not have any appreciation for what it is like to have that feeling. A manager who disciplines an employee to appease his or her own frustrations without adequate empathy for the employee's feelings is contributing to a difficult work relationship. The manager who can show empathy is better able to exercise discipline that both discourages the undesired behavior and builds a relationship of mutual respect.

The pressures of doing business and the differences that arise among people while they are doing their jobs create stress. Stress can either mobilize or inhibit desired behavior. Too little stress can lead to complacency; too much can immobilize. In between, stress can motivate. Partners should develop ways to remain sensitive to the stress level in themselves and in their company and take appropriate measures when it becomes a problem. Disruptive stress can be minimized by treating employees respectfully, considering mistakes an opportunity for learning, maintaining realistic expectations, acknowledging contributions, and initiating a constructive process for helping people deal with conflict.

Providing a quality work environment shows employees that their needs are important, and it encourages them to have a positive attitude about their work. Among the material resources that help to do that are adequate lighting, good air quality, adequate workspace, minimal noise levels, and necessary tools to perform duties. Attention to minimizing stress in the work environment also contributes to healthy work relationships. This includes providing access to computers and faxes and designing a physical layout that provides for easy communication between people who frequently communicate with one another.

ORGANIZATIONAL RESOURCES

No self-respecting organization would neglect to publish its organizational charts showing how the company functions. Those charts are limited, however, for they cannot take into account the uniqueness of the people who hold the various positions. The actual operating heart of a company is its *informal organization.* It reflects how things really happen, and it shows how the talents of the people involved are responsible for whatever occurs in a firm. On paper, the entrepreneur, or in the case of an established organization, the chief executive officer or chief operating officer, runs the company, but that does not begin to show how the company actually operates.

Theoretically, the boss's secretary has no power; in practice, he or she may wield an immense amount of power. The secretary is often the gatekeeper for the boss, ultimately deciding whom the boss sees and what information flows across his or her desk. The executive delegates a lot of responsibility to his or her secretary, thereby giving that person considerable power in the eyes of other employees.

Frequently, employees command a lot of respect and wield considerable power yet hold little or no position of power. They may not even appear on the organizational chart. Instead, their power derives from their knowledge, experience, personal relationships, or maturity. Commonly heard in firms is the comment, "If you have a problem, talk to X." People in power often turn for advice to others in their companies. Such consultants have considerable influence over what happens in a company because of their advisory position and because that position influences the way others regard what they have to say, even though they have no formal authority.

Every business requires the simultaneous performance of tasks such as managing income and expenses, producing goods, marketing, and maintenance of physical plant. The priority that executives give to these needs and their role in determining a division of labor have much to do with the likelihood of the business's success.

The division of labor is not a static state; indeed, what is useful at start-up will have to be adapted to changing circumstances through periodic review of the division of labor rather than waiting for problems to develop. That process is facilitated by encouraging employees to contribute their thoughts and is accomplished through their formal involvement in the process such as participation on a committee. Informally, it is accomplished by encouraging feedback. Some companies have suggestion boxes and award bonuses for valuable suggestions.

Defining personnel practices is a major consideration for any company. Basic to that definition is operational clarity of the objective to be accomplished. The message partners give about their company to employees is a significant determinant of how personnel policies are defined. The message may range from "You are valued, and to be successful we are all in this together" to "I'm interested in giving as little as possible to get the job done."

What responsibility should an employer assume for the welfare of his or her employees? Over the years, that responsibility has come to include providing health benefits and some combination of vacation and sick leave benefits. Each company defines its benefits individually based on its financial resources and value system as well as the message it chooses to give its employees. Companies minimize such costs by having employees share the cost and by using part-time employees or using contractors. Some companies combine vacation, sick leave, and personal time into a lump sum and allow employees to draw on this time in whatever way they choose. This system is attractive for all concerned: it is easier for administrative management, and it gives employees more flexibility.

Many established companies offer insurance (life and disability) and retirement programs. Participation in retirement programs usually requires the vesting of the employee; that is, employees must work for a certain number of years before they become eligible to participate. Many companies also provide personal days and bereavement leaves, and in 1993 Congress added its imprint by passing the parental leave bill for companies with 50 or more employees. These benefits contribute mightily to employee morale and commitment.

Another significant part of personnel practices is the management of performance and salary reviews. Morale suffers when these reviews are treated casually or when they are not done in a timely fashion. Delays in conducting them without acknowledging the need to do so to the employee and designating when the reviews will occur undermine confidence in management and lower morale.

Rituals mark the transition from one stage of development to another. In the business environment, rituals in the form of ceremonies are used to acknowledge achievements and retirement; retreats, as well as Christmas parties, encourage camaraderie and enhance morale. Some companies acknowledge birthdays and anniversaries by formally noting them at staff meetings, in newsletters, or with cards. Acknowledgment of personal milestones is another way to enhance morale and create an atmosphere in which employees are not taken for granted.

Two interdependent aspects of any business are financial viability and the ability to function effectively as a unit. Companies conduct regular financial audits ranging from quarterly to annually. Under certain circumstances, certified audits are required to independently verify the validity of income and expenses. The purpose of such measures is to ensure the company's financial viability. It would also make sense to conduct a human resources audit along with the financial audit. In that way, a company's functioning as a unit could be reviewed on a regular basis, in the same manner that a financial audit reviews the management of finances. The human resources audit can identify areas of strength and, most important, specify areas with incipient problems and need.

An organizational consultant does for human resources what the accountant does on the financial side: interviews people, observes staff meetings, interviews customers, and provides an evaluation of the overall social health of the company's human resources.

CHAPTER 7

Decision Making

A successful partnership makes joint decisions through *negotiation*, which can be defined as the product of content and the process through which agreement is reached. *Process* refers to the mechanics of how a negotiation is conducted and the way in which the participants interact with one another. When partners enter a negotiation well prepared with appropriate content, holding a respectful attitude toward one another, with the objective of a mutually acceptable solution, and following guidelines for how to conduct the negotiation, the outcome is likely to be constructive and satisfying. If, instead, partners begin to express their frustrations in insults and personal attacks, the outcome will be very different.

Differences in points of view are a natural concomitant of business relationships. Seeking a satisfactory resolution to disagreements is the first step toward harmony between partners. Inability to reach such an agreement becomes a conflict when the parties involved reach an impasse. This chapter focuses on the process of decision making in business relationships and the process of negotiating to resolve differences.

THE DECISION-MAKING PROCESS

It is not possible to avoid making a decision, for any behavior or lack of behavior signifies a decision. Decisions are usually made in some overt fashion: "I agree"; "I will buy"; "I reject"; "I disagree." Covert decision making is more subtle and takes various forms: lack of response, procrastination, avoidance, criticism, and nonparticipation. A covert decision is reached when a person takes action before he or she is aware of the decision implied in his or her behavior.

Example: Joanne and Samantha were having a discussion about the need to add a new van for their furniture business. Joanne proposed that they buy one. The conversation strayed to other issues related to managing their vehicles. Joanne took no comment to mean agreement. Samantha did not realize that by keeping silent about Joanne's proposal to buy a new company van, she gave the impression of agreement.

Daily behavior requires one to make a constant stream of decisions at various levels ranging from the routine to major, life-defining events. Some of those decisions involve the following:

- Routine daily tasks—for example, calling a meeting or making phone calls
- Decisions that affect health and safety
- Decisions about work and social relationships, work schedules, and the like
- Decisions that affect work performance and career success, or that involve coping with threatening situations
- Decisions that have a major impact on lifestyle, such as leaving a job or a significant relationship or moving to another city

Partners need to decide which decisions can be made unilaterally and which must be made jointly. They need to define the criteria that they will go by to determine that. The following commonly necessitate joint decision making: expenditures beyond a certain amount, hiring and firing, and anything that has the potential for changing company policy or goals.

Decisions usually are made on their merit. Reactive decisions are more problematic because they are based on rejecting what is proposed just to be oppositional rather than on the merit of the issue. For example, a company may react to the pressure of competition by deciding to distinguish the company's products from those of competitors rather than deciding to do so on the merit of the product. Both types of decisions involve the ability to take calculated risks and to shift course as soon as change becomes necessary. Too much hesitation can mean the difference between success and failure.

Decisions may be made at either the conceptual or the implementation level. It is often easier to reach agreement on the conceptual level. Wide differences in interpretation are possible at the implementation level. For example, two partners may agree on the need to get a bank loan but differ widely on the amount and how to approach the banker.

Productive decisions are the result of considered evaluation of appropriate information. The challenge in decision making is to determine what information is needed, the collection process, sources of information, and the best way to approach the evaluation. A singularly important first step is a patient approach to gathering information from all relevant sources.

The advent of the Internet has facilitated that process. Gathering information can become more complicated when time pressure or unavailability requires extrapolation.

Another important consideration is to ascertain who and what affects the pending decision. This includes defining relevant content, assessing how the various options will influence work relationships (inside and outside of the company), and determining any relationship problems that might occur as a result of the decision.

Partners must manage an endless number of issues requiring decisions that directly or indirectly involve employees. Common decisions that directly affect employees include decisions about hiring, firing, salaries and bonuses, personnel policies, performance reviews, and supervision. Decisions that affect employees indirectly include decisions about finances, accounting practices, contracts, marketing, and public relations. Decision makers should be knowledgeable about the direct and indirect impact of pending decisions.

Decisions are not made in a vacuum. The timing of a decision can affect its value just as much as the basis on which it is made. Many decisions are time sensitive—namely, decisions regarding the stock market, the release of a new product, and the timing of a deal. A thoughtful decision made too soon or too late can soon become a liability. When an opportunity arises that requires an immediate decision, the decision maker must decide whether the higher priority is trusting his or her instincts or postponing the decision.

As noted earlier, successful decision making requires the collection of adequate information. The qualitative evaluation of the information can inspire confidence when a tentative decision best accounts for all the available information and additional effort yields no further insight. Agreement between decision makers on both the quantitative and qualitative evaluations indicates that a responsible decision was made.

The context in which a decision is made will have major effects on outcome. The three major contexts are collegial, hierarchical, and group:

Collegial. Decision makers who are involved in resolving differences must blend their individual inclinations. In the case of partners, this usually requires consensus in decision making or some form of division of labor in which one partner delegates responsibility for the decision to the other one.

Hierarchical. The decision-making process is somewhat simplified when one person makes the final decision, even when the decision is based on input from others. This occurs in a partnership when one partner dominates decision making. The challenge here is to determine how to gain the cooperation, if not the acceptance, of those people who were dissatisfied with the decision.

Group. The decision-making process becomes more difficult if the decision requires consensus or a majority. Disputes about substantive issues are often intertwined with competition, power struggles, value conflicts, and personality differences.

As discussed in chapter 4, empathy is basic to building a constructive climate in which to resolve differences. Empathy involves the ability to hear another person's point of view without judging it, as well as a willingness to appreciate a person's viewpoint regardless of how acceptable it is to the hearer. Offers made in negotiation that reflect empathy will maximize the possibility of a constructive hearing.

Resolving differences is usually regarded as a cognitive process except for the infrequent times when emotions prevail. Strongly felt emotions often prevent a logical approach to resolving differences. The parties involved need to recognize that the context in which the decision is made influences both the content and feelings about the content.

Example: Eric and Pat were partners in the lumber business and had different opinions about whether to acquire an electrical parts business. Their accountant advised that the proposed acquisition was risky. Undeterred and calling the accountant too conservative, Eric continued to agitate for acquisition. He was absolutely convinced that his instincts were right. Pat, though in agreement with the accountant, was nonetheless willing to go along with Eric because of Eric's strong feelings about the acquisition and because their profits were running well ahead of last year and they could afford to take the risk. Negotiations for the business took place over a six-month period. But by the time they were close to negotiating the sale, a downturn in the economy developed, causing a sharp drop in their profits and increased pressure from their competition. At this point, Pat no longer endorsed Eric's deal; unswayed by the changed circumstances, Eric continued to hold to his conviction.

A partner who approaches a negotiation seeking a win-lose solution does so at the risk of destroying his or her counterpart's goodwill. The partner who chooses this approach does so with the confidence that he or she will be able maintain a win position and does not see the loss of goodwill as a significant problem. Such a person is likely to consider the benefits worth the risk.

Careful attention to similarities in and differences between negotiators' positions provides the best opportunity for finding a resolution both parties accept. It also provides another way of showing consideration for the other's point of view and invites the same in return. This effort works well as long as parties focus on finding the best solution rather than on whose point of view should prevail.

Preparation for a negotiation should include assessment of the strengths and vulnerabilities of both proponents and opponents of substantive issues, including goals and the degree of flexibility that is possible. It is also desirable to understand the politics and strategy that the other side uses in a negotiation. Careful, ongoing attention to nonverbal cues in the course of negotiation can yield information about points of vulnerability in the other side. This assessment provides material for defining the most effective strategy for maximizing the negotiation outcome.

THE NEGOTIATION PROCESS

Certain steps are basic to the negotiation of differences.

1. *Exchange of views.* An equitable decision will not likely be achieved until all parties involved understand each other's point of view. This step starts with a commonly held definition of the issue. Acknowledging what is acceptable in a discussion before focusing on disagreements improves the likelihood that both parties can be heard.

2. *Definition of operational goals and priorities.* By clearly defining operational goals, priorities, and strategies prior to negotiation, the participants build a solid base for entering discussion. The participants need flexibility to adapt these initial considerations as the negotiations proceed.

   A decision is meaningful only when it results in an acceptable outcome. For that to happen, an operational definition is essential. Disagreements will occur when the decision-making process and definition of outcome are ambiguous. There are many sources of ambiguity. To begin with, ambiguity may occur when partners fail to distinguish between the concept or content of a decision and its specific application. Conceptual differences are likely to be more difficult to resolve when they reflect differences in values and beliefs. Differences with regard to specific items more readily lend themselves to finding acceptable alternatives. For example, it is one thing to differ on the target of a marketing campaign, and it is quite another to decide which slogan should be used. The same consideration applies to the definition of outcome.

   Another source of ambiguity arises when two people believe they disagree about an issue only to find they are talking about different issues. That often happens when assumptions are treated as fact or when information is misinterpreted without checking for accuracy. By not clarifying such distortions, both parties are free to feed on their projections, distortions, and upset feelings about each other.

3. *Attempt by each party to prevail.* The goal of both parties is to be sure they understand each other. In the initial discussion, each party attempts to convince the other that his or her point of view should prevail without the judgment of the other. To do otherwise invites a power struggle.

4. *The search for a joint solution.* When neither party is willing to accept the viewpoint of the other, both should respect their differences and devote all their efforts to finding a solution. This approach works well when each party considers acceptable options that also take into account the needs of the other party. This is more than compromise; it is an investment. For this type of outcome to occur, the parties need to focus not on what each is giving up but on the positive gain that follows from a joint perspective.

5. *Implementation of the negotiated decision.* Decisions are made with different degrees of specificity ranging from the conceptual to the very concrete. For example, two partners who have decided to buy a piece of equipment may either take the time to check out all the details necessary to making the purchase or choose to make the conceptual decision and leave the details to others. The conceptual approach avoids spending a lot of time on details but runs the risk that the decision will not be carried out as intended. The alternate approach ensures that the decision will be implemented as desired but at the expense of time that would be better devoted to more important matters. The same principle applies to more complex decisions such as planning a marketing campaign, hiring a new executive, or launching a new product. An essential part of decision making is to determine how specific one will be in laying out the decision's implementation and who will put the decision into practice.

   Inadequately defined assignments are an invitation to conflict. Partners often have an easier time agreeing in principle than in determining how, when, and by whom a decision is to be carried out. Effective decision making requires agreement both at the conceptual level and in the concept's behavioral translation.

   Acting without adequate information in order to avoid a tedious process or to save time and money usually fails on all counts and leads to additional added cost. On the other hand, obsessing over how to implement a decision as an alternative approach is no more promising. Reluctance to heed lingering doubts can also be a problem.

   Example: Two partners in a swimming pool business decided to launch a new marketing campaign. While they were indulging in long debate, new products from competitors came to market and the projected campaign no longer made sense.

   Example: Phoebe and Monica, partners in a construction business, were contemplating hiring a new chief financial officer. After a protracted discussion on the pros and cons of hiring a candidate, checking references, and further deliberation, they decided on a candidate even though both still had nagging doubts about the best choice. It wasn't too long before they regretted their decision.

6. *Definition of a method for monitoring follow-through.* To ensure that the intent of a decision is carried out, the partners need to define a method for monitoring its implementation. Problems develop when people assume that once the decision is made, all the rest will follow naturally. The quality of the monitoring process is often the most critical ingredient in ensuring proper implementation of the decision.

   Example: Lloyd and Alex were partners in an appliance business. Lloyd was increasingly bothered by the frequent fallout from Alex's abrupt manner. After much struggle, Lloyd persuaded Alex to do something about his behavior. Alex decided to reserve time at the end of each day to review how he had done in managing his abruptness that day. His assessment of when he did well gave him satisfaction, encouraged him in his efforts, and gave him confidence in facing those times when he didn't succeed. Consideration of his failure helped improve his behavior. After just a few weeks of using this approach, he was able to check his behavior without having to actively focus on it.

7. *Communication of decisions.* Once closure is reached, the next step is to communicate the decision to others. Issues that need addressing include how, when, and in what manner (written or verbal, individual or group, and so on). The way in which a communication is delivered can have a major impact on how it is received. For example, indicating how suggestions were considered is likely to yield a more positive response than simply announcing the decision.

8. *Evaluation of outcome of decisions and resolution of disagreements.* A systematic effort to learn from experience will always add to one's competence. Partners can accomplish that by devoting time to a regular assessment of learning from past decisions and from experience in resolving disagreements. One approach is to set aside periodic evaluation meetings for the express purpose of reviewing gains made since the last review. The same process helps ensure that the partnership relationship continues to be harmonious.

9. *Coping with disappointing decisions.* An earlier discussion recommended that decisions be evaluated solely on the basis of adequate information that has been reasonably evaluated. Changing conditions often result in transforming what starts out as a good decision into a bad one. Partners often deal with this situation by exchanging blame. Employing the precept "Manage—don't judge" will prevent a disappointing decision from ballooning into a greater one.

CHAPTER 8

Conflict Resolution

A disagreement becomes a *conflict* when differences appear to be irreconcilable. Conflict resolution is constructive when the parties reach a mutually acceptable solution. A conflict becomes destructive when its focus shifts from issues to personal attack either in content or nonverbal behavior—through tone of voice, facial expression, or body language. It is also destructive when one party feels pressured to accept the proposed solution and gives the appearance of acceptance. Such a resolution is extremely unstable and fragile.

The parties involved must formulate an operational definition of the conflict. Otherwise, they may find that their impasse is not about a substantial disagreement but is in fact about two other, separate issues: the content of the conflict (the nature of the disagreement) and the way in which it is being discussed. It is not safe to assume that the issue underlying a given conflict is obvious.

Partners will find it easier to manage conflict resolution when they understand the following basic principles:

Judgmental behavior invites the same in return. Judging or dismissing what is important to another person invites the same behavior in return. This shifts the focus from resolving the issue to a battle for control.

Avoidance of a problem makes it worse. A person should not walk away from a troublesome situation without addressing it. Problems that are allowed to fester become more severe and more difficult to resolve. A good maxim to follow is that the sooner a problem is addressed, the easier it is likely to be solved.

Separate resolution efforts from evaluation efforts. When partners' efforts to resolve a conflict reach a stalemate, they readily adopt a pessimistic attitude regarding whether resolution is possible. That attitude undermines any effort at constructive resolution. One way to avoid that mind-set, as is the case with disagreements, is to separate resolution efforts from evaluative efforts. The parties should set aside a work period during which they devote their energies solely to resolving differences and refrain from making judgments about whether resolution is possible. They approach any disagreements with the positive presumption that success is possible. Afterward, an evaluation is made. If the parties have made sufficient progress, they may agree to another work period under the same conditions, followed by yet another evaluation. If too little progress is achieved, the resulting evaluation may end with the conclusion that the conflict cannot be resolved.

Example: Two partners had endured a difficult period in their relationship and had now reached the point where any significant disagreement led them to question whether they should end their partnership. An outside consultant was able to help them see that the constant invocation of divorce in negotiating undermined their ability to attend to constructive alternatives. Once they recognized what they were doing, they were able to agree to a three-month period during which they would approach all disagreements with the presumption that they were resolvable. During this time, no thought would be given to ending the partnership as a solution. At the end of the three-month period, they would evaluate their progress. If they had made sufficient progress, they would agree to repeat the process for another work period. If they did not feel that they were making enough progress, they would consider ending the partnership once and for all. After the second work period they decided their conflict was unresolvable and terminated their partnership.

Balance attention between accomplishments and unresolved issues. In the course of a difficult negotiation, parties often distort unresolved issues and overlook constructive accomplishments and goodwill. It is useful to periodically step back and take a macro view of both accomplishments and remaining problems. That pause provides a fresh perspective and a more constructive context for each viewpoint.

Each person controls only his or her own behavior. The natural tendency in a dispute is to focus on placing expectations on an adversary's behavior. Expecting the other person in a conflict to change only heightens resistance to constructive listening. It is more productive to start the resolution process by considering one's own contribution to the conflict. The quality of communication can never be the sole responsibility of one person. Each party has multiple options as to how he or she hears a response (constructive, hostile, judgmental, irrelevant, and more) and multiple options in how he or she responds (reactive, acknowledges what was said, offers suggestions, gets angry, blames, and more).

There is safety in expression. Successful resolution of conflict depends on clarity in defining one's position and on emotional safety in expressing one's views in an honest and open manner that respects both oneself and others. Judgment of held views or attacks on personality sabotage constructive resolution.

MANAGING CONFLICT RESOLUTION

Conflicts can be resolved in four ways (listed in order of least contentious resolution):

1. Participants negotiate their own resolution.
2. Mediation by a third party facilitates the parties' resolution (for a more detailed discussion of mediation, see chapter 20, "Troubled Partnerships").
3. Binding arbitration is initiated.
4. Management dictates a solution between conflicting subordinates.

Resolution of conflict depends on a can-do attitude. When a person approaches a task with that attitude, he or she brings energy, creativity, and commitment to it. The converse is also true: approaching a task with doubt runs the risk of creating a self-fulfilling prophecy that will affect the outcome.

One can enhance a positive attitude by engaging in the mental rehearsal process. That process helps one prepare for coping with difficult events by developing answers to difficult questions in an environment that is free of the anxiety and pressures present in the actual event. Rehearsal allows one to devote maximum energy to problem solving and developing feelings of self-confidence.

When efforts to find a common ground reach an impasse, parties often express the resulting frustration by exchanging judgments or questioning competence, motivation, integrity, and so on. One can lessen the likelihood of such a destructive exchange of emotions by unilaterally invoking a "time out."

Conflicts that appear to be substantive are sometimes based more on personality conflicts than on issues. Conflicts based on personality attacks are destructive, for they lead not to solutions but to heightened tension.

Example: Carla and Susan, partners in a food brokerage business, often expressed their frustration in personal attacks such as "You are a big nag." The other would return the compliment with "You are stubborn and bullheaded." Their lawyer helped them realize that they were not going to accomplish anything constructive by exchanging personal attacks. Their insults, she told them, only invited retaliation, leaving them little energy for resolving their differences. They were finally able to appreciate each other's frustration, and after further discussion, recognized that neither point of view was going to prevail. As a result, they were able to focus on finding a solution that made sense to both of them.

The following are common tactics partners may use to resolve conflict:

Determine whether the conflict is based on symbolic or concrete issues. Some conflicts resist resolution because the source of disagreement is based more on what a given issue represents than on the merit of the issue itself. Being able to identify the driving force behind one or the other party's rigid position is helpful in finding a solution.

Example: Ann and Walter, partners in a hat-manufacturing business, were deadlocked in a conflict about hiring a new public relations director. They were struggling between candidates, with Ann favoring Betty and Walter favoring Alex. Walter was a little puzzled by Ann's adamant position because Alex's credentials seemed clearly superior. They asked for input from their managers and learned that they all supported Alex. Under pressure from the majority, Ann reluctantly conceded. In later discussions between Ann and Walter, she became aware that part of her adamancy reflected her belief that women were more skilled in public relations.

Define a negotiating position. The negotiating position should be seen as realistic. A position that seems too unrealistic for the facts at hand suggests insincerity in serious negotiation. A realistic position should leave room for concession without unduly affecting the needed outcome.

Make concessions. Concessions have meaning when the other side experiences them as representing a victory for them. The concessions should highlight the nature of the sacrifice. Workable concessions increase the possibility of gaining similar behavior from the other side. Dramatic presentation adds credibility in leveraging a negotiating position.

Pay attention to the ongoing negotiating process for clues. When a negotiation becomes too one-sided, the party who feels he or she is losing his or her position often takes an adamant stand in an effort to regain some control. One can avoid that difficulty by permitting the other party to have some meaningful victories.

Example: Rachel and Emily were negotiating a partnership agreement. Rachel had the business experience, contacts, and financial resources, but she needed Emily's creativity. As they were working out the details of their agreement, Rachel recognized that she was dominating the negotiations. Aware that problems would develop if Emily didn't feel she had more impact on the proceeding, Rachel made a concentrated effort to have Emily's views prevail on various points she herself would have defined differently. She reserved her own assertions for the major points of concern.

Give consideration to the needs of the other party. Good will is gained when the other side is given consideration. One does that by showing sensitivity to the needs of the other side and demonstrating how the proposal being offered addresses their objectives.

Example: Tom and Henry, manufacturers of men's clothing, disagreed about the merits of Tom's proposed new line for college-age men. Henry argued that the line presented was too great a risk for the return they would get. He was also concerned that it would divert resources from other projects. Although Tom acknowledged Henry's concern, he demonstrated that the return on a college-age line would be greater than Henry thought. He also showed how this project would contribute to other company products. They ultimately agreed on a slightly modified version of Tom's original proposal.

Change the context of negotiation. Changing the context in which a subject is discussed can totally change the way that it is heard. Meaning is gained not only from the merits of a given subject but also from how it relates to other reference points. In the previous example, Tom and Henry clashed because each was arguing from a different context. Henry was speaking from the reference point of what he felt were the dangers in Tom's proposal, whereas Tom was emphasizing the ways in which the company would benefit. They resolved their conflict once Tom addressed Henry's concerns by making some modifications in his proposal.

Use the cost-benefit balance. The fact that benefits to be gained are worth the cost that it takes to get them is inherent in any negotiating position. Negotiators are likely to stand fast on their positions unless they see how modifying their position will improve the cost-benefit balance (for a more complete discussion of cost-benefit analysis see chapter 9). Tom was able to get Henry's support by showing him that his cost-benefit balance was too conservative. Contributing to this success was his ability to show that Henry had overestimated the risk involved.

Determine areas of vulnerability. Vulnerability refers to areas where arguments are weak or where a person has particular needs that may be in conflict with the subject under negotiation. Positions held in a negotiation are affected by matters unrelated to the subject at hand. Taking a firm position on a particular subject may be in support of a principle or in service of a tough image, one's ego, or personal gain. Using the knowledge of an opponent's vulnerability can be a useful tool in helping break though a stalled negotiation. Playing into the other's ego needs is a common example. Acknowledging the opponent's negotiating prowess is another. Questioning whether a party has a conflict of interest in holding to a stated position is yet another.

Heighten the stress level. A familiar negotiation tactic is to heighten the stress level with the expectation that doing so will erode the opposition's resistance. A party carries this tactic out by conducting marathon sessions, making dramatic displays of emotion, holding the negotiation in uncomfortable quarters, or conducting late-night sessions.

Use humor. A protracted period of tough negotiating can harden polarized views. Humor is useful in breaking the tension and may shift the negotiating atmosphere toward a more collaborative direction.

WHY NEGOTIATIONS FAIL

Negotiations may fail because of individual needs or because of a relationship stalemate. In some relationships, the capability for mutual problem solving erodes to the point that the viability of the relationship is undermined. The result is a business divorce. What accounts for this change in the relationship?

Successful compromise requires that two dimensions be addressed: the substantive issue and the emotional element. Two people who are comfortable in their felt competence may be able to reach a compromise primarily on the basis of substantive content. When this is not the case, the ability to effect compromise may be hampered by emotional implications. Deals are frequently made on emotional grounds, even at the expense of the substantive issue. An example is the person who enters an agreement without giving adequate consideration to his or her ability to meet his or her commitment.

If one partner is in a dominant position, the other partner will tend to be more reluctant to support his or her viewpoint because it will heighten the inequality between them and obfuscate the possibility of dealing with substantive issues.

A partner who is wedded to a particular point of view may have a hard time resolving a difference that would require a substantive change in that view. To act otherwise would require the willingness and ability to put principle and logic ahead of personal satisfaction.

Some entrepreneurs have a hard time resolving a difference because they believe resolution carries the message that they are weak or inadequate. They can avoid that problem by reframing the context in which the resolution is viewed. An alternative to seeing oneself as weak is to admire one's ability to respect the judgment of another whose recommendation is perceived as a better solution than one's own. Differences can be more readily resolved only when each participant feels enough has been gained either in substance or in image to offset whatever compromise was necessary.

If the issues involved in resolving a difference are thought to negatively reflect on the entrepreneur's reputation or competence, he or she will surely resist resolution. The problem becomes more difficult when it is addressed covertly rather than openly, an approach that often is not taken consciously. Observable clues can be detected when there appears to be a gap in the logic being argued or when there is an uncharacteristic display of emotion. In such cases, resolution of differences will elude the parties until they address the underlying issue.

An executive is likely to become flexible when being inflexible carries the prospect of losing something of considerable importance. The loss can be considered at two levels: (1) the manifest loss on the substantive issue, which would be the case if a partner has to give up a viewpoint in which he or she has an emotional commitment or one in which the partner is certain that he or she is right; and (2) whatever implications go with the loss. It may be a material loss or a loss of power, prestige, opportunity, perks, and the like.

Changes in a person's values, beliefs, or goals may also adversely affect his or her interest in continuing in the business.

Example: Fred became Chris's partner in construction with the goal of building a big business and making a lot of money in the process. Fred valued material possessions, hard work, and the challenge of growing a business. After a few years, however, he became disillusioned about the emotional and physical toll associated with becoming successful in business. He had found that a less hectic life was more important to him than the challenges of running a business. For him the emotional strain of making a partnership work was no longer worth the effort.

Difficulty in resolving differences depends on the magnitude of the consequences. Resolving a dispute that is perceived as placing the business in jeopardy can quickly lead to stalemate and can jeopardize the business relationship. The following conditions contribute to a relationship stalemate.

Inability to resolve differences. As noted earlier, the essence of a successful partnership is the ability to resolve differences to the satisfaction of both parties. Partnerships run into trouble when they fail to strike a workable balance between meeting individual needs and achieving the partnership's objective. That inability is ultimately expressed in unresolvable differences when meeting individual needs becomes the dominant priority.

Shift in priorities. Each partner enters the business with a set of priorities, but the experience of operating the business can lead the partners to develop different expectations and priorities. Inability to find common ground ultimately leads to a stalemate and business divorce. This is analogous to a marriage in which two spouses start out with similar interests and goals only to find that over time they have developed irreconcilable interests and goals. Divorce is the eventual result.

Belief that compromise will not solve the problem. When one party asserts that compromise will not solve the problem, he or she is implicitly saying that he or she has better knowledge about how to proceed than does the other party. This shifts the priority from a cooperative effort to one where energy is divided between finding a new solution and coping with an evolving power struggle. Repetition of such behavior gradually undermines the stability of both the relationship and the business.

This behavior shows that it is better to make a mistake based on a joint decision than for one party to prevail at the expense of the other's point of view. This happens in cases when the involved parties share responsibility for an error in judgment and subsequently share the task of finding acceptable solutions. Obviously, this process is preferable because it enhances the relationship and focuses collective energy on solving the problem.

Perceived loss from resolution. An entrepreneur may be adamant in his or her point of view when any joint alternative would involve the loss of money, power, prestige, or investment in a pet project. The higher the perceived stakes, the higher the likelihood of a partner having little empathy for the other party.

Hidden agenda. As the business relationship progresses, one partner may gradually develop a self-serving personal agenda. The hidden agenda is a defense against the anticipated rejection of his or her views. Once a partner embarks on this course, he or she has sown the seeds for a schism in the relationship. It may also signal the partner's feelings that his or her concerns are not being adequately considered. The hidden agenda is a way to mark time until the partner is able to leave the partnership and go off on his or her own. And if the partner instead stays on, his or her frustration may be expressed in diminished commitment to the business.

Crisis in self-esteem. Successful resolution of differences requires that both partners have self-esteem. Without self-esteem, a partner is less able to engage in constructive negotiations because self-doubt will compete with efforts to settle the task at hand. In some people, self-doubt is expressed in overly aggressive behavior that masks their underlying sense of inadequacy. This sets the stage for resentments that can become habitual and destructive.

Desire for power. The exercise of power is most productive when it considers the needs of all concerned. It becomes destructive when it serves the purposes of the person wielding the power at the expense of those providing the benefit. Flagrant examples occur in the sweatshop culture as well as in cults when a charismatic entrepreneur exploits his or her members.

Differences in a partnership become unresolvable when partners give priority to the competition for power rather than to the mission of the business. The exercise of power often becomes a way to feed an undernourished self-esteem.

Desire to sabotage the relationship. People often find themselves in a business relationship that has lost its charm. Though they become disenchanted, they feel trapped in the relationship because of their financial obligation to it, pride and refusal to admit the relationship is flawed, fear of the judgment of others, and uncertainty about alternative options. Eventually, these frustrations affect their behavior. The person who possesses such feelings may not be consciously aware of their negative connotation and will probably deny any suggestion of dissatisfaction. Ultimately, the relationship flounders without either partner being consciously aware of what he or she is doing.

Unwillingness to involve a third party for resolution. The participation of a neutral third party may be necessary to determine whether differences can be resolved. Each partner should select a person to represent his or her point of view. The two designates will then select a third party who will function as mediator. If that does not lead to resolution and the partners still desire resolution, then mandatory arbitration should be considered.

Although partners may be unwilling to utilize a third party, they should understand that an outsider might be able to help maintain the relationship. A partner with the disinclination to bring in a third party may simply be waiting for a strategic time to end the partnership.

Involving a third party may also contribute to a partner's felt sense of inadequacy, and it carries the risk of undermining a partner's negotiating position, since his or her position is now vulnerable to an outside perspective. Yet another risk is that the partner's image may be damaged in the larger community should his or her vulnerability become known.

In addition, a partner may believe that the third party's recommendations will change the business relationship or the nature of the business in an unwelcome manner. That becomes a concern if he or she is in a vulnerable position.

Change in business values, beliefs, goals, or priorities. Even though partners may start out with shared personal and business values, beliefs, goals, and priorities, the partners' views may change in different directions over time. These divergent views will give rise to problems that may elude resolution. Permitting such differences to remain unresolved will ultimately undermine the viability of the partnership.

Unresolved personal conflicts between partners. Partners who start out as friends may find their personal relationship tested. Managing a business may lead to rivalry, power struggles, and arguments as to how to conduct the business. Eventually, both the personal and the business relationship may suffer.

Loss of trust and respect. Violations of trust will undermine any budding relationship and will stress any ongoing relationship. Trust is not an all-or-nothing experience, for a person may be trusted in some areas and not in others. For example, a partner may trust his or her partner's judgment in managing employees but not in managing finances.

Trust based on an explicit agreement to behave in an agreed-upon manner leaves less room for ambiguity and is more subject to immediate accountability. In the business world, trust is ensured by committing significant expectations of behavior to formal written documentation. Not all aspects of trust in a business relationship can be committed to writing, however. There is also a need for an unwritten trust in the goodwill of both partners.

Basic to the resolution of any difference is trust that an agreement will be followed by appropriate behavior. Once either partner experiences a breech of trust, future differences will become more adversarial, and a climate more vulnerable to unresolvable differences will result.

Disagreement about work. A positive business relationship requires that the partners be comfortable with each other's work habits. Dissatisfaction in one or more areas, such as number of hours worked, tendency to procrastinate, and difficulty making decisions, leads to conflict when such differences cannot be resolved. An example is a partner who, already dissatisfied with her counterpart's short work hours, begins to call her irresponsible. Such derogatory judgments undermine their ability to work together.

Problems in perceived competence or contribution. The partners' parity in competence and contribution to the business is important to the business's stability. Stability suffers when the partnership has an unequal foundation. A familiar example is the partnership that is founded on the expertise of one partner and on the financial contribution of the other. The partner with the expertise may feel that he is making a more substantial contribution than his partner and may therefore seek more power and compensation. That is likely to lead to growing resentment in the other partner, especially if she feels that her financial contribution is essential to the survival of the business or if she feels diminished by the recognition that her partner is contributing more than she is.

CHAPTER 9

Cost-Benefit Balance

Entrepreneurs are familiar with costs and benefits in terms of dollar values; they are less familiar with the cost-benefit application in the broader context of business relationships. Such relationships are satisfying when the benefits (B) gained from them are worth their detracting aspects—cost (C). This principle is commonly violated and reflects the reality that relationships must be viewed in their totality. You can't have the desirable qualities in a relationship without the less attractive ones. That applies to the tangible as well as the intangible elements. Relationships are package deals!

The comfort level achieved in a relationship is very much a function of the cost-benefit balance (C-B balance). Although no one thinks about relationships in terms of this balance, this is what actually determines how relationships function. Even people who understand and accept the principle tend to forget this reality. When relationships become stressful, the tendency is to act as though one can just jettison anything that is uncomfortable. However, one has to accept the undesirable and learn how to deal with it to get what is desired.

Example: Karen was looking for a partner for her telemarketing firm. Sally had many of the attributes Karen needed in a partner—she was smart, assertive, knowledgeable, and experienced. On the downside, she was overly competitive, had a short fuse, and tended to be controlling. Karen's assessment of the C-B balance regarding Sally left her ambivalent as they discussed the possibility of partnership. Karen tried to work out with Sally some of the things that bothered her in their relationship. While Sally acknowledged some of her concerns, her behavior did not change materially. For her part, Sally had some objections of her own to Karen's behavior. Since both had some ambivalence about whether to risk a partnership, they eventually decided not to take the risk. They liked one another as friends but had doubts about whether a partnership could work.

People in the workplace often find themselves in relationships not of their choosing and have to find ways of coping with the C-B balance when it isn't in the desired comfort zone. This chapter focuses on variables partners should consider when defining and determining benefits and costs.

CHARACTERISTICS OF BENEFITS

A benefit is any emotional, physical, or material occurrence that is considered desirable. Benefits take the form of acquisitions, giving up something undesirable, or behaviors that help maintain the desired status quo. Acquisitions include gaining a desired relationship, money, power, material possessions, and prestige. Benefits may also include giving up undesired responsibilities, long work hours, traveling, and stress.

Knowing the context in which a behavior will occur helps determine whether and to what degree it is a benefit. In the preceding example, Karen regarded Sally's assertiveness as an asset in relation to others but saw it as a detriment in the partnership context.

Benefits may take many different forms. Here are some of the more notable:

- *Psychological.* A psychological benefit is a desired experience gained from a relationship, including feeling cared about, being consulted for advice or help, being desired as a companion or partner, and gaining respect for one's views or needs.

- *Physical.* A physical benefit is any experience that affects one's physical well-being, particularly the absence of pain, and anything that contributes to physical health, such as food, lodging, exercise, and medical care.

- *Material.* Material benefits contribute to having adequate financing and physical resources to conduct business. They include any perks that the business can provide such as country club membership, travel, and automobiles.

- *Managerial or technical.* Any experience that enhances one's ability to become a better business manager is a managerial or technical benefit.

- *Spiritual.* Any experience or frame of reference, often in a religious context, that provides an ethical context for how a person guides his or her behavior and gains a state of serenity is a spiritual benefit.

- *Immediate or delayed.* The benefits of an experience may be immediately realized or they may be gained over time. Benefits may be multiple, and many occur at different levels. A business that receives a good review in a trade magazine will derive multiple benefits: the review will bring in business, enhance the business's reputation over time, give employees added feelings of satisfaction and job security, and attract new employees.

- *Short-term, medium-term, or long-term.* Benefits vary in length from a fleeting moment to an ongoing one. Examples, in increasing duration, are having a productive phone call, having a constructive meeting, having a profitable year, and enjoying a satisfying business relationship.

- *Less or more intense.* Benefits vary in intensity from minimal to very intense. At the minimal end, the benefit barely provides a fleeting feeling of satisfaction, such as the passing amusement of a political cartoon, the satisfaction of clearing one's desk, or the pleasure of receiving a compliment. A more important benefit would result from a valued work relationship and a long-term, satisfying partnership.

- *Reciprocal.* Partners who are able to give and receive from one another gain satisfaction and stability from that balanced reciprocity.

The value one attaches to a benefit is determined not only by the substance of a relationship but also by the source of the benefit. For example, an employee may get the same compliment from a colleague and from his or her boss, but the one given by the boss will have greater value attached to it.

CHARACTERISTICS OF COSTS

A cost is whatever it takes to gain a benefit. A partner puts up with his or her counterpart's bad temper because of that person's value to the partnership. An employee recognizes that having to travel and work long hours is necessary to earn the desired salary. An additional benefit is the positive impact the job will have on his or her career. The significance of a cost may vary from trivial to prohibitive. A business may find the cost of providing employees with lunch-room facilities trivial. On the other hand, an entrepreneur may find that seeking funding from a venture capitalist is prohibitive because of the equity expectations and the degree of participation the venture capitalist expects in the business's operation. The person who bears the cost for gaining a benefit is not always readily identifiable. He or she may be the recipient of the benefit, one or more other people, or a combination of the two. The relationship between who pays and who benefits can have significant implications for working relationships and for the business, as indicated in the following examples:

- *The person receiving the benefit pays for it.* An employee gets a salary for his or her job performance and may try harder if he or she believes it will increase his or her earnings. In general, purchasing a benefit can pose a problem if the person can't afford the cost or if the expenditure is at the expense of other needed benefits. An example is the realtor who feels she needs to present an image of success by buying an expensive car she can't afford. Businesses commonly fail because entrepreneurs are unable to meet their debt obligations because they lose their perspective on the cost-benefit balance in borrowing money.

- *Someone other than the beneficiary pays for the benefit.* An example is the employee who uses a company car for personal needs. A common practice in giving gifts is the hope that it will create business—for example, free tickets to sports events, dinners, golf, free samples, and many more.

- *Both the beneficiary and others pay for the benefit.* When an entrepreneur gets a loan from a bank, he or she gets the benefit of the capital subject to the purpose for which the loan was granted. Both the entrepreneur and the bank share the risk cost.

Emotional, financial, physical, spiritual, and intellectual costs are associated with benefits:

- *Emotional.* The emotional cost includes any anxiety that may be involved in experiencing the benefit or the consequences that result from it. For example, an employee who makes a presentation for the company at a trade convention uses psychic energy and experiences anxiety about doing well. He or she may feel additional anxiety about whether the presentation accomplished the desired objective. Fear of failure in one area can consume great amounts of psychic energy, which will lead to additional anxiety when it produces diminished performance in other areas.

- *Financial.* The financial cost occurs at two levels: the direct expenditure of funds necessary for the benefit to occur and the potential loss of benefits by taking funds away from other areas. In deciding what benefits to offer its employees, a company must decide how to allocate its limited funds. That requires an assessment of the benefits gained from satisfying employee needs versus what benefits are lost in order to fund those benefits.

- *Physical.* Among the physical costs associated with start-up businesses are the long hours required. The problem is compounded when physical demands must continue for an extended period and when considerable travel is involved. Physical and emotional stresses that become chronic can create serious health problems.

- *Spiritual.* Spiritual costs emerge when an entrepreneur feels pressed to act in ways that violate his or her ethics. For example, the entrepreneur may feel the need to hide the company's financial status in order to prevent employees from leaving or to present somewhat inflated estimates of the value of the company's inventory to secure a bank loan.

- *Intellectual.* Managing a business seldom leaves enough time to pursue new knowledge relevant to the business or to continue one's personal interests. The significance of a cost may vary from trivial to prohibitive.

One cannot always know the cost of achieving a benefit in advance of receiving that benefit. In fact, sometimes that cost cannot be determined until after the benefit has ceased. This gives rise to various possibilities:

- *Cost is known before the relationship benefit is realized.* An employee is asked to complete a project and is told she will receive a bonus if it is completed in a timely fashion, but the size of the bonus or how it will be determined is not defined.
- *Cost is determined while the benefit is being experienced.* The cost-benefit balance of any work relationship is fluid and ongoing. The way an employee is viewed is the product of the employee's work productivity and his or her ability to get along with coworkers. The validation the employee gets for his or her effort depends on how hard he or she works.
- *Cost is not determined until after the benefit has ceased.* When an entrepreneur enters a partnership, he or she has only the roughest estimate of what he or she will gain from the relationship and of what will be needed to realize that. The partner can know the cost-benefit balance only after being in the relationship. Once the relationship is established, he or she must work to maintain it at a positive level. A business divorce is likely to be the result when a reasonable cost-benefit comfort level can no longer be maintained.
- *Cost is determined by the amount of time the benefit is in effect.* The cost associated with a particular benefit may be affected by the amount of time it is experienced. Entrepreneurs often find that the benefits of having their own business are overshadowed by the frustration and discomfort it takes to be successful. Over time the demands and pressures to run their businesses become increasingly wearing to the point that being in business is no longer worth it. The duration of a benefit may vary from the set time of a paid vacation to being open-ended. For example, embarrassment one feels after a bankruptcy may be carried for an indefinite period depending on the conditions that define it.
- *Cost is influenced by whether the benefit is scheduled.* The cost may also be affected by whether the benefit experienced is scheduled to occur at a particular time, is intermittent in its occurrence, or is unpredictable in occurrence. A benefit that is scheduled provides the opportunity to minimize the cost associated with having it. An example is an annual performance review, where both employee and supervisor have the opportunity to prepare for the review to maximize the benefit of the experience.

An intermittent benefit is one that will likely occur but is unpredictable as to when it will happen. An example is waiting for a promotion that depends on the current occupant retiring. The cost in this situation is an ongoing anxiety about when it will happen and the possibility that the commitment to the promotion might change over time.

An unpredictable benefit occurs when an entrepreneur is involved in developing a new product. He or she is faced with the cost of development without any assurance it will pay off. The entrepreneur has to contend with determining how much he or she can invest in the project in both time and money.

The worst case related to costs is the incurring of costs without gaining any benefit—this can be a blow to one's self-esteem in the case of a business failure. The problem is compounded when the failure leads to other costs, such as a tarnished professional reputation. In addition, partners whose business has failed tend to blame one another for the failure.

COST-BENEFIT BALANCE

Three cost-benefit assessment conditions are as follows: (1) benefits are clearly worth the cost of obtaining them—partners feel that having committed, competent, and loyal employees is well worth the cost of a good benefit plan; (2) it is unclear whether the benefits warrant the cost of getting them—partners do not know whether the continuing education program for their employees will have the desired result; and (3) the benefits are not worth the cost of getting them—partners decide that the advice they got from a consultant was not worth the financial or emotional cost in getting the requested information.

The cost-benefit balance is yet another area in which partners have to deal with difference. Each partner develops his or her own standard, which may not work for them jointly. Resolution can get complicated because the cost-benefit balance is a product of values, beliefs, and goals; however, achieving a resolution is essential to managing a successful business. Otherwise the partners would be working at cross-purposes.

CHAPTER 10

Delegation of Responsibilities

When to do a job yourself and when to delegate it is a challenge faced by any entrepreneur concerned with productivity and personal satisfaction. The ability to delegate responsibility effectively is an important part of managing a successful business. Delegation starts with the partners' ability to develop an appropriate division of labor between them. Each partner in turn needs to be able to delegate responsibility to those who report to him or her. The partner who has to do it all and be involved in every decision will soon begin to lose his or her effectiveness, or even worse, will burn out, and will lose the support of his or her staff, negatively affect the business, and undermine the goodwill necessary in keeping a productive partnership going.

Responsibility is delegated, first, *to free up the delegator's time.* Ideally, delegators make the best use of their time when they engage in activities that only they can handle and when they assign work that others can do. Second, responsibility is delegated *to bring to bear expertise that the delegator does not possess.* Delegation becomes necessary when the delegator is responsible for a particular goal but does not have the expertise to accomplish all aspects of it. Therefore, someone who possesses the needed skills will be given that responsibility. Third, responsibility is delegated *to train the delegatee.* Delegation is used in training staff and requires instruction and supervision until the new skills are learned. If the goal is training, then adequate time should be allotted for appropriate supervision. This delegation will increase the manager's workload, not reduce it. Finally, responsibility is delegated *to yield products with greater efficiency.* Such efficiency is possible only when subordinates learn to perform their assignments with minimal supervision, which is more likely to happen when employees feel they are part of a partnership.

To delegate effectively, a partner should have the following attributes:

1. *Knowledge and social skills to supervise the delegatee.* Knowledge of what needs to be done without the appropriate social skills necessary for constructive supervision will not be effective. Successful delegation depends on a constructive partner-subordinate relationship.

2. *Ability to evaluate the product of delegation when one doesn't have the skill to perform the work oneself.* Knowing how to evaluate a work product does not necessarily require being able to produce it.

3. *Ability to choose the correct subordinate to carry out the assignment.* Knowing who is a suitable candidate for a work assignment is an important part of successful delegation. Facility in this requires knowing the talents and limitations of one's staff, as well as gaining input from subordinates regarding their interest in and perceived ability to perform needed tasks.

4. *Knowledge of the delegatee's career goals.* Ideally, delegation is most useful when it simultaneously fits the needs of the partner, the work product, and the recipient of the delegation. Since that ideal is seldom possible, those variables must be prioritized, and that is most effectively accomplished with input from employees.

5. *Sensitivity to the impact of work assignments on relationships between subordinates.* A manager should recognize that delegation of work stimulates competition, cooperation, and independent effort; affects morale; and more. A manager will need to be sensitive to the effects of the delegation and will need to know how to manage those effects to ensure that work goals are achieved and that constructive work relationships are maintained.

6. *Sensitivity to overt and covert messages in delegation.* Employees need to feel respected for both their individuality and their competence, and they also need to be appreciated by their manager. The quality of work assignments is indicative of how they are viewed. Being valued for their competence gives employees a more secure position than just being liked; in the latter case, the employee is more likely to be subject to the whims of the manager. Difficult work assignments convey a double message: they give employees the opportunity to demonstrate competence but also present the possibility of diminished reputation if they fail. In addition, favored subordinates tend to get the more desirable jobs, and those out of favor the less interesting ones. The favored subordinates provide a role model for their peers and may sometimes become an object of envy or resentment. The subordinates who get the undesirable tasks serve as a negative role model. Work assignments also carry messages of competence to the company's customers, depending on how the assignments are made. Customers quickly detect how companies treat their employees by the way responsibilities are assigned. The company's goodwill with customers

is enhanced when they see company employees behaving more as partners than as employees carrying out their routine duties.

Delegation of work assignments has different political implications, depending on whether the relationships between subordinates are harmonious or conflicted. When the work assignment is a desirable one and the subordinates have harmonious relations, other subordinates may be envious but will be supportive. When the climate between subordinates is hostile, however, other employees are likely to be resentful and uncooperative, if not obstructive.

When the work assignment is an undesirable one and the employee climate is harmonious, other subordinates are likely to be sympathetic and helpful. A conflicted climate will cause the other subordinates to gloat over a peer's misfortune and, even worse, withhold cooperation or support.

7. *Awareness of how a new work assignment affects other responsibilities.* The busy partner may delegate work without paying adequate attention to the effect of the new assignment on a subordinate's other work responsibilities. If the assignment is a choice one, too little attention may be given to less desirable responsibilities. If the assignment is an onerous one, existing responsibilities may be used as the rationale for lack of adequate progress on the new assignment. Partners can avoid such problems by working with the subordinate in setting priorities between the new and old assignments. Doing so encourages accountability for work performance.

8. *Awareness of subordinates' emotional maturity.* Inadequate attention is often given to whether the subordinate has the requisite emotional maturity for the assignment. An otherwise competent subordinate may not be able to carry out his assignment because of his emotional immaturity in working with coworkers, clients, or the public. Failure may also occur when an employee is overwhelmed by the assigned task and is fearful of the consequences of unsatisfactory performance.

9. *Awareness of the need for additional supervision.* Delegation is valuable when it frees a partner to attend to higher-priority matters. Delegation that requires too much ongoing supervision obviates the very purpose of delegation when gaining additional time is desired. When delegating assignments, a partner should seek to effect a balance between benefits to be gained and the time and energy required.

THE DELEGATION PROCESS

Delegating assignments without being clear about their purpose can be negative for everyone involved. A partner who delegates work to free up time will be disappointed if he or she doesn't take into account how it will affect work responsibilities, the needs of the company, and relationships among employees. Employees who do not have adequate supervision inevitably disappoint their supervisor and themselves, and diminish the spirit of a productive partnership.

Using good judgment in making assignments can lead to greater productivity, create an equitable division of labor among subordinates, increase the skills of subordinates, and recognize employee competence. All these advantages hinge on allocating adequate time to complete assignments. Unrealistic and arbitrary deadlines will diminish effectiveness and undermine morale.

Clear communication will increase the likelihood that an assignment will be completed satisfactorily. To ensure good communication, the subordinate can be asked to repeat what he or she understands the assignment to be. Giving directions in unequivocal terms is another useful aid: follow "Give me an assessment of what happened at the meeting" with "Tell me who was at the meeting, the major points that were made, decisions made, and your judgment about the conclusions reached."

Partners encounter difficulty when they ignore or minimize the responsibilities that accompany delegation of assignments. Among those responsibilities are providing training, being available for questions (especially during the learning curve), paying equal attention to acknowledging accomplishments and giving constructive criticism, and periodically checking on the progress of long assignments.

A partner often feels conflicted when he or she must delegate assignments. For example, the partner sometimes has to delegate work assignments that he or she would prefer to do him- or herself. The creative manager handles that situation by resisting the urge to micromanage the assigned task and by using his or her supervisory responsibilities to fulfill his or her interest in the task.

CHAPTER 11

Division of Labor

Who is going to do what is an early concern in any partnership. How labor is divided up sets the tone for the partnership. A well-functioning partnership is more likely when the division of labor is mutually acceptable and complementary. The partners should clearly define their areas of responsibility, the job each will perform, and how they will communicate. They should also define when decisions need to be made jointly. Ongoing informal consultation between partners helps maintain a comfortable working relationship.

Careful attention to defining their respective areas of responsibility will help build a strong foundation for a budding partnership. In arriving at a workable division of labor, each partner should make a distinction between "want to," "able to," and "need to." Following one's preferences is often not possible. Both partners need to find a balance between what each prefers and what each has to contribute to make the partnership work. Managing the division is easiest when partners have complementary skills and more difficult when their skills are too overlapping. The situation becomes problematic when a partner has needed skills but prefers not to exercise them. If it happens that both partners lack necessary skills, one can take responsibility for filling the need by either gaining the needed expertise or recruiting someone else.

MANAGING THE DIVISION OF LABOR

Expediency tends to be the initial driving force in defining the division of labor between partners, especially in a start-up company. Labor is divided according to a combination of preferences and by determining which partner comes closest to having the needed skills and is willing to take on a given responsibility. Often overlooked are the implications of this. Responsibilities differ in the status and power they imply. The way they are divided up can influence the way the partners are viewed by employees, banks, and others.

The division of labor may be done on a temporary or indefinite basis, and its anticipated permanence will affect how it is viewed. The simplest division is one in which responsibilities match interests and capabilities. For example, one partner manages the technical area while the other handles the business area. That is likely to be the easiest arrangement, but it does not always fit what is needed. The division is more challenging when responsibilities don't match interests and capabilities. This is likely to pose less of a problem if the division is temporary. A greater problem occurs when the division is for an indefinite period and the responsibilities don't match a partner's interests or capability.

If the goal is for both partners to be well versed in all aspects of the business, the means to that end is some form of rotating division of labor. Rotation would minimize any concerns about differences in status or power that go with holding particular responsibilities. Considerations for managing the division of labor include the following:

- *Defining goals in operational terms.* Examples include producing a product for shipment by a defined date and timely management of finances.

- *Matching competence and personality with task.* Apportioning labor responsibilities is more readily accomplished by matching competence and personality with the task.

- *Periodically reviewing the division of labor.* Little is static in a growing business. What is a useful division at one time may be counterproductive at another. Partners need to develop a constructive process for managing their different expectations of one another's performance (i.e., the standards they expect performance to measure up to).

- *Facing status and power issues.* Each task in a business carries its own message of status and power. The way in which each partner carries out his or her responsibilities can add to the aura of status and power communicated. The partner who is more interested and adept in the exercise of status and power can bring tension to the partnership. That can produce an atmosphere between partners that is not in the best interest of the business.

  A division of labor that delegates the hiring process to one partner can be a problem if it is viewed as giving more status to that partner. The alternative approach—making joint decisions—can readily become cumbersome and invite struggles over control. One way to avoid that outcome is for the partners to commit to developing a joint set of criteria for all functions.

- *Rotating responsibilities.* One way to achieve parity in the division of labor is to rotate responsibilities. That minimizes competition and struggles for status and power. It also ensures that both partners are knowledgeable in performing all aspects of their business. It can work only when both partners have similar capability in performing the various tasks. The disadvantage is that spreading energies too thin may interfere with gaining more in-depth experience.

MANAGING CHANGE IN THE DIVISION OF LABOR

A business relationship must be flexible enough to provide for orderly changes in responsibilities as changing circumstances warrant. Being able to do so is essential to the continuity of the business. In making changes, each partner should periodically review and manage accountability; conducting these reviews in a timely way will minimize the possibility of slipping into a stagnant division of labor. The periodic review will help keep the division productive and provide the opportunity to adapt to changes in interests, skills, and business needs. A periodic review will also help avoid problems by anticipating what changes are needed and doing so before they develop into major problems.

Changes in the needs of the business, the interests of partners, business goals, and employee needs, as well as the partners' need for a change in responsibilities, will likely warrant modification of the division of labor between partners.

Making changes in the division of labor can be a source of conflict between partners. It starts with the question of whether a change is needed. If both partners agree on that, then the only difficulty that lies ahead is how the division of labor will be redefined. This problem becomes particularly difficult when the change requires one of the partners to give up desired responsibilities. The task becomes easier if partners are committed to the parity desired and they currently have undesired responsibilities.

Conflicts over division-of-labor issues should not be allowed to fester. When partners find that they have exhausted their own resources trying to solve division-of-labor differences, they should seek outside consultation. Procrastination only makes the problem worse.

PART II

Application of Partnership Dynamics

CHAPTER 12

Selecting a Partner

A partner should be chosen with the same care one uses to select a spouse. Choosing with care can be difficult to do, however, when a promising opportunity comes along and two entrepreneurs find themselves irresistibly drawn to one another in the glow of a shared vision of financial prosperity. This is analogous to the couple who falls in love and marries on the strength of passion without exploring whether they have the compatibility to sustain a long-term relationship. Determining prospective partners' compatibility starts with current knowledge. That knowledge reveals the significance of past history, and the accumulated information provides a basis for estimating what behavior can be expected in the future.

DESIRABLE QUALITIES IN PARTNERS

The search for a partner should be based on an evaluation of a prospective partner's general style:

- Is the person more comfortable working alone, or is he or she happier working with someone else?
- How well does the prospective partner communicate?
- Does he or she find it important to be in charge?
- How well does he or she function in a cooperative venture?
- How important is the prospective partner's vision to him or her?

Evaluating a prospective partner is somewhat like performing a physical exam. The objective is to determine the status of all the systems necessary for healthy functioning. In the case of a partner, it is important to determine whether he or she possesses the *personality characteristics* needed for a productive partnership.

A comfortable partnership depends on the compatibility of the partners' *temperaments*. Temperament refers to a person's characteristic manner of thinking, behaving, or reacting. No set combination can be guaranteed to work at all times, but complementary temperaments often work well. A partner who is not able to manage his or her emotions is a good match for one who does. A partner quick to jump to conclusions works well with one who is more considered in his or her judgments. In contrast, partners who are both inclined to be both short-tempered and impulsive are likely to have a stormy and unstable relationship. If both tend to be indecisive, they will have difficulty making timely decisions. If both are perfectionists, they will fall far short of their goals.

Incompatibility is not always obvious when one is exploring a potential partnership. Often, some aspects of temperament may apparent only under the impetus of stress or a crisis. The only way to know a person's temperament fully is to see how he or she copes with a wide variety of emotional and intellectual experiences over time.

A person who adheres to a code of values that guides his or her behavior is said to have *integrity. Trust,* on the other hand, refers to the expectation that a person can be expected to behave in a manner consistent with his or her values. Both integrity and trust are essential for effective collaboration. It takes time and experience to demonstrate these qualities, and very little violation is needed to destroy them. Once violated, they take time and effort to rebuild. Prospective partners would do well to agree on an explicit code of ethics for their relationship. Even though one may presume some things, such as honesty, to be self-evident, people have different standards regarding how honesty and other ethical values translate into behavior.

Example: Jeff, a partner in an auto dealership, professed to be honest and forthright, but he did so in a manner that irritated his partner, Charles. Jeff tended to withhold his opinion in a business conversation, thereby giving the impression of agreement. Then, just as a conclusion was about to be made, he would interject with a significant objection. This behavior infuriated Charles. They went through a protracted struggle until they were able to negotiate some clear behavioral standards with regard to honesty and forthrightness.

Accountability to oneself is a major contributor to a successful partnership. A person with self-accountability has clearly defined ethics that guide both his or her personal and business life. A positive sense of self is experienced when behavior is consistent with ethics, and conversely, a negative sense develops when ethics are violated. That negative experience should lead to behavior that corrects the deviation. A person with a strong sense of self-accountability has the ability to pursue his or her convictions in the face of criticism from others. Strong convictions are accompanied by the ability to seriously consider the views of critics. One is able to accept what seems appropriate and to reject the inappropriate. Accountability to oneself gives a person the confidence and courage to forge new directions that to others may seem inappropriate. Partners with this trait can work out their differences and thus apply their combined energies without encumbrance to the pursuit of their business.

Occasionally, pressure is exerted to make an immediate decision. *Patience* is needed in evaluating the risks of making a decision based on too little information versus the prospect of losing an attractive opportunity. The person who has confidence in his or her own judgment is better able to exercise such patience. Another essential aspect in any business effort is *long-term commitment*. A prospective partner's ability to make the desired long-term commitment should be assessed, and some attention should also be paid his or her past history of long-term commitments. This history should not be limited to business experience but should also include athletic interests, investment in organizations, and so on. It is easier to generate commitment and staying power when the partnership is believed to have the necessary emotional, material, and personnel resources to overcome the difficulties inherent in business. Insecurity and lack of self-confidence will undermine commitment and will make it difficult for the partners to stay focused in the presence of attractive but competing interests. A prospective partner's ability to maintain a commitment during difficult times must be considered.

Partners who have the wisdom to acknowledge their own *strengths and limitations* minimize their chance of getting into trouble by presuming they can do it all. This insight enables them to put their energies into areas where they will be most productive. This awareness is enhanced when they use knowledge of their limitations to either improve their own capabilities or employ people who have the needed abilities. Realistic assessment of their own and their employees' strengths and limitations can only fortify the partnership.

Venturing into any situation whose outcome is uncertain always presents risk, and risks naturally involve making mistakes. People who view making mistakes as failure will never be successful entrepreneurs. Success comes precisely from taking calculated risks and learning from one's mistakes. The hackneyed maxims "No risk, no gain" and "No pain, no gain" are reminders of a basic truism. Understanding why mistakes were made is the basis for new learning and is a stepping-stone to being successful. Of course, adequate homework must be done before taking risks so that the uncertainty, number, and severity of consequences in taking risks will be minimized. Also of concern is whether the consequences of failure are manageable and whether achieving the goal is warranted in terms of the time, money, or energy needed to accomplish it.

Example: Diane, a software engineer, was so convinced her e-commerce concept would succeed that she didn't think she needed to evaluate the risks involved. In the beginning, her prediction appeared to be correct. Success quickly evaporated, however, when a competitor produced a better product; she then went broke.

Projects that are plagued by mistakes end up in disappointment when the missteps are not offset by sufficient successes. *Persistence* is the ability to continue resolutely to pursue a particular activity in spite of obstacles. However, partners need to be able to determine when doing so is counterproductive, as happens when the need to succeed supersedes good judgment in knowing when to stop. Persistence is facilitated by dividing the ultimate goal into subgoals. Achieving each of the subgoals provides a sense of accomplishment and adds to one's confidence and desire to persevere when the ultimate objective seems far off.

Partners must be aware that moving in new directions breeds many *frustrations* that must be managed in ways that will work for them rather than create new problems. The boss who takes out her frustrations on her employees not only doesn't solve her problems but also undermines company morale and productivity. A better approach is to vent one's anger at the problem and to involve staff members in finding a solution. That tactic stimulates productive interest and focuses energy. Being made a part of the solution enhances motivation and heightens commitment.

The insecure partner has a *need for personal recognition* that gets expressed as always needing to bolster his or her self-confidence and often blurs the boundary between taking credit for company accomplishments and acknowledging those who actually did the work. That misguided practice creates tension in partner-employee relationships and ultimately harms productivity. The astute partner will soon learn that giving the appropriate kudos to others is a far better way to achieve recognition. Gaining recognition in this manner may take longer, but it is offset by a long-term gain.

The *constructive use of power,* the ability to influence, is a necessary prerequisite to successful functioning in any business or profession. Ideally, it is a skill in the service of an objective: to get customers or clients, to convince a jury, to win a contract. For some people it becomes an objective in itself. The satisfaction of being able to wield power takes precedence over the manner in which it is exercised. A person with a need for power as a priority will not make a satisfying and productive partner. The way a person relates to power is readily visible in day-to-day experiences. For example, being in charge of an activity becomes more important than getting a job done. The pursuit of winning a point becomes more important than the mutual satisfaction of those involved.

A potential partner should be evaluated based on his or her need to have power for the sake of having it, whether in service of the business objective or personal gain. One would expect and even desire a partner who seeks personal gain but only one who does so in the context of meeting partnership objectives rather than making those objectives subordinate to his or her gain.

The potential for problems related to seeking power quickly surfaces as potential partners consider joining in a business relationship. It starts with how a prospective partner goes about resolving disagreements. When mutual satisfaction is the criterion for resolution, the prospects for a good working relationship improve. The evaluator must be sensitive to indications that the need for power may be a problem. An early sign can crop up in deciding what name to give to the partnership. Competition may arise over what order should be given to names in identifying the company, as is done in law firms. Other examples include consideration of compensation, office space, and parking space and amenities. A persistent pattern in these deliberations in which personal needs supersede other considerations is a warning of conflicts to come, and it should be heeded.

Prior work history is another strong predictor of future behavior. Any of the following characteristics can be an omen of problems for the partnership:

- *A problematic relationship history.* A prospective partner will not be able to easily change established patterns of behavior, even if he or she wants to. Knowledge of success in past business relationships is a good predictor of what to expect in the partnership under consideration.

- *Questionable success in past work history.* A person may have creative ideas and the desire to succeed but may lack the skills and personality to accomplish his or her vision. A pattern of troubled or failed ventures does not bode well for a different future.

- *Difficulty making decisions.* Timely decisions, sometimes made under less-than-ideal terms, are often required for success. A history of difficulty making timely decisions can be an obstacle to a productive partnership. Equally important is learning from mistakes.

- *Trouble dealing with conflict.* Conflicts that are not promptly resolved drain productive energy from a relationship and thwart creativity. Unresolved conflict feeds on itself and increases the prospect for future conflicts. Conflict avoidance is detrimental to resolving differences.

- *Poor political skills.* Politics involves the ability to relate to other people in a partnership in a manner that is conducive to the needs of both parties. It includes having a sense of timing—that is, knowing when to deal with various subjects and how best to approach them. The absence of this ability in a partnership will be a chronic strain on the relationship.

- *Shifting priorities.* Shifting priorities too quickly and without adequate consideration wastes resources and interferes with developing the momentum necessary to achieve goals. A prospective partner's ability to manage priorities constructively can be readily tested during negotiations of the partnership agreement.

- *Checkered history in learning from experience.* A person who doesn't readily learn from experience is likely to repeat mistakes in the future.

- *Perfectionism.* High standards contribute to business success, but they are a detriment when they become an end in themselves in pursuit of unrealistic outcomes. Success—no matter how much is achieved—is always tarnished by the failure that comes from not reaching the idealized goal.

- *Conflicting responsibilities.* A partner who is otherwise desirable may not achieve his or her potential if he or she is overly encumbered with other responsibilities, such as family health issues, marital problems, financial obligations, or outside interests. Unrealistic assessment of the impact they would have on a partnership portends potential problems.

- *Difficulty following through.* Some people love starting projects but gradually lose interest and are unable to see a project through to conclusion. What may have been a satisfying and productive partnership at the beginning can soon become burdensome.

Managing Emotions

As indicated in chapter 4, productivity and comfort level will be at their highest when one's emotions and intellect are functioning in constructive unison. The situation can be quite different when one's emotions and intellect are leading one in different directions. The following behaviors may signal a problem in managing emotions:

- *Short fuse.* The conduct of any partnership is replete with crises that tax one's emotional reserve. A person who has too short a fuse in dealing with problems is less likely to make wise decisions and will create relationship problems in the process.

- *Impulsivity.* Impulsive behavior usually involves action based on insufficient consideration of what behavior is appropriate. The impulsive person treats assumptions as facts, makes costly mistakes in terms of time and money, and creates animosity in those who suffer the consequences of his or her behavior.

- *Chronic disruptive anxiety.* People who are always anxious are less productive and are distracting to others. The anxiety will become contagious, especially if the anxious person is very vocal about his or her feelings. The expression of anxiety may not always be obvious, as illustrated by the person who always needs to be busy and productive.

- *Little tolerance for frustration.* Some people do very well when their work is progressing well, but when frustration sets in, that composure quickly deteriorates. As they become less steady and reasonable, their work productivity will fall.

Low self-esteem diminishes a person's capacity to fully use his or her abilities and experience on both the intellectual and emotional level. It manifests itself in several ways:

- *Need for excessive acknowledgment.* Difficulty trusting one's own judgment requires frequent acknowledgment of accomplishments. This may seem odd when it occurs in someone who regularly demonstrates considerable competence. It poses a problem when the need for acknowledgment distracts attention from the task at hand.

- *Poor self-discipline.* Setting unrealistic goals contributes to poor discipline, which gets expressed in substandard performance and further reinforces feelings of inadequacy. Vulnerability to distractions is another indication of self-discipline problems. It results in lost focus, substandard performance, and missed deadlines.

- *Need for power and control.* Self-esteem derives from feeling powerful and in control. The preoccupation with power becomes a priority to the extent that it can get expressed in substandard behavior, which reinforces low self-esteem.

- *Name dropping.* People with low self-esteem gain confidence by making reference to the people of stature and prominence with whom they have had some experience. People with great competence often have low self-esteem. In this apparent contradiction, accomplishments apparently do not influence underlying self-esteem.

- *Difficulty acknowledging competence in others.* For some, acknowledging the competence of others serves as a reminder of their own felt inadequacy.

One has to be accountable for one's behavior and follow through on commitments. Difficulty maintaining *accountability* occurs in various forms:

- *Use of double standard.* A person may set one standard of performance for him- or herself and another one for others, so that more tolerance is shown for one's mistakes than for ones other people make. Owning up to mistakes or accepting constructive criticism becomes very difficult for this person..

- *Quickness to blame others.* A person who has difficulty accepting responsibility for his or her own behavior is quick to hold others responsible when things go wrong.

- *Insensitivity to needs of others.* A person who is preoccupied with his or her own needs will have less energy or interest available to respond to the needs of others.

- *Lack of compatible values.* Partners have difficulty maintaining accountability when there is an incompatibility in their values.

- *Lack of compatible beliefs.* Holding one another accountable is difficult when the partners have different perceptions of what has occurred. Nevertheless, a partner who perceives a problem exists should be accountable for behaving in a responsible way consistent with his or her belief.

- *Failure to provide personal resources.* Problems in accountability occur when partners do not follow through on their commitment to provide certain resources (intellectual, emotional, financial, and political). They should be accountable for maintaining an ongoing assessment of whether they have the resources they are pledged to contribute.

Successful partnerships depend on the partners' ability to *engage in constructive relationships*. A creative vision supported by plentiful funding will go for naught if the partners do not have the ability to participate in productive relationships between themselves and with others—employees, banks, lawyers, and more.

Communication Skills

Communication skills are one of the more critical determinants of success in a partnership, serving as the cement that binds the parts of a business effort into a productive whole. A good prospective partner

- uses "I" instead of "You are" statements ("You are wrong" as opposed to "I disagree with you" or "You are making me mad" versus "I get mad when you behave that way");
- communicates in a thoughtful, caring manner, giving attention to particular behavior and not to the person as a whole;
- bestows positive acknowledgment appropriately;
- is predictable and stable in his or her ethical behavior;
- shows patience, commitment, and respect for the feelings and views of others;
- makes constructive use of power;
- displays a collaborative decision-making style;
- checks out assumptions before acting on them;
- listens attentively, making regular and sympathetic eye contact, using body language (i.e., sitting upright and with slight inclination toward the speaker, looking attentive), uttering periodic vocal affirmations, and requesting information or clarification;
- possesses an active speaking ability characterized by eye contact, an engaging manner, validation of the listener, and use of stories that attract the listener's attention;
- displays behavior that enhances communication, such as constructive feedback, affirmation of accomplishments, and respect for others' opinions; and
- eschews behavior that impedes effective communication, notably using silence, teasing and sarcasm, joking, and making decisions for others.

A partner demonstrates competence by the way he or she accepts feedback from peers and subordinates. The insecure partner, upon hearing negative feedback reflecting on his or her competence, is likely to turn the problem back on the subordinate. In contrast, the secure partner accepts the negative feedback by addressing the issue presented and uses it as an opportunity to enhance his or her relationship with the subordinate. This partner shows appreciation for valid criticism or gives reasons why he or she thinks the feedback is not wholly warranted. As a secondary benefit, this person presents a model for accepting feedback.

A partner can best educate employees by demonstrating desired behavior through example. The partner also gains respect by holding him- or herself to the same standard he or she imposes on others. This modeling encourages commitment to performance and bolsters morale.

Respecting contributions by one's partner also strengthens the partnership and provides an added incentive for employees to be committed to their work. There are a myriad of ways to demonstrate respect for others' contributions. One can affirm positive behavior, provide critical feedback in a respectful manner, value opinions, accept criticism graciously, and be sensitive to employee illnesses or personal crises. These methods will encourage employees to develop and utilize their creativity and commit themselves to their work.

Another necessary component of a working relationship is respect and sensitivity for the feelings and views of others. Attention to how a prospective partner managed relationships in the past and does so in the present will give ample indication of how he or she respects the views and feelings of others.

A question for prospective partners to consider is whether both partners are comfortable with and respect contrary views. This ability is an outgrowth of the partners' good sense of their own competence and recognition of the benefit to be gained from collaboration. This collaboration occurs when the focus is on reconciling differences rather than on competing for who will prevail. The objective is to adopt a win-win approach to resolving differences.

As noted earlier, differing views in a partnership can be both an asset and a liability. Differences are an asset when partners can find a way to incorporate the benefits of their respective views to their joint satisfaction. Differences become a liability when they are so divisive that they interfere with the partners' ability to constructively pursue jointly defined business goals. Some individuals have the capacity to deal with conflict when acting alone but are unable to do so in a partnership.

Example: Gregory, Jeffrey, and Michael's enthusiastic, jointly held vision led to the formation of their partnership without their giving adequate consideration to the compatibility of their personalities. They just presumed that the merit of their plans would override whatever difficulties they would face in their interpersonal relationships. The impact of that oversight was not long in coming. The major personality incompatibility occurred between Gregory and his two partners. Gregory was quick tempered and impulsive, and often failed to control his anger. Though very bright, he found it difficult to attend to the views of others, especially when they clashed with his own. Jeffrey and Michael were more alike temperamentally but had problems of their own. Jeffrey created problems in the partnership because of his inconsistent work habits, and Michael got into difficulty because of his tendency to procrastinate. Jeffrey was also dishonest. In addition, none of them was an effective decision maker.

Frequently, they would approach decisions by lobbying with one partner behind the scenes to coerce the other partner to accept a given point of view. If they had made the effort to evaluate the compatibility of their personalities, the partnership likely would never have been formed. However, they did form a partnership, and it failed.

Values, beliefs, and goals and compatibility of goals were discussed fully in chapter 2, but they apply to partner selection, as the next two subsections show.

Value-Belief Discrepancy

When a significant discrepancy exists between a value one holds and the belief that one has related to it, a state of tension exists. One can handle the discrepancy by changing the value to match the belief, changing the existing conditions that give rise to the belief so that the belief matches its associated value, or learning to live with the discrepancy.

Dealing with the value-belief discrepancy becomes more complicated when it involves two partners. Each person has to deal with the discrepancy within him- or herself and then with the discrepancies with his or her partner's differing views. Suppose that a widget maker decides he needs a partner and finds that his prospective partner has a different view about the relationship between quality of product and profit. The prospective partner holds the value that they should organize their business around the principle of profit as the priority and the quality of the product as secondary, while the widget maker holds the opposite view. These views reflect differences in their beliefs about how the marketplace functions and in their values about the quality of their product. The widget maker wants to feel good about his product even if it reduces profits; the second partner views quality as important only insofar as it doesn't affect profits. Their relationship will flourish only if they can find a common value and belief system that is realistic in the marketplace.

Stress develops in the presence of a significant discrepancy between a given value and a belief about it. If the value is honesty in communication and the belief is that a partner is not being honest, the resulting stress will need to be addressed. Doing nothing will only add to the tension, which will at some point surface inappropriately and create a new problem and still not resolve the original issue. If the discrepancy is taken care of at the time it is relevant, constructive resolution becomes possible. Failing this, there is still clarity about an unresolved issue between partners.

Values, beliefs, and goals are like links in a chain: the chain is no stronger than its weakest link. A partnership can have compatibility of values and beliefs and all the other resources necessary for success but may encounter major problems if the partners do not pursue the same goal. It is not sufficient to have a general goal such as making money. The partnership requires observably stated goals so that all needed resources can be properly focused without ambiguity.

Compatibility of Priorities

Once goals are mutually defined, the remaining task is to determine agreement on priorities among goals. These are not fixed but should be viewed as a first approximation. Flexibility is needed in modifying priorities as circumstances and experience dictate. The partners' ability to define and modify priorities in a compatible manner inspires confidence in achieving a viable business relationship.

The following observations provide useful information in understanding the relationship capability of a prospective partner:

- How does the prospective partner relate to his or her spouse?
- How does the prospective partner relate to his or her children?
- How sensitive is he or she to the needs of others?
- How does he or she relate in a social situation?
- How do the characteristics observed in the work context compare to those observed in a social situation?

It is easy to commit to the concept that differences need to be managed constructively, but it is another thing to have the ability and commitment to follow through in behavior. Partners need to be sure that they both possess that ability. A person who needs to "win" will have a poor prognosis for constructively addressing differences.

Social Context

Partnerships do not exist in a vacuum. They exist in the larger social and physical context that includes personal habits; work habits; lifestyle; a stable and supportive personal life; and commitment of time, energy, and resources.

Personal habits such as promptness, attention to appearance, and manners, as well as addictions such as smoking, drinking, or drug taking, play a major role in determining the compatibility of partners. Potential partners should get to know each other well enough to determine whether personal habits might negatively affect a working relationship. The presence of such problems has only a minimal impact when the partners are able to acknowledge their existence and make an appropriate accommodation.

Having compatible *work habits* is also necessary. Examples include maintaining predictable work hours, organization, timeliness in following through on commitments, decisiveness, promptness, skill in time management, sensitivity to the effect of one's behavior on others, willingness to share in routine tasks, adherence to jointly agreed-upon procedures, and promptness. Knowledge of work habits can be gained prior to considering a business relationship, and a useful approximation can be gained while the partnership is being explored. Negotiation of the prospective relationship should include discussion of work habits, keeping in mind that words do not necessarily translate into behavior.

Lifestyle becomes important when it impinges on the partnership. A person whose outside interests are likely to interfere with the needs of the partnership becomes a potential problem, especially when such interests conflict with partnership duties. For example, a person may become very involved in community activities, believing such activities will enhance the image of the business relationship. That lifestyle, however, may interfere with carrying out work responsibilities. Similar problems arise when one partner has extensive family responsibilities or when excessive substance abuse or gambling are involved. These behaviors do not inspire much trust within the business relationship or among clients.

The demands of conducting business require the concentrated attention of all the partners. A partner who is having severe personal difficulties is vulnerable to distraction and ultimately to poor judgment. Some weight should be given to the possibility that a prospective partner's personal life might interfere with his or her work performance. Such concerns are best assessed by viewing a person's current situation in the context of past history and evaluating the implications of current circumstances for the future.

Specific attention should be paid to determining how supportive a prospective partner's spouse is likely to be when the demands of the partnership forbid much family time. Also worthy of interest is whether there is a history of personal or family problems and whether they are likely to continue. A history of marital problems, or the existence of a chronic debilitating illness affecting a parent, spouse, or child, are examples of situations that warrant attention. Although such an evaluation may be considered invasive, unnecessary, unreliable, and awkward, it should still be made. The guiding principle is to determine the probability that any personal problem is likely to chronically interfere with the partnership.

It is one thing to have a vision, but quite another to make the total commitment needed to make it happen. This is particularly true with start-ups, and in such cases, that level of commitment will likely continue until the business achieves enough stability to permit a more balanced commitment.

To be successful, partners need to be willing to invest all the resources required to accomplish their goals. During the start-up phase of their business, they face many demands on their physical stamina and suffer emotional stress. This stage is better tackled when they have the support of their families. The long hours at work and the partner's unavailability to spouse and children, both physically and emotionally, will strain family relations unless family members are made aware of the sacrifices that a new business requires. Sometimes the spouse will have to play the role of both parents. He or she will therefore have to know that his or her concerns are understood and will have some impact on what happens.

The partners will have to make time on a regular basis for family commitments. The spouse also needs to be party to the financial risks involved. Without such interaction, a partner will be caught between the competing demands of business and family. Being unexpectedly confronted with the potential loss of all family assets, including one's home, is a real threat to a marital relationship. This would be the case when personal signatures are given as collateral for business loans.

The potential for family problems increases when the partners' family needs are quite different from each other or when one partner is unmarried. An unmarried partner, unable to fully appreciate the pressure of divided loyalties that a married partner faces, may expect his or her partner to devote undivided attention to the partnership.

Once the business has been established and has stabilized, the impact on family diminishes and the partners will need to maintain a continuing balance between their commitment to business and family. That need becomes a greater challenge when marital or family problems are downplayed in the interest of business demands. The unwary businessperson may wind up with a thriving business, poor family relationships, and possibly a marital divorce.

Of particular importance is that the partners are compatible in how they manage differences in their commitment of time, energy, and resources. Any chronic imbalance left unattended for very long will breed resentment and ultimately threaten the partnership's viability.

Business Matters

Does the prospective partner have the motivation and physical ability to put in the hard work and long hours required? Does he or she have the appropriate relationship experience? Is he or she able to cope with the emotional challenges of risk, stress, conflict, and uncertainty?

Since past history is the best single predictor of future behavior, prospective partners should assess the resources each partner would bring to the relationship—notably intellectual, emotional, and political assets; business and partnership experience; technical knowledge; people, time management, and delegation skills; and the ability to adapt.

Do the partners collectively have the *intellectual skills* needed to engage in the partnership? Are they intellectually curious? Are they intuitive or creative? Do they prefer working in a structured environment, or are they more comfortable in a more flexible environment?

Parties to any business venture need to understand that the venture will face many challenges that will tax the partners' *emotional resources.* This will involve the partners' ability to control their anger and frustration when all their instincts compel them to lash out at the offending source. An assessment of an individual's past experience in dealing with such issues will give some indication of what might be expected should such circumstances occur in the future.

The business relationship will need to assess the extent to which it can gain access to political contacts, namely, potential referral sources for customers or clients, legislators, community contacts, and the like. A review of a prospective partner's past experience will indicate what resources might be available in the future.

Do the partners have the necessary business experience? Do they have adequate knowledge of business management—specifically, finance, marketing, strategic and tactical planning, and personnel management? What can past business experience teach that would be relevant for the future?

Example: A major handicap for the members of the Management Consulting Firm was their lack of experience in running a business, although they were well versed in the technical areas of management consulting, expertise they had gained by working in consulting firms. They had little experience in the mechanics of running their own business, however. In addition, none of the partners had previous partnership experience. In the excitement of starting a new business, they got along comfortably, but the comfort level began to diminish as the realities of running a business set in.

What prior *partnership experience* do the prospective partners have? How well do they relate to business, social, and family contacts? Each of these situations can provide clues that can be applied in evaluating the business relationship.

Do the partners have the *technical know-how* required for conducting their responsibilities in the business? In addition, a preliminary assessment should be made of whether they can obtain the financial resources needed to launch the business relationship. Financial viability is a final determinant in developing the business plan.

Example: The Management Consulting Firm's major asset was its intellectual resources—its ideas, knowledge, and ability to help others solve their problems. Members of the company also had excellent political skills, including good contacts, skill in networking, and knowledge of the business community and professional organizations. Their major disadvantage in the area of personal resources was their inability to maintain the necessary financing to conduct the partnership. Although they managed to acquire sufficient financing to get the business going, their preoccupation with the technical side of the business, at the expense of insufficient attention to business practices concerning collections, payables, and contracts with associates, led to problems. Ultimately, it resulted in the dissolution of the original partnership.

Partners, like symphony orchestra conductors, guide a group to work effectively together in order to accomplish their objective—be it a stirring performance or some product or service. They must relate to their subordinates in a way that will motivate them to make the most effective use of their energies. To accomplish that end, they must, first, *respect the employee's boundary between work and family.* A surefire way to generate tension in a relationship with partners or employees is to make excessive work demands on them. When this problem becomes chronic, problems in family relationships are the result. And when a person is regularly pressed to choose between work and family responsibilities, the inevitable result is lowered morale and diminished productivity or even the loss of the employee. It is in the partnership's interest to respect this boundary and be ever conscious that families are in a sense a silent partner. Keeping them happy is simply good business. When excessive time demands cannot be avoided, some form of concrete acknowledgment in the form of a day off, a bonus, or a special event can help minimize stress.

Second, partners must *set realistic expectations.* With the pressures of a start-up or of running a going business, expectations tend to be guided by what is needed rather than by what is realistic. When the distinction between the two begins to blur, frustration develops in all concerned, and criticism of management begins. The result can also be burnout. In such cases, the short-term gain becomes a long-term loss. A collaborative feeling can quickly give rise to an exchange of criticisms to account for the shortfall. Setting realistic expectations that can be met will have the opposite effect.

Third, partners should *focus criticism on behavior, not on the person.* "What is the matter with you?," "You're a liar," "Don't be stupid," "You have a lousy sense of humor," and "You're insensitive and selfish" are better left unsaid. Far more effective are "You made a mistake," "I'm angry at what you did," or "I don't agree with what you said." Shaming employees is destructive and will be reflected in their work; it is especially destructive when done in the presence of other people. Witnesses to such an experience are also affected because they naturally conclude that they could be the next target.

A characteristic useful in selecting a partner is *time management skills.* These skills are important both in the partner relationship and in educating employees to manage their time. Time management is a common source of stress in the workplace. Partners need to ensure that before projects are launched, they have given adequate consideration to how much time they realistically will take and how well they fit in with existing commitments. The overloaded employee feels overwhelmed and fears he or she will never catch up. Additional stress is felt when tight deadlines have to be met. The result is often burnout. To get their employees to be as efficient as possible, the partners need to apply basic time management principles. This effort can be managed from a relationship point of view, as follows.

Problems develop between partners and subordinates when objectives are defined in *conceptual* rather than *behavioral* terms. People can agree on a given objective but have different views about how to behave to accomplish it. Without a concrete statement of a work objective, it is unclear when the objective is reached. The likely result will be an annoyed partner and a frustrated employee, whose satisfaction in doing a good job is shattered by the manager's displeasure. The partnership can avoid this problem when manager and employee understand what observable behavior is required—for example, generating a certain amount of income, building a particular object, or getting a certain number of clients.

Another consideration is for partners to *prioritize work objectives.* Employees will impose their own priorities unless the manager and employee agree on priorities. The manager must be careful not to let the employee get caught in the cross fire; otherwise everybody loses.

Partners should also *set realistic estimates* of the time needed for task completion. Stressed relationships between managers and employees often result from the unrealistic time estimates they set. A manager will do well to teach his or her employees how to set realistic time estimates. An employee gets into trouble making unrealistic time commitments in the hope of impressing his or her boss, only to have the reverse happen when the employee isn't able to realize his or her objective. That is less likely to happen when an employee learns to make time estimates that start with the ending of another task and include the time needed to complete it. The new task is considered completed only after the workspace is cleared for the next one. Employees will benefit from the often-used rule of thumb of doubling one's best estimate.

Helping an employee learn to manage his or her time benefits both manager and employee. The effort starts with helping the employee set up a Monday-through-Friday calendar, and that includes fixed commitments such as lunch hours and meetings. The remaining hours form the time bank for allocating time to work projects. Employees sometimes do not recognize that borrowing from the bank is not an option; once the available time has been allocated, no new work commitments should be undertaken. To attempt to do so is to invite stress, diminished work performance, lowered efficiency ratings, and missed deadlines. The employee has to learn to avoid the temptation to accept new responsibilities even if he or she is presented with a desirable new task, unless the new task warrants bumping a lower-priority task or an existing commitment is delayed.

Interruptions are the nemesis of efficiency. Partners can improve their relationship with employees by helping them deal with interruptions in their work and creating an efficient work environment in which an employee is respectful of his or her fellow employees' work patterns. Major culprits are phone calls, visits from people wanting to chat, and an inability to say no to requests for time.

A ringing telephone, rarely, portends a great opportunity waiting, but the price for picking it up is most often lost time and lost concentration. Either a negative or positive call will make it difficult to resume one's work. The more calls one takes, the less chance one can accomplish much concentrated work. An ideal way to deal with phone calls is simply to allocate a fixed time of the day for calls, a routine that one must pass on to potential callers. One may not be able to follow that routine perfectly; however, the principle is to recognize the importance of managing phone calls in a more efficient manner. The potential of reducing incidents of telephone tag is an added incentive for dealing with phone calls in a more structured way. A great deal of discipline is required to carry out and maintain such a schedule despite the anxiety it may cause.

Employees need to understand that an open door is an invitation to interruption; it is a signal that it is okay to interrupt. Employees who share a workspace usually set up guidelines for interaction. The person who negotiates and insists on the conditions under which he or she can be interrupted will be more productive and will develop better work relationships. Fear of offending people will not be a problem if the interruptee makes his or her needs known in a congenial, respectful manner. Those who are reluctant to set limits on interruptions to avoid offending usually communicate their discomfort nonverbally and so reveal the very message they attempt to keep hidden.

A closed door signals "do not disturb" and is not an offensive approach. Posting a "Do not disturb" sign is even more effective in setting limits on interruptions.

Fending off disruptions by saying no is complicated when one fears the implications of doing so. Can you in effect say no to a supervisor, board member, major client, or customer? It is more easily done than one would expect, if the other party can be made to see its usefulness to him or her. Aggravation can be avoided and more work accomplished simply by finding a comfortable way to say no and tempering it with an alternative: "I'm sorry I can't talk now, how about meeting in an hour?"

Employees often need help learning how to avoid feeling overwhelmed. Sensitivity to an employee's existing work commitments is helpful when a new assignment needs to be given. Many approaches can be used to organize work tasks, including keeping up-to-date lists of jobs pending and prioritizing what needs to be done, starting with the more difficult items. Some problems result from putting off the most difficult or unpleasant tasks: such procrastination will get employees in trouble with their supervisors.

Achieving a satisfactory level of productivity depends on understanding how effectively one can work. Research by Rossi (1991) and others has demonstrated that people can work at maximum efficiency for just 90 minutes to two hours at a time. Work continued beyond that point usually results in decreased efficiency: jobs begin to take longer and to be less fully completed. Rossi recommends a 15-to-20-minute break every 90 minutes to two hours. Lost productivity during these breaks is more than made up for by the increased productivity achieved after resuming work. How the break time is used is the key to effectiveness. Ideally, the break should take some form of quiet time—meditation, a walk, a power nap, or fresh air. Talking with a colleague about work over coffee or otherwise being involved in work-related matters is not helpful. The guiding principle should always be to relax the mind. The application of these findings will benefit the relationship between partners and employees.

Example: A managing partner of a law firm was chronically frustrated because the stream of interruptions limited his productivity. When he began to treat all interruptions as equally important requiring immediate attention, he decided to engage a consultant. The consultant recommended that he set aside two-hour blocks when he was not available except for emergencies, which were rare. The partner also accepted a similar suggestion for managing phone calls. The managing partner followed the prescribed suggestions and was pleasantly surprised at how much more he was able to accomplish by applying these suggestions.

Balance between Strategic and Tactical Functioning

Success in business depends on the ability of partners to strike an appropriate balance between strategic and tactical functioning. The selection of a partner should take this understanding into account.

A partnership venture starts with a vision, which is the beginning of strategic thinking, leading to a consideration of how the vision can be made a reality. Next, tactical considerations are established to make it happen. The strategic plan should be reviewed and modified periodically as circumstances in both the company and the marketplace change. Partners must recognize that a team effort will be more successful when all of the players understand the long-term goals and understand how their immediate effort contributes to achieving them. They need to achieve a balance between strategic and tactical functioning and to learn how to involve their employees for the benefit of all concerned.

Understanding the relationship between structure and function is helpful in creating an effective partnership. A clearly defined organizational structure facilitates accomplishing the business mission. That definition includes a table of organization, job descriptions, a marketing plan, and the like. The table of organization should be designed with enough flexibility to permit adaptation to changing needs. Sometimes the comfort and convenience of doing business in a certain way becomes a goal in itself. When that happens, the convenience of operating in a familiar way competes with the need to adapt the existing structure to changing goals and market conditions. Resistance to changing the structure may result from fear of loss of power, uncertainty about the future, or reluctance to take on undesirable responsibilities or give up desirable ones. This resistance runs the risk of inhibiting the successful pursuit of business objectives. A prospective partner's ability to keep structure subordinate to function can be evaluated by reviewing the partner's track record. Many a business fails when partners are unable to adjust their familiar way of doing business in response to changes in demands of the marketplace

A prospective partner needs to be skilled in delegating authority. No partner can do everything by him- or herself. Skill in delegating work and responsibility to others therefore not only relieves the partner's workload but also gives managerial depth to his or her company. (See chapter 10 for a discussion of delegation.)

Making timely decisions is another essential component of success. Whereas chapter 7 discusses the principles involved in decision making, the present discussion focuses on the appreciation of a prospective partner's decision-making style. Of particular concern is whether the prospect has a history of difficulty in making decisions. Observing the process of exploring a partnership will provide one a perspective on the prospective partner's current decision-making style.

Decisions don't always work out the way they were intended. An important aspect of relationships among partners is how they react to mistakes. Too little tolerance of mistakes, either one's own or those of one's partners, creates an aversive environment that breeds anxiety destructive to the partnership. Decisions should be judged not on the basis of outcome but on the process through which they were made. This position is warranted because the decision outcome generally involves variables that may be unknown at the time the decision was made. It is also relevant that the person making the decision has no control over such variables even if they are known. The fairest way to evaluate a decision is to determine whether it was based on having relevant information and on making an appropriate evaluation. Judging the merits of a decision based on information that was not available at the time it was made is an injustice to all concerned and runs the risk of undermining a person's confidence in his or her judgment.

There are two kinds of entrepreneurs: those who like to build businesses and those who like to run them. *Builders* thrive on meeting the challenges of the unknown and enjoy handling the many changes needed to get a business started. Comfortable in adapting to change, they are not threatened by the uncertainties that go with it. *Runners* are more comfortable with the greater stability that issues from having a business that is up and running. They too need to adapt to change, but they do not have to face as much uncertainty as their builder counterparts.

The success of both types of entrepreneurs depends on their ability to form relationships that support their missions. Builders do best when they can recruit creative people who identify with their vision and are comfortable taking risks. Runners depend more on people who are more comfortable with a stable working situation. Both builders and runners face the challenge of keeping employees motivated.

EVALUATING THE COMPATIBILITY OF PARTNER ATTRIBUTES

Those considering a partnership would do well to review the skills desired in a prospective partner relative to their importance in making a choice. The most obvious place to begin this evaluation is with current knowledge, for that will give some direction as to which priority must be pursued in learning about the candidate's past history. On this basis it becomes possible to estimate what behavior can be expected in the future.

Useful additional information can be gathered through experiences with a prospective partner in social situations, particularly with his or her family. Such settings can reveal traits that might not be as evident in the business context. This happens because a person is less on guard in familiar social settings, where there is likely to be less at stake.

Guidelines for Conducting a Prepartnership Evaluation

A prospective partner should be evaluated according to each of the following characteristics, using the questions that follow this listing.

- *Temperament*—the partner's characteristic mode of emotional response, including emotional sensitivity, degree of irritability, expression of emotions, inclination toward impulsivity versus reflectivity, and other behaviors.
- *Personal habits*—predictable work hours, skill in time management, follow-through on commitments, decisiveness, promptness, sensitivity to the impact of one's behavior on others, and comfort in working with others.
- *Lifestyle*—attention to personal health, which includes achieving balance in one's work and personal life, practicing good nutrition, working regular hours, and not abusing drugs or alcohol.
- *Communication skills*—capability in active listening, shown in the use of "I" instead of "You are" statements, balance in the ability to communicate with thinking and feeling, attention to particular behavior and not to the person as a whole, ability to give positive acknowledgment appropriately, predictability

and stability in ethical behavior, patience, commitment, respect for the feelings and views of others, self-awareness, use of power, and decision-making style.

- *Values*—the values that are important for a satisfying and productive partnership. (Are the prospective partners' values mutually compatible?)
- *Beliefs*—the way the prospective partner perceives existing conditions that are pertinent to an effective partnership. (Are the prospective partners' beliefs mutually compatible?)
- *Goals*—goals for the partnership and the business, including those related to finances, personal satisfaction, and lifestyle. (Are the prospective partners' goals mutually compatible?)
- *Priorities*—priorities relative to how the partners will achieve their common goals. (Are the prospective partners' goals mutually compatible?)
- *Past business or professional experience*—past business and professional experience, including management skills, technical knowledge, relationship skills, and business experience.
- *Personal resources*—intellectual, emotional, financial, and political resources.
- *Ability and commitment to cope with differences*—the prospective partner's ability to respect differences and commit to finding solutions that reflect the concerns of both partners. A person who needs to "win" to feel successful will not make a good partner.

The following questions relate to the preceding characteristics:

1. Do significant differences exist between you and the prospective partner regarding the characteristic?
2. How important are those differences?
3. Are the differences likely to present a problem for the relationship?
4. If the answer to question 3 is yes, how resolvable are they?
5. How important is this characteristic to the success of the relationship?

Once each specific characteristic has been evaluated, the characteristics need to be considered as a group. Are the assets of sufficient magnitude to offset the deficiencies? Although it is easy to focus on the desirable traits and minimize the negatives, you should remember that a relationship can work only when you can relate to the total person (and he or she to you) and not just to the desired characteristics.

REFERENCE

Rossi, E. L. (1991). *The 20 minute break*. New York: Putnam.

CHAPTER 13

Development of the Business Culture

Partnerships are like plants. They will thrive depending both on the quality of both the seed (vision) and the environment that supports its growth. Each type of partnership described in Part III of this book has its own business culture, which is the product of the various influences related to forming and managing a partnership. Defining the work culture designed to accomplish the partnership's mission involves a value system, performance expectations, and guidelines for behavior. Partners need guidelines for relating to their employees and the outside world—suppliers, customers, banks, and so forth.

Role theory in social psychology provides a perspective on how relationships are defined. The starting point for defining relationships is the two contexts in which they occur. The first context is made up of formal positions that serve social needs such as police officer, doctor, lawyer, and bus driver. Formal positions carry clear definitions of appropriate behavior needed to carry out their function. The second context encompasses the informal positions of friend, manager, employee, and more. The appropriate behaviors for these positions are defined by the participants in each situation within the broad limits defined by society, such as not breaking the law. In the business context, these positions are defined by the company's organizational chart, such as chief executive officer, chief financial officer, vice president, manager, supervisor, and secretary. The code of behavior for both formal and informal positions is defined in three categories of behavior—required, prohibited, and permitted. Behaviors are assigned in the required and prohibited categories based on the belief that the success of their partnership relationship and the business requires such a designation. For example, the partners may explicitly or implicitly define these behaviors in the following way for their partnership relationship:

- *Required behavior.* For example, a partner must be honest and meet his or her commitments.
- *Prohibited behavior.* Partners may decide that making unilateral financial commitments for the partnership is prohibited and that forthright communication is required.
- *Permitted behavior.* All behavior not accounted for in required or prohibited categories is permitted, for example, the way a partner organizes his schedule or runs a meeting.

The preceding behavior allocations are not static; a certain behavior may move from one category to another as the need dictates.

EVOLUTION OF THE BUSINESS CULTURE

The partnership culture evolves through a series of developmental phases similar to the phases that characterize a marriage: exploration, engagement, marriage, stabilization, and eventual termination through closing the business, business divorce, illness, or death.

The Exploratory Phase

Figure 13.1 illustrates the process involved in beginning a partnership. One entrepreneur approaches another with the prospect of forming a partnership. They explore their respective visions and whether their personalities are compatible. Each brings to the initial meeting a professional culture that is the composite of his or her personal culture, education, and professional work experience. The personal culture, a product of the value system and experiences the prospective partners had in growing up, provides the intellectual and emotional tools with which they venture forth into the world. The addition of training and experience evolves into the professional culture and is the basis of their partnership. Their compatibility is a function of how well their combined personal and work histories mesh. Of special importance is how their education and experience result in defined values, beliefs, attitudes, and skills in pursuing their occupation. Each job further refines their perspective. The exploratory phase ends when the prospective partners conclude that a partnership is or is not viable.

The Engagement Phase

The engagement phase starts when the prospective partners decide they are compatible enough and that they can now design a business plan

Figure 13.1
Start of a Business Partnership

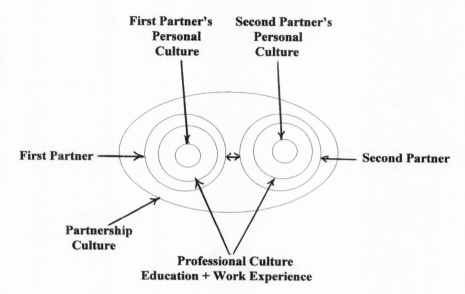

Evolving Business Partnership

satisfactory to both. This process will be successful when they consider how they will relate to and be affected by the external influences (business climate, marketplace, availability of funding, and more) that affect their success. The interaction between internal and external considerations will define the business culture for the partnership.

The Marriage/Merger Phase

The marriage, or merger, starts with an agreed-upon business plan and partnership agreement. Figure 13.2 shows in schematic form the various components of the partnership process. The objective in the marriage phase is to develop and implement a going business that includes a productive and acceptable division of labor for the partners. The division of labor will permit them to devote their energies to management of their business within the company and in relationship to the community they serve.

To survive, the partnership must adjust to the changing needs and circumstances of the business culture, including changes in market conditions, competition, and the economy. Other issues that need attention are personnel practices and the quality of the work environment. Guidelines for developing and maintaining a successful partnership and business culture include the following:

- Each participant should acknowledge the needs of other participants—entrepreneurs and employees, manager and subordinates, company and customers.
- All participants should understand the rules for interaction.
- The business should operate a safe environment that supports self-expression.
- All people involved should understand the mission of the business and their part in making it happen.
- Disagreements should focus on issues and should not devolve into personal attack.
- All participants should be kept informed of company progress and be acknowledged for their own achievements.
- Employees of the company should be respectful of differences.
- The partnership should provide constructive tools for resolving conflicts that are respectful of all concerned.
- All participants should pay attention to cultural background and to the biases that may result from gender differences.
- Those influences that may affect the partnership should be determined, and accommodations should be made to ensure that they have a positive effect on the business.
- The partnership should heed the changing needs of those institutions and cultures that affect the operation of the business. For example, shifts may take place

Figure 13.2
Development of a Partnership/Business

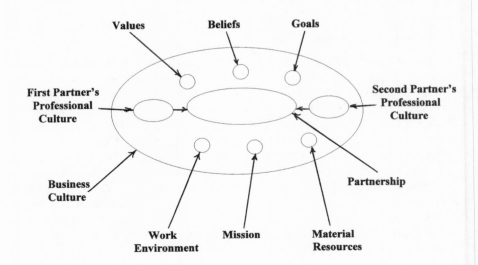

Partnership Relationship

in the composition of the customer base, in laws, and in environmental concerns.

- External parties should be asked to advise on matters that affect the business. For example, an advisory board or focus groups can be used.

The Stabilizing Phase

During the stabilizing phase the work accomplished in the exploratory phase is reinforced as kinks in functioning are corrected. Procedures that were initially unfamiliar have become familiar, practiced, and well established. Increasing amounts of energy are now expressed in productive and satisfying relationships. The continued success of the business depends on the company's ability to adapt to changing circumstances in technology and in the marketplace without adversely affecting the quality of these relationships.

Figure 13.3 illustrates that external influences on the business affect the definition of its business culture. As noted earlier, the business culture must be flexible enough to adjust to changes owing to pressures from both within and outside the business. For example, changes in interest rates, in marketplace competition, or in the company's product can all have a profound effect on working relationships. Specifically, the cost of providing employee benefits has increased to the point that some employers are devising ways to avoid or minimize those costs. The resulting strain between management and employees may lead to diminished employee morale and loyalty.

Figure 13.3
External Influences on the Partnership/Business

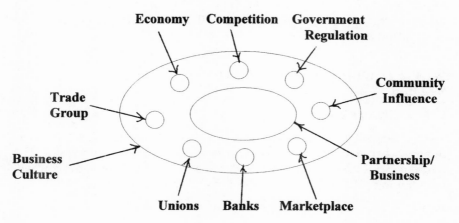

Business Culture

To survive, a business must maintain its profitability. Business cultures undergo developmental stages much as humans do, including infancy, latency, adolescence, young adulthood, adulthood, middle age, and old age. But unlike humans, a business need never "die." Analogies drawn from human development are useful in understanding the business life cycle. For example, familiarity with the adolescent struggle between dependence and independence can be helpful to partners in managing employees who want to have more independence in how they perform their responsibilities before they may be ready to do so. Partners who struggle with retirement face some of the same issues in principle as an elderly person who is coming to grips with aging.

Mind-set is another important consideration in developing a business culture. Once a given behavior has been learned, it no longer requires conscious management and it becomes an automatic behavior, which Langer (1989) refers to as *mindless*. Conversely, behaviors that require conscious monitoring are referred to as *mindful* behavior.

From this vantage point, developing a business culture involves moving partners and employees from the mindless behavior of their familiar world to the mindful behavior required in establishing a new business. The partners must therefore be aware of the mind-sets that both they and employees bring to the new work environment. Many new behaviors will have to be learned that involve shifting undesirable mindless behaviors useful in other situations to mindful awareness, so that they can be adapted to the needs of the current business venture. For example, an employee in sales may need to change his or her way of selling from what was appropriate in a former job to one that fits the current business. Having to make too many changes in mind-set at the same time affects employees' ability to absorb new information and may lead them to repeat old counterproductive patterns. That can undermine self-confidence and morale, which interferes with productivity. A major function of the stabilization phase is to establish basic work procedures that will shift the need from mindful attention to mindless behavior where possible. That will free up psychic energy, which people can then divert to meeting both the physical and emotional demands of new situations.

WHEN THE BUSINESS CULTURE IS NO LONGER VIABLE

The Closure Phase

Even the best use of resources may not always be enough to develop the quality work relationships necessary to make a business successful. The particular business culture involved, a disappearing market, difficulty in maintaining healthy work relationships, changing economic conditions, or competition may all be factors in preventing success. Upon the business's failure, the partners are left to cope with the vanishing dream on both an emotional and a business basis. They will also need to learn from the experience to increase their chance of success in the future.

REFERENCE

Langer, E. J. (1989). *Mindfulness.* New York: Addison-Wesley.

CHAPTER 14

Transitions

A vacation starts with the excitement of planning and the prospect of realizing one's fantasy. This experience is heightened with the onset of the actual event. Eventually, the experience ends and one has to adjust to the return to daily routines. Fond memories of the trip help one make the transition. As one ventures forth, thoughts are of the learning gained and the way to apply it in daily life and in planning the next vacation.

The same process occurs in a partner relationship with the added complexity that one has to deal with multiple "trips" at the same time (production, sales, finances, etc.), each of which has its own transitional needs.

A partnership starts with the excitement of anticipating what the experience will bring. That is followed by the experience of forming a new relationship, which is followed by developing a way to manage the partnership on an ongoing basis. Eventually, the relationship has to come to an end, and the partners are faced with the consequences resulting from the ending.

That is one example of the myriad transitions the partners will face in the course of their relationship. Each project—developing a new contract, starting a marketing project, hiring a new executive, running a meeting—has its own transition path to follow. The duration of the transition may be a very short period or may last for the life of the partnership. Each case starts with anticipating a forthcoming event, coping with its onset, and managing it until it is no longer relevant. One then has to deal with the meaning and consequences of each experience. The success of the partnership is the cumulative result of the partners' success in managing the broad range of transitions.

This chapter focuses on the challenges partners face in coping with transitions from one partnership experience to another. These transitional phases may be markedly different in that the partners will need different intellectual, emotional, and material resources to accomplish their objectives. Awareness of that will help partners understand what resources they require to successfully manage each project as well as how to most prudently allocate resources among the various projects that are ongoing at a particular time. It will also help them determine when projects should start or end depending on existing priorities.

Management of transitions (from anticipation through adaptation, maintenance, termination, and integration) involves the following:

- *Mastering the skills needed in each phase of transition.* Each phase has a particular need for certain skills. The anticipation phase benefits from clarity of the vision, creativity, and organizational ability to plan for the desired event. Coping in the adaptation phase requires the ability to be creative and decisive and to quickly assess and respond to changes. Maintenance requires a steady hand that is comfortable in managing an established relationship. Termination calls for the ability to determine when an experience needs to end and to do so efficiently, even when emotions run high.

- *Coping with the transition events in combination.* A partnership involves managing multiple relationships at different levels that put varying demands on emotions and intellect. For example, in the early phases of a start-up business, partners are under pressure to cope with anticipating and starting many new relationships—with employees, customers, lawyers, accountants, bankers, and others. At the same time, they need to manage existing relationships and cope with the varying demands of managing a business.

- *Balancing resources among transitional periods.* A successful business needs to strike a balance between resources devoted to anticipating new events, maintaining existing events, and handling the ending of other events.

- *Learning from each phase of an experience.* Often the press of dealing with immediate needs leaves one no time to reflect on what one can learn from each experience. No sooner does one handle one situation than one's attention must shift to other demands. Valuable learning will be lost if one doesn't make the effort to reflect on the lessons gained from current experience. To fail to reflect is to repeat one's mistakes. One useful approach is to reserve time at the beginning or end of each day to reflect on what was learned. It is also a good idea to commit this examination to writing. Otherwise, important insights may become the victim of fleeting memories.

THE ANTICIPATION PERIOD

By anticipating a forthcoming event, whether desired or undesired, and its impact on existing relationships, a person can prepare for its occurrence or, if need be, prevent its occurrence. A couple approaches one such event—marriage—with joyful anticipation. Those who are realistic in planning have a greater chance of putting their plans into practice smoothly. Analogously, business partners enjoy the excitement of planning for the launching of their business, and the more they can anticipate, the better their chance of getting their business off to a smooth start. This includes the ability to manage differences of opinion in a useful way.

Although future events can never be fully anticipated, one can minimize the unexpected by preparing for likely possibilities. Some relationship experiences can be anticipated—offending a partner, losing a trusted employee, being maligned, a change in the marketplace, and others. Understanding what is involved in this period can help prepare for many eventualities.

Anticipation of a problem does not take place in a vacuum; rather it is a function of what else is happening in the partnership's life space. It also depends on the likelihood that the problem will occur, its potential consequences, and the probability that something can be done to heighten or diminish the consequences depending on whether they are viewed as desirable or undesirable. If little or nothing can be done to cope with negative outcomes, then the evolving anxiety will likely be expressed in maladaptive behavior such as denying that the event will occur or developing disruptive anxiety. When that happens, a partner's capacity to function effectively will be significantly diminished by this preoccupation.

People approach an anticipated event in various ways: they ignore it; they deny that it will occur; they minimize the impact of its occurrence; they make preliminary and detailed preparations; or, in the extreme case, they become obsessed with preparation. Making such assessments involves both emotional and intellectual preparation for anticipating a potential relationship problem and the attendant assessment of how to cope with it. The emotional preparation includes what feelings the prospective problem arouses and whether those feelings will impede one's ability to handle other responsibilities. The intellectual process involves an evaluation of all the elements involved in determining what is likely to happen, what resources are needed to deal with it, and the perceived ability to do so. Also of concern is how severe the potential consequences are likely to be. What can be done to change or control the severity of the consequences, and what is the likelihood of accomplishing that?

One can facilitate the anticipatory process by using the mental rehearsal model proposed by Arnold Lazarus (1984). Success will depend on keeping one's anxiety at a level that does not interfere with the described analytical process. According to Lazarus, mental rehearsal requires the motivation and discipline to adequately rehearse coping strategies in preparation for forthcoming events. Among the benefits of successful rehearsal is skill in coping with the anticipated event at a level that approximates actual performance of the behavior.

This increases the probability of a successful outcome and in turn enhances one's self-confidence and one's ability to handle other problems. Each successful experience increases one's repertoire of resources. If the rehearsal is unsuccessful and the forthcoming event is significant, one's anxiety level will likely increase greatly, which will interfere with adaptation to the event.

When an Event Can Be Anticipated

There are a number of considerations that one can address that can help to better prepare for an anticipated event:

- *Does it matter whether the event occurs?* If it does matter, is any action indicated and by whom? Consider the situation of an entrepreneur who believes he should confront his partner about a decision he feels reflected poor judgment. He is concerned that avoiding the issue will undermine his trust in his partner. This leaves him focused on how and when to talk to him so that it will be constructive for both the relationship and the business.

- *What resources are needed to handle the forthcoming event—the confrontation—and are the resources available?* For this partner's confrontation to work, he will need to be sure of his facts and must be free of assumptions. He will need to present his concerns in a nonjudgmental fashion that focuses on issues and does not involve a personal attack. This anticipatory work should help him deal with anger so that it doesn't come out in a destructive way.

- *How would the forthcoming confrontation affect the partner relationship?*
  - *If the event is desired,* then addressing his concerns before they leak out and create other problems will help the partner keep his psychic energies focused on business matters. Paying prompt attention to his concerns will also bolster his self-confidence and build up the partnership rather than threaten it.
  - *If the event is undesired,* that is, if the partner has great doubts about confronting his counterpart with his concerns, he will find a way to rationalize not doing it. He might convince himself that his partner couldn't handle it and that it might lead to the breakup of their arrangement. He might also convince himself that the problem isn't such a big deal and that he will get over his anger. These are risky assumptions that in all likelihood will eventually backfire.

    The prospect of having to face an upcoming uncomfortable relationship problem such as confronting one's partner, having to go to court, or having to explain questionable projections to the bank can result in feeling impotent or refusing to do anything about the problem because of the anticipated discomfort in doing so. This often happens in a partnership when one partner knows he has to confront the other, as in the current example.
  - *Preparing for the confrontation.* The partner's recognition that he has to confront his partner leads him to outline a strategy for coping with the event. The process starts with the broad outline of how to proceed, followed by fine-tuning the details. Once he has formulated a satisfactory strategy for

confronting his partner, he shifts his attention to the details of how to best implement it. Mental rehearsal of what will be said and how difficult responses will be managed improves the chances of success in implementing his plans. This will help prevent mental blockage that sometimes occurs under stress.

When an Event Cannot Be Anticipated

There are a number of considerations that one can address that can help to better prepare for an event that cannot be anticipated:

- *The event is desired.* The occurrence of an event comes as a pleasant surprise, providing it does not negatively affect relationships or conflict with current or anticipated events. For example, a company that unexpectedly receives an achievement award from the government will be delighted by the honor and the benefits it will provide. The only consideration will be to anticipate the impact of this unexpected event. It could have the positive effect of increasing business, and in that case the company would have to prepare for the forthcoming event. There also may be concern about the partnership's ability to maintain its reputation if it should fail to properly conduct the anticipatory work.

- *The event is not desired.* An unexpected, unwelcome event, such as the sudden departure of two key employees who leave to set up their own business, will test the partnership's ability to face a sudden twist—in this case, to overcome the loss. Here, the partnership would need to do some damage control in replacing the employees, dealing with any negative impact on morale, and protecting its customer base.

Problems Associated with the Anticipation Period

Here are some pitfalls to be avoided in the anticipation phase:

Insufficient anticipation. Giving too little attention to anticipating potential problems in the partnership can unnecessarily stress the relationship. This problem can be avoided if each partner respects the other's values and issues.

Being overzealous. Being overzealous in anticipatory work unnecessarily drains resources and detracts attention from other issues. The partners run the risk of overemphasizing anticipatory work and thereby creating a new set of problems.

The potential for developing new problems increases when both partners are excessive or insufficient in the same direction. It is better for them to err in opposite directions and to gain perspective from one another's view.

When one is anxious about a problem, preparation for its occurrence can completely absorb one's energies. Overanticipation can seriously distract attention from current work responsibilities, thus creating other problems.

Partners differ in their approach to anticipation. Four differences in approach are noted here. (1) The partners *place different values on anticipatory work.* One partner may feel that too much energy is being expended on things that may not even happen and prefers to trust both partners' ability to deal with issues as the need arises. The other partner thinks that dealing in the moment leaves too much room for miscalculations. (2) The partners *agree in concept on giving attention to anticipatory work but disagree in how to implement the anticipatory work.* This can be resolved by one partner accepting responsibility to attend to the needed anticipatory work with consultation from the other partner. (3) The partners *differ in whether attending to anticipatory work interferes with other issues that need attention.* (4) The partners *differ as to the degree of anticipatory work that is warranted.* One partner may be satisfied with the anticipatory work in general, leaving the details to be ironed out as the need evolves, while the other partner may want to work out all the details ahead of time. The first partner potentially errs in too little preparation, and the other partner errs in the direction of too much. One way to resolve the difference is to include working out the details as part of the interested partner's responsibility. In that way, they agree on how much attention to devote to anticipatory work. The partner concerned with anticipatory work will make it his or her priority, and the other will not have to deal with something he or she doesn't value. If this arrangement doesn't work, they need to renegotiate their priorities regarding allocation of psychic energies.

THE ADAPTATION PHASE

The task in the adaptation phase, adjusting to launching the partnership, involves the partners' ability to receive information, assess it, and behave appropriately on an ongoing basis as the partnership and the business begin actual operation. Once the expected demands of launching the partnership occur, the anticipatory work of the partners is tested for the accuracy of its planning and their ability to adjust to unexpected events. For example, anticipatory planning may not take into account the amount of training employees will need or the number of people that should be hired to meet the needs of customers. Success occurs when the partnership is able to satisfactorily respond to an event in a manner consistent with its objectives. Adapting to an event is likely to be easier if the partners have had the opportunity to anticipate its occurrence.

Options in Coping with Adaptation

Adjusting, resisting, ignoring, or becoming immobilized are ways in which partners may respond to the need for adaptation.

Adjusting. The occurrence of a problem requires a strategy for coping with it that doesn't unduly interfere with attending to other responsibilities. Multiple demands on partners' attention require them to do a cost-benefit evaluation to determine which issues get priority and in what order. Partners' capacity will break down when too many demands overwhelm their resources.

Resisting. Resisting is a behavior that tries to prevent the event from happening or at least to minimize its negative impact. For example, partners might try to discourage a valued employee from leaving, while making alternative plans in case he does leave.

Ignoring. The option to ignore is utilized when the relationship issue or its consequences are of low priority or irrelevant. For example, the partners do not pay much attention to the departure of an employee when it has little to no impact.

Becoming immobilized. When partners become immobilized in their efforts to correct their problem, the ultimate result is a business divorce.

Example: Two partners had a successful business for many years. They had successfully weathered many storms. Their partnership was challenged when they were confronted with multiple crises at the same time: one of the partners developed a serious chronic illness, the other partner was going through a divorce, one key employee retired, another left for another job, and the business was faced with economic recession. The partners' diminished resources left them unable to cope with these multiple problems. They became immobilized, ultimately resulting in termination of the business and their partnership.

Adaptation is more challenging when anticipatory work does not occur. Without it one needs to obtain required information while having to deal with ongoing events. The following steps may be helpful:

- As quickly as possible after the onset of the event, determine what information is needed to set priorities.
- Establish priorities and the order in which they need to be addressed.
- Gather needed information and apply it.
- Periodically review progress and make appropriate adjustments.
- Avoid the temptation to react without adequate information.
- When it becomes necessary to take action without sufficient information, trust one's instincts. As soon as possible, evaluate and make appropriate adjustments.

Partner Differences in Dealing with Adaptation

Response Time in Coping with Change

Partners are likely to differ in the way they respond to new events, especially when they haven't prepared for them. The partner who tends to respond faster than his or her colleague will tend to have an advantage in managing the situation. This can become a problem if it becomes a competition for power.

Stress Tolerance

Having to cope with change will increase stress, especially when one is anticipating problems caused by the change. Under such conditions, it becomes tempting for partners to take their anxiety out on one another. People often release their pent-up anxiety in the presence of some established connection, as in a trusted family relationship or business partnership. The safety in these relationships will deteriorate if the expression of anxiety is not balanced by behaviors that enhance the relationship. Partners can minimize this problem when they agree on ways to manage it that will work for both of them. One possibility involves partners learning to vent their frustration on issues rather than on personal attack. That increases the probability of constructive action and avoids stressing the partnership relationship.

Being Defeated by Mistakes

Having to adapt to situations without preparation is likely to lead to mistakes. Self-confidence can easily suffer if mistakes are allowed to undermine faith in one's judgment. Partners can make the most of mistakes by learning to view them as an opportunity to learn rather than as a judgment about their competence. Partners can help each other maintain this positive perspective.

Endurance

The demands of change often exceed the emotional and physical tolerances of partners, who are likely to differ in their capacity to deal with either the emotional or physical aspects, or both. Partners can avoid this problem by being realistic about their tolerances without being judgmental about the differences between them. Good results occur when partners develop a strategy that takes into account their respective limits and differences.

THE MAINTENANCE PERIOD

To achieve a satisfactory operating state is the task partners face in the maintenance period. This period has two concurrent parts: (1) to ensure that the necessary resources are available to accomplish what is needed, such as maintaining high morale and quickly resolving any conflicts that may occur; and (2) to prevent disruptive influences or interpersonal conflicts from interfering with stabilizing the partnership relationship and the business operation. Once the partnership has achieved a modicum of stability in both aspects, it faces the challenge of maintaining its profitability.

Once partners have adapted to a new situation, they should work to stabilize the change in order to ensure a satisfactory level of continuing performance. This effort involves instituting the process and content needed for how the partnership will be conducted, as reflected in their business plan and partnership agreement.

As discussed earlier, partnerships are a product of a shared vision and the efforts to make that vision a reality (anticipation and adaptation). The partner relationship will be further tested once the venture enters the maintenance period. Getting a business up and running and keeping it running have different requirements. Partners are likely to find that they need to renegotiate the basis of their relationships as the needs of the business change—from the intensity of starting a new business to the less tumultuous and more routine experience of maintaining it.

The demands of business are always in flux; some fall within the range of the expected variations of doing business and some necessitate substantive changes. To be successful, a partnership must take care of both the normal variations and the unusual and unexpected ones, which may involve major adjustments and innovations.

Successful businesses tend to start simply and with success grow increasingly complex. Companies therefore get involved with repeated cycles of anticipation, adaptation, and maintenance as new situations evolve. That can place heavy physical and emotional demands on the partnership, which can strain any partnership relationship unless the partners are realistic in building the capacity to deal with the stress of various demands.

Problems in the Maintenance Period

Many events may disrupt a partnership's transition to a maintenance period, including relationship problems and business-related problems. Relationship problems include

- disagreements over how to manage transition to the maintenance period;
- differences in goals resulting from the adaptation period;
- difficulty adjusting to needed changes in the division of labor as the partnership enters the maintenance period; and
- partners having different levels of interest in adjusting to new situations versus ongoing management situations.

Business-related problems include

- differences in how partners want to deal with the hiring and management of personnel;

- differences in the partners' perception of the need to change the mission, goals, or priorities resulting from experience in the adaptation period;
- differences in how partners wish to define personnel practices; and
- problems in personnel practices—changes in benefits, performance reviews, and salary increases will create tension with management and negatively impact morale, and other changes may raise job-security issues, depending on the context in which they are presented.

Avoiding or resolving such problems will be a test of whether the partners favor reaching consensus or pursuing individual priorities.

THE TERMINATION PERIOD

Experiences end by accident or design—the goal is to terminate the experience in a constructive manner that respects how the event affects the people involved. The ending of the business partnership is always dramatic, marking the end of a vision. The partners must cope with the lost vision and all of the consequences that go with that—financial losses, tarnished reputations, and lost and conflicted relationships.

Termination marks the end of a partnership; it has its own set of consequences and feelings. The consequences of termination in general range from the inconsequential to the heartrending: from the lingering calm of a just-finished cigarette to the end of a beautiful sunset to the loss of a job to the death of a loved one. Termination may signal a temporary or a permanent loss; the person may or may not have a choice in experiencing the change. It may seem odd to view the end of a negative experience as a loss. But, for example, a person may be happy to be released from prison but mourn the loss of friendships he had there. Partners may be happy to be out of a troubled partnership but mourn the loss of good feelings they had when they began the partnership. The significance of the loss is a function of several things: whether it was voluntary, its severity, one's ability to cope with it, and how severely one misses the comfort of dealing with familiar circumstances.

By recounting memories of the loss and one's feelings pertaining to the experience, one tries to adjust to absence, feelings that result from the change, judgments about why the change resulted, and who has responsibility for the loss occurring. Termination does not usually end when the physical experience ends but when one finds emotional closure. However, it may end immediately if the event no longer has emotional significance. In reality, it can take any length of time, and in some situations it never ends. One sometimes hears that a person dies of a broken heart after the death of a beloved spouse. Likewise, a partner who loses his or her business may never get over the loss.

Rituals can help one adjust to significant losses. Christians hold wakes and Jews sit shiva (a formal mourning period followed by entertainment restrictions for a defined period after burial). Rituals mark other kinds of passages as well. Retirement parties mark the end of a career, just as graduation signals the end of college and facing the reality of adulthood.

The intensity and difficulty one encounters in dealing with the termination period depend on whether it occurs through choice or accident and whether it is anticipated. Mourning that results from choice, such as resigning from a job, carries the positive feeling of having had control over the event. That facilitates adjustment to a loss, even when the choice was an ambivalent or undesirable one.

Unexpected loss is generally the most debilitating and can be totally disruptive in all aspects of the life space. Being fired from a desired job for cause could have many ramifications: embarrassment among colleagues, friends, and family; problems getting a reference; and the need to look for a new job. Similar experiences can result from a bankruptcy, which has the additional problem of affecting one's business life and credit standing for a number of years.

When a loss can be anticipated, one can prepare for the event and thus experience a less painful adjustment. Partners who recognize that their business is likely to fail can take actions that will minimize the loss. A fired employee has an easier time handling the loss when he knows that his performance was deficient; he therefore has time to anticipate how to deal with the loss.

Adjustment to the loss of a partnership is more difficult when one has uncertainty about the future. That might occur when there is a question about whether a new partner can be found. Adjustment will also be difficult when one has doubts about being able to replace lost income or when the ending of the partnership means the loss of meaningful relationships one considers irreplaceable.

A number of considerations affect a person's ability to cope with the termination of a partnership:

- *Permanence of the loss.* A long-standing partnership with a considerable positive history is likely to leave a large emotional vacuum in a partner's life. The loss will be greater if the termination occurs at a time when the personal relationship is positive. The loss might be felt keenly even when the parting is not so amicable, bringing to an end a lifestyle that has dominated a large part of a person's life.

- *Speed of onset.* As noted earlier, losses that develop gradually provide an opportunity to anticipate how to adjust to them. It becomes much easier for partners to live with bankruptcy when the process evolves over a period of time than when it happens suddenly. A partnership that deteriorates gradually is easier to deal with than one in which one's partner announces, quite unexpectedly, that he or she wants to end the partnership.

- *Ambiguity of the loss.* Loss experiences are not always clearly defined. A person may believe that his or her reputation has been tarnished but be unclear about how or to what extent it occurred, or a partner may have the feeling that something has changed in his or her relationship with another partner but not know quite what it is.

- *Centrality of the loss.* The more a loss is confined to one segment of a partner's experience, the less impact it is likely to have. The death or significant health problem of one's partner will have far more impact than the loss of an employee.

- *Severity of the loss.* Reaction to a loss is affected by how deeply it is felt. The impact of losing a partner with whom one has had a close and long-standing relationship may be much like that of losing a spouse.

  Another dimension of severity is the length of time one is exposed to a loss. An entrepreneur will have greater difficulty dealing with the mourning the longer it takes him or her to find a replacement.

  A partner's diminished capacity to perform his or her job also contributes to the severity of the loss. The other partner will have to struggle between loyalty to his or her partner and significant financial consequences.

  For many people, aging or a decrease in physical capabilities becomes a significant loss because their identity depends on having a youthful appearance and abilities. Thus, the partner who could work 13-hour workdays and enjoy it is depressed when she finds that an 8-hour day saps her energy.

- *Meaning attached to the loss.* Many people attach symbolic meaning to things or events that may be routine to other people. For some people, their identity is intertwined with their feelings of self-worth. Losing a job or a business can feel like losing their identity.

- *Context in which the loss is experienced.* One's reaction to a loss is affected by the context in which it occurs. Often a given loss experienced under one set of conditions will be experienced differently under another set. A partner whose partnership fails will experience the loss differently if he or she is not able to find a needed replacement.

Example: Alex and John had a rocky time during most of their 10-year partnership in a box-manufacturing business and so considered terminating the partnership on several occasions. They never did so because it seemed easier to put up with their periodic struggle than to go through the stress of dissolving the partnership. The end finally came when Alex decided he had had enough of the box business. John vowed that he would give up the business before he would consider getting another partner.

The way a person views the consequences of a loss forms the context for how he or she relates to it. If a loss is viewed as irretrievable and its occurrence is devastating to one's lifestyle, self-worth, or the survival of the partnership, then it is seen as a traumatic event. This in turn is likely to interfere with functioning in other areas, which only adds to the impact of the loss. If one sees the loss as more manageable, it leads only to temporary disruptions and disappointments.

The entrepreneur who views the failure of his or her business partnership as conclusive evidence that he or she could not handle a partnership will view the loss as devastating. The result could have a major impact on how the person relates to his or her family, perhaps precipitating relationship problems that might ultimately threaten his or her marriage. Some people turn to suicide when they suffer a loss that is too hard too bear. Others may view the same experience quite differently, seeing it merely as a learning experience, however disappointing.

Coping with Losses

Partners overcome losses in a number ways, including the following:

- *Opportunity.* Being mired in a difficult partnership requires all of one's energies between efforts to keep it afloat or figuring out how to terminate it with the least amount of damage. Once the partnership has ended these energies can be applied to considering new opportunities. The ease with which new possibilities are identified and achieved will have a major impact on how loss of the partnership is experienced.

- *Receiving and giving support.* Emotional support is critical in overcoming a loss. Supporting one another after a loss is essential for the health of the relationship. A loss may be of a personal or professional nature. One partner's failure to gain a much-needed contract would be very disconcerting on both a personal level and a business level.

- *Preserving confidence.* Confidence fuels the energy needed to take the risks that may lead to success. One gains self-confidence by learning from past experiences, including losses. Such losses must therefore be viewed in a balanced way, paying as much attention to what went right as to what went wrong. This will afford the partners confidence and optimism that they will not repeat the same mistakes.

- *Regaining analytical ability.* Analytical ability is essential in discriminating between what works and what doesn't. After suffering a loss, people need time to mourn before they can regain this ability. Partners should not judge their analytical competence during the mourning period because the loss often causes things to appear distorted.

- *Preserving physical capacity.* Partners can easily ignore their physical limitations under the pressure of a start-up or a crisis. Pushing the limits of physical exertion increases the chances that partners will turn on one another. Sometimes attending to physical needs should take precedence even at the risk of having a negative impact on the business. Pressing beyond one's limits may resolve an immediate crisis but result in a more serious problem if the resulting illness requires an extended absence from the business. That would put added pressure on the other partner, who could become ill him- or herself or resent the first partner for not attending to his or her health.

- *Preserving one's vision.* Vision is the lifeblood of entrepreneurial life. Coping with a failed vision can be devastating, depending on its degree of significant financial, emotional, and physical impact. It becomes more devastating when it destroys self-confidence and has long-term impact. Partners are challenged to keep their perspective and learn from their mistakes; the task becomes more difficult if their despair feeds off one another.

- *Retaining one's ethics.* Ethics serve as the moral compass for partners, keeping them focused on how to behave in pursuit of their vision. When they sacrifice ethics for a momentary gain, they may well lose the trust of those who depend on them. Once trust has been lost, there is no quick way to recover it. Ultimately, the price the entrepreneur pays is the lost support needed for success of his or her venture. It becomes easy for partners to take their frustrations out on one another, unnecessarily creating a new problem and making the task of regaining trust all the more difficult.
- *Coping with mixed feelings.* Loss may be experienced in a positive or negative light, or both. Positive feelings occur when negative experiences end; a loss may also have positive consequences.

  Many situations involve both feelings. A partner may be happy to end a conflicted partnership but may then have to assume the added responsibility carried by his or her partner. Or consider the entrepreneur who loses a valuable employee who has a difficult personality. The entrepreneur will miss the employee's valued contributions but will be happy not to have to deal with him or her. The overriding experience of a loss is determined by the balance between the positive and negative resultant feelings. The loss experience is more complicated when the two contrasting feelings are approximately equal. In that situation, the depth of the loss will depend on whether positive or negative feelings are dominant at the moment.
- *Coping with a history of loss.* A person who has survived many losses over his or her lifetime is likely to handle a new loss more successfully than a person who has had little such experience. Failure to come to terms with prior losses can exacerbate one's reaction to a new one, with the additional complication that one cannot determine how much of the current reaction is due to the present situation and how much is due to the memory of a previous loss. The accumulation of too many losses, resolved or unresolved, without sufficient counterbalancing experiences, can seriously damage one's self-confidence and may discourage one from investing in another relationship. As a result, a partner with a history of painful losses may decide to work alone and to have only formal and minimal dealings with others. That becomes his or her way of protecting him- or herself from further losses. An entrepreneur considering a partnership would do well to consider the loss history of a prospective partner.
- *Coping with a combination of losses.* When multiple losses occur so quickly that there is too little time to adjust, the effect may become overwhelming, leading to diminished capacity or even immobilization. Additional losses may ensue in a domino effect. Partners have an advantage over individual entrepreneurs because they are there to help each other mobilize the needed perspective to prevent existing losses from leading to other losses.

The Mourning Process

The mourning process associated with death provides useful insights into how partners can handle major losses. The traditional mourning process serves three functions: it shows respect for the deceased, it provides an outlet for feelings of loss, and it marks a transition to a replacement of the loss.

Kubler-Ross's (1979) well-known articulation of the stages a person experiences when faced with impending death—shock, denial and isolation, then anger, bargaining, depression, and finally, acceptance—has its business counterpart. The person experiencing the loss of a significant business relationship also experiences these stages.

That person feels shock when the loss is unexpected, as in the case of an unanticipated firing. Denial may follow as a defense against the resulting loss. Once the denial wears off, the person may express anger at the cause of the loss. The person will feel guilt to the extent that he or she takes responsibility for contributing to the loss in some way. An employer may feel guilty about an employee's physical breakdown, wondering whether the pressure she put on her employee in the preceding months to meet a product deadline was a contributing factor.

Sadness may lead to depression as the full impact of the loss is experienced. As the person adapts to the reality of the loss, his or her attention gradually turns to acceptance, and from this resignation emerges the realization of how to cope with the resulting changes. This process is facilitated once the mourner is able to develop ways to deal with the loss.

Understanding the mourning process can help partners deal with losses and aid one another. One partner may be going through a personal loss or may be having more difficulty dealing with a business loss than the other partner. A troubled partner who seems overly angry at a loss may be reacting more to the emotional impact than to the material assessment of his or her loss. Recognition of that by the other partner can help the partner in mourning and avoid a conflict that would likely occur if the partner's comments were taken at face value.

A number of factors affect the success of the mourning process:

- *Centrality of the loss to the entrepreneur.* The more a person is affected by the loss experience, the greater will be the difficulty in managing the mourning process.

- *Familiar versus the unknown.* A loss involves the end of something familiar. One is better able to adjust to the loss when other familiar experiences can replace what has been lost. Fear of whether replacement is possible may delay the progression of mourning, and partners may view bankruptcy as the ultimate disaster.

- *Risk of further losses.* After suffering a significant loss, partners may not want to become vulnerable again and risk yet another loss. Accepting replacement for what has been lost occurs once an adjustment has been made to accepting the reality of the loss.

- *Inability to accept a loss.* The length of the mourning period varies according to how much the loss has meant and the availability of a replacement. As noted earlier, in extreme cases, the mourning process may never end.

- *Reminders of losses.* After the period of acute mourning has ended, people may re-experience the loss through reminders of it. People who have died are often remembered on special occasions such as holidays, birthdays, weddings, anniversaries, and graduations or at other events where the absence of the deceased person's presence is felt. Such occasions are not limited to deaths. Similar feelings can occur regarding a business loss. In a partnership relationship, special occasions include anniversaries of the partnership's beginning, of going public, and of grossing its first million. Each anniversary may be a reminder of the loss(es).

- *Ability to replace what has been lost.* Marking the anniversary becomes less intense over time, depending on its meaning and the time it takes to find a replacement for what has been lost.

A person in mourning usually shares the experience with others or goes through the process with the help of a supportive environment. A significant loss is likely to affect one's functioning in other areas of life as well. Too many losses experienced at the same time can overload one's emotional system and impair one's ability to deal with any of them. The problem gets worse when a new loss situation triggers memories of past losses.

There are some added considerations in coping with mourning when a partnership is involved in mourning a shared loss and there is little or no ability for partners to support one another in their grieving. Under such circumstances, the mourning is complicated by one partner's grief only intensifying the experience of the other.

Problems in the Termination Period

A person is likely to resist the termination phase of transition when no viable alternative is available. The inability to find a replacement for something that has been lost can lead to chronic impairment and preoccupation with the loss. A partner may also have difficulty dealing with a lost partnership when he or she had little in life other than work.

Termination will be even more difficult if the stress of it compromises one's ability to communicate. It will also be difficult if one partner sees the flawed performance of the other partner as responsible for the termination.

An event can be said to have two levels of meaning: the literal meaning of a given event and what the given event symbolizes. The ending of a partnership is an example. The relationship has literally come to an end, and the partners attach positive or negative significance to it. A failed partnership can be experienced as failure and incompetence. Holding that view could have a profound impact on a partner's ability to approach any future effort.

THE INTEGRATION PERIOD

The goal in the integration period is to apply learning gained from experience to future ventures. People who don't take the time to learn from their experience run a greater probability of repeating the same mistakes in future ventures.

Ideally, the learning gained from the other phases of transition—anticipation, adaptation, maintenance, and termination—is reinforced during the integration period, but contrary to common wisdom, people do not always automatically learn from their experiences. For new learning to become part of a person's way of thinking and acting, the new behavior must be sufficiently practiced to become automatic. Just as some people repeat the same mistakes in relationships or marriages, so some entrepreneurs go from one failed venture to another, repeating the same errors. A partner would be wise to evaluate what he or she has learned and how to incorporate it into daily practice until the new learning becomes integrated into his or her life. To do otherwise is to invite repetition of past mistakes. One approach to integration is based on the idea that redundancy helps new learning become automatic behavior. Here are the steps that will facilitate integration:

1. Schedule time each day to review the day's new learning. This would include new insights and what can be learned from mistakes.

2. Summarize the learning on a weekly or monthly basis.

3. On a semiannual basis, review the accumulated learning, showing how it applies to a company's mission. (This review will concern application of general principles gained from the more detailed reviews.)

4. Design a specific program for the integration of learning that fits the unique needs of the business.

The reviews should be written down to facilitate periodic review. The cumulative impact of the reviews will ensure that learning derived from past experiences will not be lost. In addition, the partners will benefit from the process being joint as well as individual. Each partner is likely to take different things from the experience, depending on individual needs.

REFERENCES

Kubler-Ross, E. (1979). *On death and dying.* New York: Macmillan.

Lazarus, A. (1984). *In the mind's eye: The power of imagery for personal enrichment.* New York: Guilford Press.

CHAPTER 15

Managing External Relationships

Businesses periodically need the services of outside agents, such as accountants, lawyers, or other consultants who deal with finance, human resources, compensation and benefits management, insurance, public relations, and organizational issues. The combination of consultants needed varies from business to business.

The word *consultant* is a familiar one, but it means different things to different people. Generally, this agent can be described as a person with expertise in a particular area who is usually an independent contractor. He or she may be involved on a full-time, part-time, or as-needed basis, and he or she may or may not have formal authority. In recent years, consultants have been used in line positions. This arrangement suits the employer because it does not involve payment of benefits and carries no long-term commitment to employment. It suits the consultant because it allows him or her to have greater control of his or her work. The consultant's responsibilities may range from making recommendations to assuming line authority and responsibilities.

Businesses use consultants (1) to provide skills that are not found within the permanent workforce, (2) to oversee a special project that requires unusual security and limited exposure of sensitive material to employees, or (3) to evaluate the operation of a project or department or provide an independent assessment of a work product. Such a consultant can give feedback without fear of retaliation and without the bias of protecting a special interest.

Consultants are hired through referrals from colleagues, headhunters, professional organizations, professional schools at universities, and retirees, and through ads in newspapers and professional journals. Consultants, like most employees, are ultimately chosen on the basis of their resumes, recommendations, interviews, and past demonstrations of competence.

The resume of a prospective consultant should indicate (1) the applicant's range of experience, which may be either directly or indirectly relevant to the needed task, and (2) experience in doing the kind of task needed, not only with regard to the content of the work but also to the kind of work relationships involved. A consultant may have a lot of experience working on solo projects but limited experience working with others or in certain kinds of environments. How a person fits into a particular environment can be as important as the content of the work.

Another consideration in the hiring process is the length of the project for which the consultant is being considered. Some people do better with short-term projects, and others prefer longer ones. Finally, the consultant should account for time, employment gaps, or experiences that the resume omits or minimizes. Unsatisfactory experiences often do not appear or are not explained clearly on the resume.

Recommendations from previous clients can be helpful if they provide a balanced view of the candidate. The only way to determine a true picture of that balance is through conversations with previous clients. Given the current litigious climate in the United States, people are very cautious about what they put in writing. Conversations can produce nonverbal cues about what was written. A consultant's excellence will be reflected in the recommender's tone of voice, enthusiasm or lack of it, overcautious demeanor, and freedom with which he or she offers comments. Guarded and restricted comments may suggest limited satisfaction.

The nature of the recommender's relationship with the consultant can also be gleaned through such conversations. Whether the recommender had firsthand experience or whether his or her views are based on the report of others will soon be apparent, as will the degree to which the relationship was solely professional or personal. A recommendation that comes from a friend will of course need to be evaluated for bias. A talk with the interviewee should also indicate whether the applicant has strengths in the needed areas. It is quite possible to get a glowing recommendation that may not be related to needed skills. Speaking to the recommender may reveal relevant information that was not reflected in the written recommendation or resume. Conversations are a more likely venue to learn about limitations or problems than written communication. Clues can be gained from the recommender's explicit statements and qualifying comments or from his or her explaining why a situation was problematic.

A minimum of three candidates should be selected for interviewing; this will give a good basis for comparison. Interviews are the only way an employer can determine whether there is suitable "chemistry" or a good match in the working relationship. Specifically, the interviews should explore how the consultant's work style would fit with the people with whom he or she would be working and the company's culture. They should also determine the interviewee's ability to communicate, especially if he or she would be working with others or would be involved in instructing others. Being an instructor mandates more than technical experience; it also requires patience, organization, respect and sensitivity for different levels of capability, an understanding of how people learn, supportiveness, and the ability to establish a good balance between presenting concepts and concrete examples. A combination of individual and group interviews by several people is an effective way to gain needed information. The group interview provides an opportunity to see how the candidate handles the added stress and how different interviewers assess the same behavior.

An interview conducted by a single interviewer is useful in the initial screening as a means of reviewing background and filling in any gaps, screening for personality compatibility with the company, determining whether proceeding further is warranted, and providing an opportunity for more in-depth interviewing for the person with whom the interviewee would be working. Such individual interviews may also be needed since information gained in that format provides a better sense of how the person communicates on a one-to-one basis. Partners may find it useful to interview separately in order to provide a better two-dimensional perspective than if they did it together.

Group interviewing is an economical way to have multiple people participate in the interview process. It gives perspective on how the interviewee deals with the pressure of a group interview; it avoids the possibility of the interviewee giving different messages to different people; and it provides a common base of information for a group evaluation of the candidate. The consultant should be asked how he or she would handle certain situations. It is best to include both substantive and relationship issues, as well as circumstances that might interfere with the consultant's work.

In addition to interviews, the prospective consultant should be given an opportunity to demonstrate his or her competence, either by giving a lecture or working with a staff member for a brief period of time. Once the prospective consultant's expertise and skills have been established and recommendations have been checked, the final decision should be made, with major weight given to the opinion of the person with whom the consultant will be working. This increases the benefit to be gained from the consultation.

The company should provide the consultant it chooses with a written contract or letter of agreement that states the objective to be accomplished in behavioral terms, including standards for assessing performance; whether a written report is required, in what form, and when due; the time frame for delivery of services and whether any penalties are to be imposed for not meeting defined objectives; the amount of compensation and when it will be paid; any confidentiality requirements; the conditions under which either party may terminate the agreement; and any other conditions deemed necessary by either the company or the consultant.

The consultant should be given the opportunity to refine the objective and method for accomplishing his or her assignment, thereby maximizing the benefit the company will derive from the consultant's expertise and creativity. In addition, consideration should be given to whether more will be gained by giving the consultant current thinking before he or she does the work or letting the consultant do the work before sharing any current thinking. These approaches have both pros and cons. Providing the thinking ahead of time has the advantage that the consultant will not go over ground that has already been covered. The disadvantage is that it may bias the consultant's approach to the problem. Getting a fresh perspective may be one reason for the consultation. Revealing the company's current thinking after the consultant presents his or her views provides a better chance of getting a fresh perspective. The disadvantage is that work already done may be repeated; however, on the positive side, it may affirm the work already done.

Potential benefits from the consultation can be lost if the focus is limited to getting a particular project accomplished. The greater benefit from a consultation may come from understanding the thought process that went into the project rather than from the outcome itself. Gaining the benefit of the thought process can be accomplished by building into the consultation agreement a means of gaining that information—for example, through demonstrations, lectures, or seminars or by having relevant people work with the consultant. The company should emphasize that the consultant is to provide the basis of his or her thinking.

CONSULTANT SERVICES

When consultants are called in because of an uncertain situation or a perceived inadequacy in a company, it is easy to give them more power than may be good for the business. The consultants may collude in this process when it serves their own needs, even when they recognize it may not be in the business's best interests. A good consultant is therefore one who doesn't accept more power than is needed. Entrepreneurs must remember that they will have to live with the results of any consultation, so they should not accept any advice that doesn't make sense to them. They should be extremely wary of the consultant who responds to questions with "Trust me" or with demeaning comments such as "This is too complicated to explain" in place of valid explanations. Always remember that the consultant works for the entrepreneur, and not the other way around.

In soliciting a consultant, an entrepreneur should be aware that it is cost-effective to engage one who is familiar with a business similar to that of the entrepreneur. Otherwise, the entrepreneur will have to pay to educate the consultant in his or her business. It is prudent to select a consultant with whom the chemistry feels right for the entrepreneur. One should therefore speak with two or three consultants to guarantee the best fit possible. This exploratory process should include a discussion of what the consultant and the entrepreneur expect of each other. Finally, it is essential to check out the prospective consultant's reputation, background, and experience. Getting recommendations will simplify the process.

Accountants

Accountants' services are necessary to comply with the complexities of state and federal requirements and tax laws. Companies that are too small to have in-house accountants use bookkeepers, who provide day-to-day financial information and prepare information for the accountant. Businesses that have loans from banks are most likely to need the services of these consultants.

Accountants design and provide broad financial services, including assisting new businesses in establishing systems for managing their finances, providing regular and as-needed financial statements, conducting audits as needed, consulting on the merits of purchases and investments, consulting on tax matters, and preparing tax returns. Frequently, they are given power of attorney in businesses that are undergoing a tax audit. Periodically, accountants and lawyers work together on tax questions and examine the merit of purchases and investments.

Accountants tend to be conservative and to emphasize caution. They help entrepreneurs understand available options and the financial consequences of proposals so that entrepreneurs can decide how much risk is tolerable.

Lawyers

Lawyers provide formal documents such as agreements, contracts, partnership agreements, articles of incorporation, bylaws, and other documents necessary to give an organization its legal definition. They consult on tax-related issues and represent companies in dealings with the IRS; initiate legal action on behalf of their client or defend against actions brought against the business; serve as mediators in disputes between partners; provide legal services related to the sale and purchase of real estate and other entities; assist businesses in relationships with banks concerned with loans and legal issues; consult on patent, copyright, and other intellectual property matters; consult on matters related to filing or avoiding bankruptcy; assist in the dissolution of businesses; consult on the general boundaries of legal behavior; and consult on labor-related issues.

The lawyer is the legal counterpart of the accountant. When entrepreneurs select an attorney, they base their choice on the kind of legal needs they anticipate. That determines whether they will opt for a firm that can handle any conceivable need or whether a small firm will be sufficient. When a partnership engages a large law firm, the partners will probably be serviced by an associate under the supervision of a senior partner unless the partnership is a high-profile client. As a result, the partners are less likely to have a personal relationship with the senior partner. In contrast, a more personal relationship is likely when dealing with smaller firms, as is the chance that the partnership's work will be done by a partner.

The attorney's usefulness depends on whether the partnership fully discloses information regarding any action in which he or she may become involved. Withholding information because of embarrassment or fear of judgment will likely create more serious problems than it will avoid.

Financial Consultants

Businesses periodically need to consult about how to finance or refinance the business, and for that service they hire a financial consultant, whose services overlap those provided by accountants and lawyers. Financial consultants may also be useful in raising investment capital for business expansion, for new product development, or for acquisitions or mergers. They provide a more unique service than raising capital: they broker loans, mergers, purchases, and sales of businesses or property, and they consult on restructuring a company.

A partnership should hire a financial consultant through a process similar to the one described for selecting accountants and lawyers, taking into account reputation, experience, familiarity with the entrepreneurs' area of need, and comfort level in the relationship.

Human Resources Consultants

A human resources consultant provides services on matters relating to personnel recruitment and management, specifically establishing recruitment, hiring, and firing policies and procedures; defining personnel practices and policies; managing problem situations; complying with federal and state laws regarding personnel matters; handling environmental

issues; establishing grievance procedures; formulating compensation policies; and defining policies and procedures for performance reviews.

A human resources consultant is very helpful in dealing with start-up
planning and should be retained until the business gets large enough to
warrant an in-house employee. Investment in this consultation from the
beginning helps the entrepreneur avoid problems that can become costly.

Compensation and Benefits Management Consultants

Entrepreneurs compensate themselves and their employees through a
combination of salary, benefits, perks, and bonuses. The kind of benefits
package they choose for their employees is an important business consideration. Consultants in this area have the expertise to help a company
determine the benefits that will best suit its needs and financial capability;
particularly relevant are pension plans. Establishing compensation guidelines is especially helpful when competition with other companies is a
consideration. These consultant services include designing and implementing compensation and benefits programs, monitoring programs for
modifications, providing actuarial information as needed, and distributing information on standards in the marketplace.

A business needs such consultation when it becomes sufficiently established to require attention to developing a sound compensation and benefits program. The nature of the program will depend on the kind of culture
the company wishes to define for its employees. The selection of a consultant should be compatible with this point of view.

Insurance Consultants

Insurance consultants provide information on how a company may
protect itself from financial disasters. Such consultants should not be the
same persons who sell the insurance unless that will not compromise the
business's best interest. Businesses have a variety of insurance needs,
some of which are mandatory and others voluntary. Workmen's compensation insurance, for example, is required of all businesses. Other examples of insurance are the banks' requirement of insurance to protect their
loans and the insurance of business owners to protect themselves from fire
or property damage and liability for accidents on their premises. Insurance also protects companies from theft or embezzlement by employees
who have access to finances. Often, the business insures principals and
critical employees as protection against their death or disability. In addition, a common insurance benefit package today may include some combination of medical, dental, life, and disability insurance. In the current
climate of cost reduction, consultants have devised various ways to help
companies reduce or limit such coverage, such as the following:

- Helping companies determine what insurance is needed and in what amounts. This includes making recommendations on defining levels of deductibles.
- Assisting in finding the best carriers. Entrepreneurs must make sure this doesn't involve some form of kickback to the consultant. Getting the names of more than one possible carrier sometimes helps deal with that possibility.
- Advising companies of changes or developments in the insurance industry. This might involve changing companies or the type of insurance selected, as well as changes in laws that might have an impact on insurance.
- Periodically reviewing a company's insurance program to ensure that it continues to meet company objectives.

The insurance consultant should be flexible enough to adapt insurance coverage to the business's changing needs. Such a consultant should view his or her relationship to a firm over the long term, recommending increases or decreases in coverage depending on the business's needs and educating his or her client about how to use insurance, rather than just being willing to sell it.

Marketing Consultants

Marketing consultants provide an outside perspective on the company's marketing program, assist the house marketing staff in developing new markets or marketing strategies, and participate in hiring marketing personnel. They are especially helpful in the early stages of start-up and at points along the way when in-house capabilities are inadequate or special projects have to be launched.

Public Relations Consultants

Public relations consultants help a company develop its best image and present it to the outside world. They also help recruit and hire public relations personnel, recommend and assist in the preparation of materials, prepare press releases and press conferences, make presentations on the company's behalf, lobby for the company, and act as spokesperson for the company. The company that can present itself in a unique and creative way has a better prospect for success. The public relations consultant must be personable, effective in communication in both written and oral media, and creative.

Organizational Consultants

Organizational consultants generally consult for companies in more than one capacity. These consultants may carry the same label, but they can perform distinctly different services. As a result, a company may find it has a need for more than one type of consultant. Consultants provide services in the following areas:

- *Organizational development and structure.* Changing business conditions or a decrease in profits can lead management to change the company's organization and structure. An organizational consultant with an outside perspective and no vested interest in the company may help facilitate this process.

- *Management practices.* A change in organizational structure is likely to be accompanied by modifications in managing skills to meet changing needs and objectives. Executives may seek help in changing their management style; specifically, they may change the way decisions are made, modify job descriptions, develop new positions, or eliminate others.

- *Personnel issues.* A company may need help with personnel-related issues, especially morale problems, conflict-management skills, stress reduction, incentives for performance, and team building.

- *Strategic and tactical planning.* A company's long-term success may depend on its ability to balance the needs of its day-to-day operation with those of strategic and tactical planning. Getting an outside perspective may sometimes be helpful in this regard, especially when areas of special expertise are needed.

Organizational consultants are generally in contact with many people in the company. They should therefore understand the culture of the company, be sensitive to issues of confidentiality, and possess good communication skills.

RELATIONSHIP TO CUSTOMERS

Customers should be seen first as people who can be persuaded to buy as much of the entrepreneur's product as possible. The idea is to maximize sales without regard to whether the customer needs the product. The salesperson does not take into account how this approach to selling affects the customer. Second, customers are those who can benefit from one's product, and in this way the salesperson is one who helps the customer fill an unmet need. Third, customers are potential partners; the customer and salesperson work as a partnership, with the salesperson's product solving the customer's problem. Fourth, customers contribute to the success of the business; the business therefore places value on having good relationships with customers in the long term.

These views are not mutually exclusive. Basically, the salesperson should recognize that he or she is there to be of service to the customer in one form or another. The customer is not there to take care of the salesperson. The customer's needs and those of the business are not mutually exclusive. When the relationship to the customer is handled properly, the needs of both will be met. The prospect of developing a long-term relationship with a customer will be enhanced when he or she experiences that the sales person attends to his or her needs even when it results in a smaller sale than might have been otherwise possible.

PROFESSIONAL ORGANIZATIONS

There are two categories of membership in professional organizations. One involves membership in organizations in the entrepreneur's own field and can help him or her establish connections. This membership also serves a continuing education function, enabling an executive to keep up with development in his or her field as well as recruit new partners or employees.

The other category is membership in organizations related to the company's business; such membership is very useful in establishing visibility in the community. Such organizations include chambers of commerce, the American Business Association, and specialty organizations relevant to the entrepreneur's business. These memberships can help build goodwill for the company and produce new business.

COMMUNITY RESOURCES

A company is part of a community, and the entrepreneur can relate to the community in either a compatible or an antagonistic manner. Choosing the compatible route will create a good environment. For example, the company can show concern about how its business may affect the community by instituting policies regarding noise, traffic, or air quality. In turn, the community will be motivated to be supportive of its neighbor.

In contrast, taking the antagonistic route invites an adversarial response by the community, drains resources from the company, and creates ill will instead of goodwill. Not surprisingly, when such a business makes expansion plans that require community approval, the community may respond with delays and resistance.

COMPETITORS

Although competitors are adversaries, they are also resources; that is, competitors can learn from one another and at times even cooperate in ventures of common interest. For example, a number of competitors involved in manufacturing machine parts were upset at the Occupational Safety and Health Administration (OSHA) for imposing safety and health requirements they felt were excessive. By banding together in a group, the manufacturers were able to negotiate modification of these standards. In addition, competitors routinely learn from one another at trade shows and meetings; these meetings afford them the opportunity to demonstrate their competence without divulging proprietary information.

PRO BONO INVOLVEMENT

For many companies, pro bono contributions to community efforts, organizations, or other causes serve as an investment that at the very least creates goodwill. Many companies view such investments as marketing. Lawyers have elevated this to an art form. They serve in organizations and community projects, knowing that the personal contact will pay off when people need a lawyer. Indeed, they know that it is much easier to turn to a known entity than to the yellow pages. The same applies to businesses that donate their product; familiarity with a product leads to increased sales.

RELATIONSHIP TO BANKS

Traditionally banks are leery of supporting new, unproven ventures. Therefore, a company's best chance for bank support is to craft its proposal and application very carefully, taking into account how the bank evaluates applications. The bank's primary objective is to make money, which it accomplishes by making loans to low-risk ventures. The challenge to the aspiring entrepreneur is to demonstrate why his or her company is not a high risk for the bank; he or she can do so in the following ways:

- *Pay attention to surface credibility.* By surface credibility is meant one's physical appearance, radiation of self-confidence, and manner of speaking. Dressing in conservative attire suggests to bankers that you are part of the community and understand what is expected. Uncertainty or hesitation in presenting the application suggests self-doubt, which feeds their doubt. Communicating self-confidence and speaking in a language familiar to bankers will encourage their attention.

- *Prepare a solid business plan.* Surface credibility will get you in the door, but a solid business plan will get you the loan. All elements of a business should be thought through in detail; you must provide as much backup data as possible to support the assumptions that are being made. The most difficult area to deal with is the projection of income, which will receive close scrutiny. Bankers are very aware that projections can represent more hope than realistic likelihood. Therefore, the more the projections can be substantiated, the better; it will add to the banker's confidence that the entrepreneur is a good risk.

- *Supply letters of recommendation.* Although letters will not make up for a problematic business plan, they can help materially in borderline situations. Recommendations have greater impact when they come from influential people or from people who have personal relationships to the bank.

Getting the loan is only the first step. Maintaining credibility with the bank is an ongoing process. Bankers don't like to be surprised. The relationship will be strengthened when the bank is informed of any events that may affect the loan. It is best for the banker to learn of problems from the customer rather than from the community or other departments of the bank. Once a loan has been given, the supervising banker has a stake in your partnership's success, since failure will reflect badly on him or her. Prompt payment of all obligations will help keep the relationship constructive; a breech of trust can take a long time to be repaired, and often trust is irretrievable.

RELATIONSHIP TO GOVERNMENT AGENCIES

Government involvement with businesses is nearly always negative. Especially to be avoided is any attention from the Internal Revenue Service. For example, unwary entrepreneurs with cash-flow problems may be tempted to use withholding taxes as a temporary banker. The IRS does not take kindly to such behavior and can be very punitive; it may ultimately padlock the company's door and seize its assets. Once a company is accused of that transgression, the business becomes an ongoing target of scrutiny. States are no less forgiving, although their punishment is somewhat more negotiable.

The Labor Department can be another source of problems with the government when dissatisfied employees seek the department's help. Conditions surrounding firings, working conditions, and other dissatisfactions can become causes for seeking the Labor Department's involvement. Companies can keep such problems to a minimum, however, by clearly stating working conditions and personnel policies and applying those policies scrupulously, as well as by documenting their actions.

Injuries suffered in the workplace are worker's compensation issues. Disputes about whether injuries are related to work often lead to litigation—which can go on for years, causing legal costs to pile up. Knowing the emotional distraction and financial cost involved, many companies opt for early settlement even when the price seems excessive because they know it will be cheaper in the long run. Keeping accurate records about every work injury can have a major impact on the outcome of a dispute. Such records should include the time, place, and circumstances surrounding the injury, the company's response, and the names of any witnesses to the event.

Safety and environmental issues can mean the uninvited involvement of government, notably of OSHA and the Environmental Protection Agency. Prevention is the best approach to avoid problems with these agencies. Accordingly, companies should avoid any action that might bring them to their doorstep. Seeking advice from them proactively can prevent future costly problems.

THE INTERNET

The Internet continues its explosive growth, and although still maturing, it is already generating business in the billions of dollars. E-commerce has expanded the potential for new markets. No business today should neglect to consider whether and how to use this electronic resource. Proper exploitation of the Internet may create a global marketplace for a business. The executive him- or herself should be well versed in the use of the Internet and in addition should have technical support staff to keep up with the rapid rate of technological innovation. For example, wireless technology provides new flexibility in communication and in the use of computers and greater access to the Internet's resources. The Internet is not a panacea for success, however; like any tool, it should be used with caution and with an understanding of what it can and cannot do.

CHAPTER 16

Stages of Partnership Development

A partnership relationship, once created, proceeds through a series of developmental stages: formalizing the partnership, developing a business plan, implementing the partnership agreement, strategic planning, financing the business plan, implementing the organizational structure, establishing physical facilities, and defining personnel practices and guidelines. These developmental stages grow in complexity as they mature. Complexity brings increasing competition for the partners' attention. The lifeblood of the partnership relationship and the business it serves depends on the judicious expenditure of the partners' finite psychic energy, which has to be balanced between the needs of the partner relationship, self, and family.

This chapter discusses the developmental stages a partnership moves through from the first glow of the vision through making the partnership a reality and coping with its eventual ending.

HOW TO PROCEED WITH THE BUSINESS VISION

How to proceed once one has a business vision depends on the answers to the following questions: Can the entrepreneur achieve his or her goal alone? Does he or she have the needed technical knowledge, financial resources, business acumen, time, energy, and personality suited to such an effort? And even if he or she has that capability, does the entrepreneur want to do it all by him- or herself? The alternative to having a partner is to employ people with the requisite skills, but several critical employees are not likely to have the same commitment that a partner would have.

There is also the possibility that senior employees may use their experience to launch their own competitive enterprise.

Once the decision to have a partner is made, the next step is to decide when to do so. A partner can be named at the beginning of the business or acquired after the business has been established. The demands of the business may require more than the sole entrepreneur is able to do on his or her own, and he or she will need to have someone share the responsibilities of managing it. Or it may become lonely managing the business alone. Bringing a partner into an established business has the advantage of defining the partnership in a way that might not have been possible at the business's start-up.

A third option may arise out of necessity. It may be necessary to secure a partner and his or her resources to save a failing business. Gaining a partner under such conditions sometimes leaves the entrepreneur vulnerable to commitments made while under pressure that he or she would not have accepted under normal conditions. An entrepreneur who is pressed to seek a partner under such conditions should consult an objective third party (a lawyer, an accountant, or another professional) to guard against making unnecessary commitments.

Once the decision has been made to take on a partner, consideration must be given to the form a partnership agreement should take. To proceed without this agreement in the glow of blind trust creates vulnerability that may well lead to future problems. For example, a partnership is formed with a longstanding close friend, but the business relationship adds new dimensions to a friendship. The amiability that works in a friendship may not carry over into the business relationship.

The process of negotiating the partnership agreement demonstrates the viability of the working relationship. It is a trial run of the partners' ability to relate to their business and individual needs. A critical part of this effort will test their ability to constructively work out differences, if any. Often, the difficulties that such a negotiation naturally entails are minimized or rationalized under the pressure and excitement of starting a new business. Warning signs, such as differences of opinion about ownership interest, management control, and financial contributions and responsibilities, that go unheeded become a "time bomb" waiting to go off. As in two lovers' whirlwind romance that results in a quick marriage before the couple can learn whether they are compatible, a rashly formed partnership will have a heightened probability of divorce.

FORMALIZING THE PARTNERSHIP

A formally executed partnership agreement is a requirement for a successful, long-lasting partnership. Preferably, both partners should have independent legal representation in drafting or at least reviewing the agreement. The process of formalizing a partnership agreement is the final step in evaluating the viability of the prospective partnership.

A partnership agreement defines a workable structure for the relationship, making explicit what the partners expect of one another and how they will manage the relationship. The agreement spells out what each partner is contributing to start the partnership. One can anticipate that this will be relatively easily done when the partners are each contributing similar amounts of money, time, energy, knowledge, and the like. More difficulty can be anticipated when their contributions are not so proportionate. There is likely to be some struggle about how different contributions are equated, which in turn will lead to the issue of how ownership is divided if that is to be done unequally. Each partner needs to anticipate how this issue will be addressed. Plus, they need to reach agreement on what their initial product will be and the timetable to be followed in launching the partnership. This process provides an opportunity to test their ability to negotiate a common set of guidelines for how they will work together. An early consideration is naming the partnership. Coming to an agreement on a name is easier when something other than the partners' names are used; otherwise, there is potential for competition and struggle to be the lead partner.

The agreement should stipulate how decisions will be made, outline the appropriate division of labor, include an organizational chart, and address how negotiating differences is to be anticipated. Discussion of each of these areas will provide further information on how well the partners work together. Difficulties the partners encounter in any of these areas should give them pause for reflection on the quality of their working relationship. Any concerns should be made explicit; increased risk of failure will result unless these concerns are addressed satisfactorily.

Partnerships benefit from applying the concept of a business plan to forming the partnership. Generally a partnership agreement should include the terms for forming the partnership ("getting married"), for ending it ("getting divorced") and for what is expected of one another in between.

Specifically, a partnership agreement should include the *mission statement* of the partnership, which provides a reference point that helps partners clarify what they ultimately wish to accomplish. The mission statement also gives the outside world a general idea of what the partnership expects to accomplish.

Financial considerations are more complicated. The arrangement should include definitive language stating each partner's initial financial contribution and how profits and losses will be managed. A distinction needs to be made between ownership and leadership. Ownership is defined by equity contribution to the business, whereas leadership is provided by whoever provides direction for the company. Leadership may be defined formally or informally—formally by the occupant's position (e.g., as president and chief executive officer) and informally through the force of personality, expertise, or a vacuum in formal leadership independent of formal position. Problems that arise between formal and informal leadership are ultimately resolved by majority ownership.

How do the partners determine ownership? Usually, the decision is based on the relative capital contribution of each partner. Other variables that influence this decision include time invested, expertise, creative input, political connections, patents, copyrights, and leadership qualities. An early challenge to the partnership relationship is to decide how to value the partners' resources when determining the ownership split. A split that may make sense when based on the contribution of assets may be materially altered when delegated authority or force of personality enters the picture. For example, the combination of a dominating and charismatic partner and a laid-back partner may lead to a troubled business relationship if these differences are not adequately addressed.

Determination of each partner's compensation is based on some combination of active participation in operating the business and other forms of contribution that include money invested, expertise, time invested, political and business contacts, and so on. This determination starts with what each brings to the start of the partnership. Setting the compensation is easy if both partners feel they are making an equal contribution in each area: creativity, time, money, and so on. It is more difficult to set when they make different kinds of contributions. A source of difficulty can arise in how to equate equity in different contributions. How can creativity, time invested, business skills, and capital be equated? This ongoing issue can become more challenging over time. If one partner feels that he or she is making more of a contribution than the other, he or she will likely want to have that reflected in their relative compensation. This is likely to stress the partnership unless the partners develop a way to address this issue before it becomes a problem. Often this issue results in an impasse. An efficient way to avoid this problem is to have an outside consultant help resolve the issue. Otherwise, it is likely to fester and lead to bigger problems—to the point that personality issues obscure business needs.

Another potential source of difficulty between partners is when they have different value systems as a guide to management of profits. A partner who will do whatever it takes to maximize profits will be at odds with a partner who is satisfied with limiting profits in the service of employee or customer relationships. In addition, one partner may want to invest profits in growing the business. Partners who agree in principle on how to deal with profits before they occur may feel differently when the profits are available. A firm and consistent position is to avoid the pitfalls of arguing about money, a rule some marriages follow. Also to be considered is the ability to adapt as changes in circumstances warrant.

Example: The Management Consulting Company did not develop a business plan but instead launched its business on the basis of financial projections. It proposed to provide a range of services but did not adequately define how to develop them. As a result, it invested its limited resources in too many products, resulting in its failure to provide the proposed services in a timely and satisfactory way. Contributing to that failure was the partners' inability to agree on how to utilize resources.

Example: The Sporting Goods Company's goals for expansion were unrealistic for the resources and market it served. Its purchase of merchandise was not consistent with its sales and line of credit. A business plan would have prevented the major problems it later encountered.

The partnership agreement should also address the following relationship considerations:

- Make a full description of each partner's responsibilities in operating the business, including who has responsibility for such matters as hiring and firing, tax issues, and purchasing.

- Prepare a detailed process for resolving disputes.

- Define a procedure for a regular review of partnership functioning.

- Clearly define critical issues at the start of the business relationship, particularly if one partner is aggressive and assertive and the other is laid back. While such qualities may be advantageous in managing the business, the laid-back partner may find it difficult to make the necessary impact in the relationship. It is helpful at the outset to establish mutually desirable ways to communicate and make decisions.

- Set out an unambiguous policy on nepotism. Hiring family members in a partnership is a frequent source of problems, creating conflict among partners regarding their commitments to the business and to family members. A clearly defined policy on nepotism can reduce the problem, but it is not likely to completely eliminate it because emotional commitments do not easily yield to logic. Problems related to hiring family members, for example, can be minimized by having the hiree report to someone other than a family member. Another consideration is that the partner whose family member is involved will not veto any decision involving that person. Hiring and dealing with family members is a very tall order and is likely to test the best resolve of all parties.

A partner with an employed family member may feel that in a particular instance the family member was not treated appropriately, but the partner may decide not to interfere by virtue of the partnership's nepotism agreement. However, his or her resentment is likely to come out indirectly in one form or another. The result often is increased tension without understanding where it is coming from. This could be minimized if the partner were free to express his or her concerns without assuming it will change the outcome.

Example: Ernie and Jerry were brothers and partners in a construction company. They were getting on in years and began to think about preparing the next generation to take over. This led to giving Ernie's son managerial control. Almost immediately, however, problems developed because the son, Marshall, did not take advantage of his father's and uncle's experience. His desire to prove himself prevented him from getting their help. Ernie's desire to give his son a chance led him to give him more latitude than he should have. Meanwhile Jerry was getting increasingly upset as he saw disaster approaching. Jerry's efforts to be heard were minimized or ignored. It took his threatening to sue his brother that got Ernie to realize the gravity of the situation and the need to take corrective action.

Problems that occur when dual roles (e.g., brothers and business partners) are combined are most readily seen in family businesses. Business judgments are often unduly influenced by emotional connections to family members. This can be reinforced by pressure from other family members. In one family business, a mother who was not formally a participant in the business was continually pressuring her husband to treat their son in a manner not consistent with his performance. The mother's involvement created a situation that was not good for the son, the marital relationship, or the business.

- Prepare a "prenuptial" agreement, which is just as relevant in business as it is in marriage, that is separate from the partnership agreement. For example, partners may have assets they do not wish to commit to the partnership. They may be willing to use these resources in the business only upon the understanding that the assets are loaned or leased to the partnership and are not part of the partnership's capital contribution.

- Develop a process for holding partners and subordinates accountable for fulfilling their commitments. This will contribute to productivity and provide a sense of stability and safety. It will also provide some assurance as to what people can expect from one another and trust that management is doing its job. Modeling accountability by partners is an effective way to encourage the same in others. Specifically, (1) partners should define the means for reviewing each other's performance; (2) each partner should have an operational job description that specifies his or her responsibilities; and (3) partners should develop a code of ethics to carry out job responsibilities defined in item 2.

- Partners enter their relationship presuming that they share a common code of ethics. When they discover significant differences, they often have to resolve them in the heat of an issue, which is far more difficult to handle than at the start of the business relationship. Although not all significant differences can be anticipated, establishing a principle of respect for such differences and a process for dealing with them is likely to make dealing with unanticipated issues easier to resolve.

The impact of such problems can be diminished by establishing standards of behavior that will guide all aspects of the business relationship. Among such standards are those for making decisions, resolving conflicts, and dealing with relationships within the company and the outside business community. A mechanism also needs to be put in place to deal with violations of this code. When partners reach an impasse in dealing with differences, they should hire an outside consultant.

- Delineate buy/sell provisions in the event one partner wants out, and spell out how the value of the business will be determined in this situation, as well as how a buyout will be executed.

- Make provisions for continuing the business in the event of death, disability, or withdrawal of one of the partners.

- Prohibit either partner from becoming involved in another competing business.

DEVELOPING A BUSINESS PLAN

Traveling is very rewarding when the travelers have a clear destination and a map that shows how to get there. The same is true in business. A business plan contains both elements: a vision destination and a business plan map for arriving at the vision. The goal of the partnership also benefits from having a map—the partnership agreement. It is essential to formulate a business plan for both the partnership and the business. This is needed because the partnership may apply to more than one business.

The process starts with the development of a mission statement in both conceptual and operational terms. The operational definition is necessary to ensure that both partners agree on how to translate the conceptual mission statement into actual practice.

Partners need to pay careful attention to the details of how the business will be organized and managed. This requires considerable thought about what needs to be done on what kind of timetable. Anticipating likely problems and how to cope with them can help minimize the stress associated with a start-up. Key to success in this process is to keep one's energies focused on implementing one's plans and solving problems. Partners would do well to avoid expressing their frustrations in personality struggles between one another.

Implementing the Partnership Agreement

Two requirements necessary for defining the blueprint for how the partners will approach realizing their shared vision are the mechanics (management, finances, physical plant, marketing, and so on) of implementing their vision and their ability to work together as an effective team. The current focus is on what it takes for two partners to be an effective team. As indicated, this process starts with the development of a business plan that serves both as a guide for creating the business and for meeting the requirements of banks or investors. Thus, the mission statement becomes the guide the partnership will follow in accomplishing its objective.

Among the goals of the business is to keep the expenditure of company resources—labor and finance—focused. That can happen only when the partners share the same operational definition of goals.

The situation is very similar to what can happen in marriage. Two romantic people may decide to get married with the goal of finding happiness and starting a family. But if they overlook issues of compatibility and how they propose to achieve their goal, the marriage will be at high risk. In like manner, a successful partnership depends on the partners' ability to address the following questions:

- Is there a clear definition of the product or service?
- Is there an operationally defined goal?
- Is there a realistic time frame for achieving the goal?
- How can one determine when the goal is achieved?
- What standards will the partnership use to measure success: quality and quantity of product or monetary return?
- What standards will determine which service or product is offered to what market?
- What capital do the participants need to contribute, and how much needs to be borrowed?
- Is the partnership committed to a periodic review of goals?

Although partners may have little difficulty agreeing on the conceptual framework of their business, reaching a consensus on implementing various aspects of the business—for example, marketing, production, and hiring—may be more difficult. A subtle undercurrent of such deliberations may be a sense of competition between the partners and the need of each to feel that he or she is carrying his or her own weight. This process becomes more complicated if the need for control is an issue in the partnership. Partners have different needs and abilities, and the evolution of the business may play to the strengths of one more than the other; that can stimulate tension between partners and sabotage their partnership.

Strategic Planning

Achieving balance between strategic planning and tactical management strengthens the partnership's chances for success. This balance involves attention to short-term goals (tactical management) in a manner that is consistent with achieving long-term goals (strategic planning). It also requires discipline to keep focused on how time and resources are apportioned for both needs. Partners often differ, however, in how to balance their energies between tactical and strategic management. The press of immediate needs may lead them to dismiss strategic planning with the attitude "We'll worry about that when we get to it." One of the difficulties associated with strategic planning is learning how to manage all the uncertainties in planning for future events over a period of years. Accomplishing this task requires that at least one of the partners be comfortable dealing with incomplete data and that the best judgment be made with the data that are available. Being right is less important than being able to adapt to changing information and circumstances.

The business plan becomes the first test of whether the vision behind the partnership is a viable one. The partners must consider every aspect required for a successful business—expenses, income, staffing, marketing, competition—and make a realistic assessment of them. Partners must also learn to manage their differences in a way that does not compromise the goals of their business.

Financing the Business Plan

In financing a business plan, partners must be willing to undertake the needed financial commitment. Specifically, they must be willing to give their personal signatures to guarantee a loan and make other personal financial commitments as needed, have confidence that the business will be successful, be willing to take all required risks, and accept the consequences if the business fails.

If the partners' net worth is significantly different, that is likely to be a problem because the consequences of failure will affect the partners quite differently. For the partner who has considerable assets, failure may be inconvenient and distasteful, but it will not have as major an impact on his or her lifestyle as it will on the less affluent partner.

Projection of income in the business plan poses a major challenge. The desire to succeed can cause the partners to fit income projections to need rather than to realistic aims. The task is further complicated by having to project when the income will be realized in addition to how much it will be. The business plan gives the partners a sense of how well they can work together, including sharing ideas and managing differences. Work done on the plan provides an opportunity to ferret out and resolve problems before they develop significantly.

The partners may differ in willingness to take risks because they have different financial vulnerabilities and different comfort levels when dealing with uncertainty. The first difference can be managed by finding a way to tolerate risk. The comfort-level difference, however, is more problematic because it has to do with a personality characteristic that is not easily modified. More than that, its presence should raise serious questions about the viability of the partnership.

Money in business, as in marriage, is an ongoing high-priority issue that often stresses the partnership relationship. People's attitudes toward managing finances are often at odds. Moreover, battles about money often mask underlying struggles over control and insecurity. Success in developing collateral partnerships with banks depends on the banks' confidence in the partners' experience in managing differences with regard to generating income and managing finances.

Partners pursuing their dream must face the cold reality of what is fiscally sound. Some enterprises, especially busy start-up companies, are distracted from attending to financial matters because they are overloaded with demands from all directions. Finding a disciplined way to monitor finances helps minimize such problems. One solution can be found through the division-of-labor route: one partner deals with creative matters and the other with the business management. Fiscal management gets difficult when creative needs conflict with fiscal restraints and when control and competence issues are also involved.

IMPLEMENTING ORGANIZATIONAL STRUCTURE

Organizational structure, the blueprint for managing working relationships, defines the communication hierarchy and the attendant responsibilities necessary to attain the business objectives. Organizational structures vary from a rigid structure to a loosely defined structure that is guided more by function than by hierarchy. Numerous possible variations lie between these polarities. Each partnership needs to decide on the kind of organizational structure that best suits their personalities and the requirements for achieving their business objectives.

Careful attention to detail will determine the best way to organize and manage the partnership as well as the needed timetable. Anticipating likely problems and formulating ways to cope can help minimize the stress that goes with a start-up. Success in this endeavor lies in keeping one's energies focused on the business plan and solving problems with a can-do attitude. Both partners should avoid permitting their frustrations to be expressed in personality struggles.

Employees also have different preferences for the organizational structure in which to work. For example, a *product partnership*—collaboration between an employer and employee to produce a product or service—should take into account both the partners' and the employees' preferences. By developing a mutually compatible structure, partners should avoid creating an environment of unhappy employees that in the end will negatively affect the partnership's chances of success.

Example: Organizational structure was a problem for both the Management Consulting Company and the Nursing Home Company. The partners in the Management Consulting Company did not have a well-defined structural relationship. On the contrary, they often functioned separately on various matters relating to the company. As a result, they frequently disagreed about how things should be done and often duplicated efforts. Their inability to define areas of responsibility was wrapped up in their deep-seated competition for power and control. Not surprisingly, the partnership dissolved at an early date.

The Nursing Home Company suffered similar competition problems. The partners seemingly operated in a more congenial manner than was the case in the Management Consulting Company. Informally, one partner was the more influential because of his greater financial resources and the force of his personality. This informal functioning worked satisfactorily in the early years of the company, but as the company grew the partners became more competitive and their priorities shifted from the common one to their individual goals.

Physical Facilities

Locating and developing the necessary physical facilities is an early consideration for partners in pursuit of their business vision. One partner may feel that a physical facility should reflect a certain image of the company, while the other partner may focus more on financial practicality. Resolution will depend on the partners' ability to avoid expressing their frustrations in personal judgments of one another.

Another potential source of difficulty is who gets the more desirable office or workspace—the corner office, the better parking space, and so on. This struggle can become intense when one or both partners are insecure and need the symbolic reinforcement that prime space represents.

Hiring of Staff and Job Descriptions

Determining staffing needs and training programs is an ongoing process, but it is particularly important at the beginning of the partnership. Determining what skills are necessary among the staff and what criteria the partners will use in selecting staff requires careful thought and often requires a delicate balancing act between the higher cost of skilled help and the lower cost of inexperienced staff. The partners also need to formulate a mutually acceptable process for making decisions. Their successes in this area will further affect the way their relationship is defined.

Efficiency and productivity will be at their highest if job descriptions are realistic. Partners should attend to operational statements of what can be achieved in an allotted time and when carrying out one responsibility conflicts with another.

Job descriptions are an integral part of a successful product partnership and should be appropriately defined. They should include what is expected of a person occupying a position and provide information about how a given position affects other positions. Inadequately defined job descriptions can lead to many problems. A too-vaguely defined job description leaves the employee confused about what is expected of him or her and distracts the employee from attending to his or her work. Such an employee will question whether he is doing what he is supposed to be doing and whether he will get into trouble if he guesses wrong.

Similarly, job descriptions often do not present realistic expectations of the time required to perform all of one's job duties. Accordingly, the employee chronically fails to meet deadlines, which undermines his or her self-confidence and raises concern about how supervisors will view his or her performance.

On occasion, the job description will delineate conflicting responsibilities. This can result from pressure to produce as much work as possible while expecting high standards of quality.

When different parts of the job involve reporting to different people, the employee is put in the tenuous position of trying to meet the job expectations of two people who may have different or, even worse, contradictory standards. Such an employee will get into trouble with both people no matter what he or she does. The problem is exacerbated when the people to whom he or she reports are in conflict with each other. The employee pays—and so does the work product.

Often the same responsibilities are given to different people without clarifying how their efforts relate. That may lead to destructive conflict and power struggles between employees.

In many companies, job descriptions are merely a formality, and the company makes little or no effort to hold employees accountable for adhering to them. When used properly, job descriptions can be a valuable tool for crafting a well-functioning organization. Otherwise, they can be a source of conflict and a useless waste of time and resources for all concerned.

Job descriptions are more useful when they are written with the personality and skills of the employee holding the job in mind. The job description should include accountability for meeting job expectations.

Job descriptions are needed as much for the partners as for the employees. As noted earlier, a good working partnership is promoted by clearly setting out the responsibilities to be undertaken by each partner. In the absence of that clarity, dissent and conflict are likely. Enough unavoidable differences exist without adding those that can be prevented.

Clear job descriptions for the partners become critical once a company expands. Ambiguity as to the partners' responsibilities translates directly into confusion and ambiguity among employees. Partners will give conflicting orders, which will result in inefficiency and low company morale.

Admittedly, the pressures of getting a business started leave the partners little psychic energy to devote to the details of job descriptions. However, use of broad and ambiguous terms in the descriptions will simply create an environment in which differences flourish; if they escape detection, they will surely surface in some other form.

Personnel Practices

Personnel practices are a strong statement about how the partners regard their employees. Their concern for employees will be communicated between the consistency in partners' stated values and how they are implemented in personnel practices. Personnel manuals help employees understand the nature of their jobs and elucidate company operating policies with regard to working hours, vacations, sick leave, insurance, personal days, and educational opportunities. In addition, they may outline procedures required in their job performance. How these policies are defined and implemented directly affects employee morale and productivity. Employees' participation in defining these practices plays a major role in defining a product partnership.

Example: Inadequate definition of personnel practices contributed to problems in the Management Consulting Company and the Nursing Home Company. In the Management Consulting Company, the partners described medical benefits in an ambiguous manner that allowed employees to believe that they were eligible for more comprehensive benefits than was intended. This was an embarrassment to the partners and created resentment when the employees found that the benefits weren't what they had been led to believe.

The partners in the Nursing Home Company started the company with the vision of treating their employees as though they were a form of partner. In their enthusiasm they defined a benefit package that was unrealistic for their resources, and they didn't realize their mistake until benefits began to be used. They found themselves in the embarrassing position of having to renege on their initial commitments.

Managing Start-Up Stress

Until an operation develops some stability, the partnership's ability to manage multiple tasks simultaneously—some anticipated and many that are not—will be tested. The partners will have to learn to manage their anxieties while solving problems and avoid the natural tendency to take out their anxieties on one another or on their employees. Much the same situation obtains in families: it is easier to take out frustrations on family members than on strangers.

Terminating Projects

Also needed are criteria and structures for deciding when to terminate a given effort or project. It is often difficult to give up on an effort once one has made a commitment to it, much as the losing gambler continues to keep playing with the thought that through continued effort he or she will ultimately recover the losses. Partners who have strong differences are often in conflict. Protecting one's ego can become very expensive.

Periodic Review of Operations

Once some semblance of stability has been achieved in the business operation, the partners will have time to review what is working and what is not and to make adjustments accordingly. Partners must keep abreast of changing situations on many fronts simultaneously, including the political and economic climate, market conditions, interest rates, and changes in competition. A change on any one of these fronts is a problem in itself. Often the seductive thought emerges that pursuing a failing project just a little further will bring the desired success. Unfortunately, however, the problem is likely only to worsen.

The situation becomes more complex when changes occur in more than one variable at the same time. The pressure of managing a business often results in postponing problems until they *must* be faced. Partners can minimize these problems by regularly reviewing the status of their relationship; this includes addressing any tensions that have developed and resolving them before they become totally destructive. This will ensure that the partners' psychic energies remain focused on business matters. Partners need to know that they can express their concerns to one another in a way that will center on resolution rather than on defense of their own behavior. Periodic reviews will identify problems early, when correcting them is easier and less costly.

CHAPTER 17

Keeping the Partnership Healthy

Once the business is a going entity, the partners need to switch from a start-up frame of mind to one of managing a business over time. Not every partner is comfortable managing both the start-up phase and the ongoing operation. Most can handle just one or the other of these stages comfortably. It may help for one partner to gain expertise in one area and the other partner to gain expertise in another area.

MANAGING A HEALTHY PARTNERSHIP

Once started, a partnership is a "living entity," and to survive it needs to be nurtured; the partners must function effectively both individually and in concert. Failure to diagnose and correct deficiencies in their individual or collective behavior will erode the effectiveness of the partnership.

To function profitably, a partnership must regularly monitor its vital signs. How effective that monitoring is depends on the partners' agreement on how it will be accomplished. The monitoring process involves five steps:

1. Define desirable behavioral criteria. For example, partners resolve differences by focusing on issues, not on the person.
2. Determine whether the current level of functioning in the partnership is satisfactory.
3. If that level of functioning is not satisfactory, define a course of action for going from the present level to the desired level of functioning.

4. Determine what resources are needed to modify relationship problems. The partners need to make a judgment about whether they can manage the problem themselves or they need to engage outside resources (e.g., use an organizational consultant or seek outside counseling).

5. Define a process for ensuring that the needed changes do occur. This involves some form of tracking to see that problematic behavior has improved.

The vital signs include values, beliefs, and goals; leadership; communication; power; resources; decision making; conflict resolution; cost-benefit balance; delegation; division of labor; adaptation to change; compensation; working conditions; opportunity for advancement; acknowledgment of contributions; respectful treatment; value placed on company product; and the monitoring of satisfaction. Since all of these signs (except monitoring satisfaction) have been fully discussed in previous chapters, only monitoring satisfaction is singled out here.

MONITORING SATISFACTION

Ongoing relationships develop a characteristic pattern when they reach a satisfactory level. Often it is easier to endure living with an unsatisfactory relationship than it is to face the uncertainties and bother of changing it. Parties in a relationship will accept change when the discomfort of continuing the status quo becomes more painful than the anticipated difficulty of changing it. Healthy partner relationships can be achieved by periodic evaluation of the following:

Level of satisfaction in the partnership. Is the business relationship sufficiently satisfying to warrant a full emotional and intellectual commitment? Are partners respectful of one another? Can they constructively resolve their differences and meet personal needs through their business relationship?

Satisfaction with the level of profitability. Is the business making sufficient profit to warrant continued commitment to the business relationship? In some cases the business relationship is viable, but the level of profitability is not sufficient to support continuing the relationship, and the likelihood of changing it is not good. If this situation is not addressed quickly, both the business and the relationship will begin to erode to the point where neither is viable.

Satisfaction in managing the business. Although people may be comfortable in their working relationship, they may lose interest in managing their business because they have decided to pursue other interests or because economic conditions or personal circumstances have changed. When such changes occur, it becomes too easy to assume that the feeling or need will pass. The discomfort of facing a situation early, however, is much less acute than the discomfort of allowing it to linger until conditions force it to be addressed.

Adequate resources for nurturing the partner relationship. All types of part-nerships thrive on mutual respect and concern for each other's needs. The partners must ensure that a constructive process exists that affords them the safety and freedom to manage different points of view. The partners need to understand the importance of devoting time and energy to main-taining their relationship.

Impact of partners' relationship on employees. How the partners act in their relationship serves as a role model for employees to follow and con-tributes to how the partnership is viewed. A stable, positive partner rela-tionship promotes employees' confidence and feelings of security about the company. The opposite occurs when partners battle and employees take sides—a process very similar to the dynamic that operates in battling families. Feelings of security get threatened when the parents are in con-flict. This often results in children getting into trouble and thereby dis-tracting the parents from their conflict. Employees are likely to respond in a similar way.

Impact of partners' relationship on consumers. The same concerns apply to customers and clients. When customers or clients are involved in conflict between partners, it undermines the collateral partnership as well as the company's image and the public's confidence in the company. There is also the risk that the tarnished image will spread to the larger business community.

Relationship of partners to employees. The best of visions may never become reality without the workforce to make it happen. The business's chances of success improve when employees regard their work product as more than a means to a paycheck. Encouraging and recognizing their con-tributions may result in employees who are committed to their jobs beyond requirements and who take pride in their work.

HELPFUL BUSINESS TOOLS

Meetings are an effective way to coordinate the partnership's efforts; they also affect the quality of the partners' relationship. Following recom-mended guidelines for the conduct of meetings, including setting an objective, will positively affect the work relationships of those involved. The primary purposes of holding a meeting are to exchange ideas and to make collective decisions. A meeting that is devoted mainly to lengthy presentations is not a cost-effective use of time and stresses the partner-ship relationship.

Speakers may lessen the tedium of a lengthy presentation by distributing written material at a sufficient time prior to the meeting to permit prepara-tion. In this way, each partner, or whoever else participates in the meeting, can review the material in his or her own fashion, which may involve mul-tiple readings and time for thoughtful reflection. The meeting itself should be devoted primarily to the exchange of ideas, culminating in decisions.

Meetings are likely to be most productive when partners are fresh and alert and the agenda focuses on an exchange of ideas. Early mornings usually bring out the best in participants; after lunch is the worst time, as the presenter has to compete with the lull that follows a meal.

A clearly focused agenda and a leader with the ability to parry any distractions from the meeting's established objective are essential. Difficulty sticking to the agenda may result for a number of reasons. Here are some of the more notable:

- *Participants have individual interests.* A participant may believe he or she has a more pressing concern and so may attempt to preempt the official agenda.
- *The agenda may become a vehicle for expressing conflict.* Conflict in a work relationship may be expressed at a meeting. It is not always easy to distinguish whether people are honestly disagreeing over the substance of an issue or whether they are angry over some previous issue or are merely competing with another participant.
- *There is a struggle for power.* A meeting may reflect a power struggle. It may provide an opportunity for a participant to challenge the authority of the leader, either directly or indirectly.
- *Participants are trying to avoid an agenda item.* A participant may express his or her reluctance to deal with an agenda item by introducing items of greater relative comfort or concern.
- *The chairperson has difficulty leading the meeting.* A chairperson who is ill prepared or uncomfortable in his or her position can stir restlessness, mistrust, and discomfort in the participants and may so affect the constructive level of their participation.
- *It is difficult to maintain attention.* The meeting's success depends on holding participants' attention. The concept of *ultradian rhythm* (Rossi, 1991) does for work activity what the circadian rhythm does for biological activity. According to research, the average person can maintain a focused concentration span for only one and a half to two hours in one sitting. Continued maximum concentration is generally possible if a 20-minute break is taken every hour and a half to two hours. Such breaks are not effective, however, if they involve continued discussion of business. Ideally the break should involve some form of relaxation—taking a walk, getting a bit of fresh air, sitting quietly with eyes closed, and the like. Rossi reports that such breaks have been shown to increase productivity rather than slow it down. The renewed efficiency that derives from the break more than makes up for any lost productivity it may cause.
- *The chairperson cannot manage the agenda.* Responsibility for managing the agenda is only one facet of conducting a satisfactory meeting. It is the joint responsibility of both the chairperson and the participants to maintain respectful interaction, thereby permitting different points of view to be expressed.
- *Performance and contributions are not acknowledged.* Just as food is nourishment for the body, acknowledgment of one's contribution feeds work relationships. Acknowledging contributions encourages motivated and creative employees.

Such acknowledgments can be made both privately and publicly; they often take the form of financial rewards; promotions; new responsibilities; perks such as time off and special privileges; or nonverbal acknowledgment such as a smile, a pat on the back, or a show of respect for opinions.

Conflict Management

Managing a business is not a democratic process. Participants may not like the decisions that are made but must still adhere to them. What matters is that they are consulted on matters that affect them. Essential to a constructive resolution of differences is that each person feels that his or her point of view has been given serious consideration. Even when someone's desires are not met, the person should be given the courtesy of an explanation of why that is so.

A stalemate occurs when a resolution requires the agreement of both partners and a satisfactory solution cannot be achieved. Binding arbitration may be a solution. One approach is for each partner to select a representative for his or her point of view, and for the two representatives to select a third member. The recommendation of this group then becomes binding on both partners. This process provides a way for the partners to deal with issues they cannot resolve by themselves and addresses them in a constructive way before they cause serious rifts in their relationship. Binding arbitration is a tedious process and becomes a relationship-threatening one if called upon too frequently.

An alternative approach is to appoint a board of directors that has an odd number of members in order to avoid the possibility of a tie. This has the advantage of providing an in-place mechanism for resolving conflict. Its potential downside is to dilute power by having people other than the partners making policy. That disadvantage is in part offset by appointing board members other than partners to defined terms of office.

One of the greatest drains on a relationship is to permit unresolved conflict to fester. When that happens, energy is increasingly dissipated in wasteful tension and less energy is therefore available for constructive efforts. The longer an issue remains unresolved, the more entrenched positions become. There is the risk that such entrenchment will become irreversible.

Managing Transitions

Proper management of the five phases involved in managing transitions as described in chapter 14, "Transitions," is very relevant for maintaining a healthy partnership. The five phases are briefly summarized here; they are (1) anticipation of a forthcoming event, (2) adaptation to a situation, (3) stabilization and maintenance, (4) termination and closings, and (5) learning from experience.

Anticipation of a Forthcoming Event

Anticipation provides one the opportunity to adequately prepare for the forthcoming event or situation. This, of course, is what we call planning, be it short-term, long-term, strategic, or tactical planning. Determining what resources are needed in planning for an event requires judgment. Too much planning can be wasteful, and too little can be disastrous. Anticipation requires talent and vision in estimating the range of events and needs that will require attention. The healthy business is the one with the capacity to anticipate and prepare for future events. For some businesses, their very survival may depend on their ability to anticipate. This is particularly the case in highly volatile industries, as we have seen in the high-tech industry.

Adaptation to a Situation

Adaptation signifies performance time: the time to implement plans, start a contract, provide a service, and begin production. It involves implementing recommendations called for in the planning, as well as organizational skill and coordination of people and resources. The challenge is to cope with unexpected events that can elude even the best of plans. Adaptation requires good diagnostic skills and the ability to think critically and decisively in the midst of tension and emotion when the unexpected occurs. The problem is heightened when one must adhere to a designated timetable or when staying within the budget is paramount.

Stabilization and Maintenance

Once a business is operative, the focus shifts to functioning profitably on a day-to-day basis. This involves anticipating and preventing potential problems. For those problems that do occur, the task is to resolve them efficiently in order to limit any negative impact on the business. In this phase, managing also requires effecting a balance between coping with the short term and planning for the long term. In large organizations such responsibilities are divided between the chief executive officer and the chief operating officer.

Terminations and Closings

Terminations and closings occur at two levels: (1) the ending of a contract or a product, service, or program or any change in the work environment; and (2) the end of the entire business.

Business ventures end mainly because of poor management, conflicted relationships, changing market conditions, obsolete products, insufficient capital, retirement, acquisition by another company, and health or personal problems. Such endings may be accompanied by feelings of happiness or sadness, and sometimes they include feelings of failure. Although each of these reasons has its own unique implications, they all have one thing in common: everyone involved will have to cope on an emotional and financial level. The situation becomes more devastating when financial ruin is a consequence. Shutting down a business is a complex task, especially when it occurs involuntarily.

Also part of keeping a business healthy is the ability to terminate any part that is no longer operating profitably or is negatively affecting profitability in other areas of the business. An inability in this area may spell the company's downfall. It may involve reluctance to give up on a favorite project and difficulty in reducing staff because of emotional involvements that give rise to conflict between survival of the business and unrealistic financial responsibilities for these employees.

Learning from Experience

Closings that are difficult or traumatic can leave emotional scars that interfere with learning from the experience. This problem is most likely to occur when the closing is experienced in a very personal way that affects an entrepreneur's feelings of competence and self-worth. Necessary for success in any future endeavor is the ability to learn from the terminated experience.

Managing Multiple Projects

No one has unlimited energies. The undisciplined person who takes on too many projects at the same time can quickly get into trouble. Underestimating a given project's emotional and physical investment can also be a problem. For that reason, adequate assessment of project requirements is essential. To make such an assessment, one needs to appreciate what a given project will require and to understand how investment in a given project may affect other ongoing projects.

Each project has a beginning, undergoes development, and at some point comes to an end. The greatest drain on resources is likely to occur during the anticipation and adaptation phases. Once a project is viable, the demand on resources will diminish to some steady state except when a problem or crisis requires heightened attention.

Most projects start simply and become more complex over time. The greater the complexity, the greater the drain on resources. A crisis develops when too many projects demand a company's resources at the same time. A business remains healthy when it makes a careful evaluation of the resources needed in both the immediate future and the long term. In addition, the healthy company has an effective way of dealing with the allocation of resources when unforeseen circumstances create an overload.

Managing multiple projects occurs at three levels, depending on their size and complexity: the company, the individual departments, and the individual. One challenge in management is to juggle the multiple involvements of all department members so that they perform without interfering with the productivity of other people or departments. The person who is very productive at the expense of another is not truly productive.

Managing multiple projects can be difficult when the demands of an employee's personal life unduly interfere with productivity. This becomes a significant problem only when the drain occurs over an extended period of time and becomes chronic. At such times, the company must decide how long it can tolerate the situation without harming company operations. The degree of sensitivity used to manage this decision will not only affect the relationship between the company and the individual but will also carry a message to other employees.

Cost-Benefit Influence on Behavior

Cost-benefit considerations apply not only to the purchase of material goods but also to all aspects of human behavior. This is discussed in more detail in chapter 9, "Cost-Benefit Balance." Rational decision making involves considering the cost involved in gaining a desired benefit. Entrepreneurs are constantly faced with balancing benefits against costs in employee relationships. The dollar cost for benefits is easily determined; determining how that evaluation affects morale, motivation, and commitment to the company is much more difficult.

The desire for a given benefit may become so great that the implications of the attached cost are overlooked. The implications of attached cost can also be overlooked when an error is made in assessing the cost or when the cost changes over time owing to unforeseen circumstances.

Paramount in a healthy business is careful attention to the cost and benefit of an investment in physical and financial commitments or in the people it employs. Businesses get into trouble when their enthusiasm for a pet project clouds their assessment of fiscal and marketplace realities. The assessment becomes more difficult when the cost is not readily assessable. The resulting judgment can be highly vulnerable to distortion because of the emotional investment.

REGULAR REVIEWS OF PARTNERSHIP

Staying healthy means that a business must commit to regular reviews of all aspects of its operations. These reviews enable management to avert problems or to catch them in the early stages when they are more easily correctable.

Who Should Conduct Reviews and How Often

Who should conduct such a review? It is best conducted by an outside source who will bring a fresh perspective that avoids established mind-sets, favored involvements, and the politics of established relationships. Businesses that are volatile and subject to rapid change are likely to need more frequent reviews; conversely, those that are more stable are likely to need them less often. Commonly, six-month or annual reviews are suffi-cient.

How to Conduct Reviews

The most productive reviews are those that follow a formally defined procedure so that all participants know what is expected of them. These reviews should be seen as a constructive tool rather than as an intrusion.

The items to be covered in the review depend on the business plan and the items described earlier in this chapter. Of particular importance is an assessment of the partners' relationship. Special attention should be paid to determining whether adequate resources exist for nurturing the part-nership. Also deserving of attention is the partners' ability to keep per-sonal problems from interfering with the business relationship.

The general objective of the review is to provide a status report on the operation of the company as a whole and for each of its subdivisions and departments. Also included should be an identification of those subdivi-sions showing notable performance and those whose performance is seri-ously lacking. The report should make recommendations for needed changes and give some indication of the company's perceived ability and commitment to accomplish those changes.

Investment in a more empirical review provides detailed assessment of all aspects of personal qualities, partners' relationship, and business sta-tus. It also provides a basis for tracing performance over time, permitting the early detection of incipient problems and prompt remedial action. The frequency of such reviews follows the same logic as for financial reviews. A good starting point would be quarterly reviews. At each review, the partners should make the following assessments: (1) evaluation of each partner's personal qualities as outlined in chapter 12, "Selecting a Part-ner"; (2) evaluation of the partner relationship; and (3) evaluation of the performance of the business. Each item in these categories should be eval-uated on a scale along each of two dimensions: the priority attached to the importance of each item and the satisfaction with which it is achieved.

The partners should initially make the assessments individually. They should then follow up with a joint review of their respective ratings, which will point to areas of strength and deficiency. This closely parallels what would be done in a financial review.

The partners' first reaction to the empirical evaluation might well be that it is cumbersome, too time consuming, and perhaps too threatening because they will have to look at themselves and each other in ways that might be uncomfortable. But there is no way to know the benefit unless it is tried. Its benefits would range from self-improvement to a satisfying partnership and a healthy business. The details for implementing the empirical evaluation are described in Appendix B, "Schedule for Monitoring Partnership Health."

REFERENCE

Rossi, E. L. (1991). *The 20 minute break.* New York: Putnam.

CHAPTER 18

Signs of Trouble

Developing an "early-warning" system can help reveal relationship problems before they become serious enough to affect the partnership. Such a system identifies developing problems at a time before adversaries become entrenched in their positions and when the means for resolving them are more readily available. When ignored, relationship problems can take priority over attention to conducting the matters of business. Two partners may get into a power struggle so fierce that winning soon takes precedence over the health of their business. The signs of a troubled partnership take a variety of forms:

- *Boredom with subjects that used to command interest and enthusiasm.*
- *Increased investment in outside activities at the expense of work responsibilities.*
- *A decreased level of energy and enthusiasm, accompanied by a distracted appearance.*
- *Negative comments about one's partner to employees and others.* Such comments implicitly invite the employee to takes sides against the other partner.
- *Change in work habits.* A partner gradually decreases the hours worked, participates less in meetings, and lets other job-related performance slack off.
- *Changes in the way of relating.* Such changes include irritability, overreacting to undesirable events, procrastination, a diminished sense of humor, and becoming hypercritical.
- *Increase in minor illnesses.* One way dissatisfaction gets expressed is in physical complaints, minor illnesses, and injuries.
- *Complaints about the work environment.* The partner expresses chronic dissatisfaction with his or her workspace and the quality of the work environment.

- *Drop in attention to conflict.* One's ability to resolve conflict is tested early in the development of a partnership. Successful resolution involves subordinating individual needs to the partnership's needs. When the initial capacity to resolve differences deteriorates into unpleasantness, the result is psychic drain and increased risk to the partnership.

- *Letting personal or relationship problems get in the way of the partnership.* Differences between partners can originate from personal problems stemming from family or health crises. This situation is particularly difficult for the unaffected partner, who must now balance the needs of the business and his or her compassion for the troubled partner. Solving this problem without threatening the partners' personal relationship poses a challenge to one's maturity. Relations between partners can also deteriorate when shared business goals need to change and the partners are unable to adapt their relationship to meet the changes. The challenge they now face is to prevent their dispute from unduly affecting the business. This process can be facilitated once they agree on revised goals while working out their differences in how to get there.

- *Problems agreeing on responses to changes in the business environment.* Changing business conditions often require the partnership to adjust goals and its approach to doing business. An inability to create and implement different approaches for dealing with such changes gives notice that the partnership is headed for trouble; a solution needs to be found quickly. A partner who enlists the support of an employee to buttress his or her argument with the other partner only reveals a felt weakness in his or her position and a diminished confidence in being able to negotiate difference.

MANAGEMENT-EMPLOYEE RELATIONSHIPS

Problems with Personnel Practices

Partners' inability to agree on personnel practices reflects their value and belief differences and will ultimately affect their employees, exacerbating the conflict between partners. Some differences revolve around differences in how to treat employees. Those differences may escape detection until personnel practices need to be defined. Belief differences, on the other hand, reflect disagreement as to what impact personnel policies are likely to have on employees.

Partners may disagree on how to respond to employee contributions. Holding different philosophies on the matter—such as virtue is its own reward, compensation is adequate acknowledgment, people should know when they are contributing, or employees shouldn't have to be recognized for everything they do—is not only a source of conflict between partners but is also likely to affect how the partners acknowledge each other's contributions.

Inadequate Communication

Partners may disagree on both the form and content of what is communicated to employees. One partner may prefer to give employees information on a need-to-know basis, while the other may believe that an informed employee is a more productive one. Difficulty or inconsistency in resolving this difference is likely to affect the company's productivity and undermine a productive partnership. It may also create problems when the more open-minded partner begins to wonder whether the same philosophy is being practiced in his or her relationship with the other partner.

Managing compensation is demanding enough when partners are in agreement; it becomes all the more difficult when partners disagree on how it should be handled. Employees are likely to pick up on the conflict, which will only increase the tension between partners, especially when employees side with the partner viewed as more sympathetic to their needs.

Employee Status

An employee's job satisfaction depends largely on how he or she is viewed by the employer. Partners who disagree on performance standards and on how they should be communicated will see that disagreements negatively affect employee satisfaction. Often the conservative partner will view his or her counterpart as coddling the employees, whereas the more liberal partner will feel the other is insensitive to employee needs. Dissatisfied employees do not of course give their best effort. Partners who cannot agree on how to motivate employees will ultimately wind up blaming each other for the problem, thereby reinforcing the negative effect on motivation.

Unrealistic productivity expectations are a frequent source of dispute between employers and employees. The problem intensifies when the partners are not able to agree on what is reasonable and express their differences in ways that only heighten existing tensions.

Employee Relationships

Destructive competition between employees is intensified when partners take sides in the conflict. Their ability to constructively deal with such issues is confounded when they do this and especially when their sympathies differ and it becomes a source of conflict between them. Partners will get involved in this manner when they use such occasions to further their own interpersonal struggles.

Impact of Personal Pressures

Every employer must at some time face the question of how to balance personal pressures (sick family member, marital conflict, troubled children, or children in need of parental presence) against business needs. It is easy to set up policies; implementing them is difficult, especially when dealing with a person in trouble. This situation becomes considerably more difficult when partners do not agree on how to set limits. Tensions between partners increase when one partner has a relationship with an employee who has a problem and therefore wants to be accommodating. The uninvolved partner usually takes a harder line. The involved partner is then in the unenviable position of choosing between his or her commitment to the other partner and his or her desire to be responsive to the employee. Resolving this conflict becomes more difficult when the partners are already experiencing tensions in their relationship.

MARKETPLACE PHENOMENA

Decreased Sales

A protracted decrease in sales is usually the product of many factors. Blaming one another or outside forces such as an economic downturn may be a way for partners to vent their frustrations, but it is a useless exercise. Not only does it not address the problem; it also undermines constructive problem resolution. The more effective approach is to figure out how best to adjust to changed circumstances.

Complaints from Customers or Clients

The easiest way to handle unpleasant situations such as customer complaints is to blame somebody or something else. But partners who are quick to blame one another when a problem arises are already in trouble. Blaming prevents finding a constructive solution and undermines the partnership. Problems with customers can be turned to advantages when customers feel their concerns have been taken seriously. This can happen even if customers aren't able to get what they wanted. Such situations demonstrate the power that comes when one feels acknowledged.

IN-HOUSE CONCERNS

Finances

Creating financial projections can be another test of partners' ability to deal with difference, especially when one partner is a realist and the other is an idealist. The challenge for both is to put the best face on their business, especially if the projections are needed to secure financing.

Persistent cash-flow problems are of concern for two reasons: first, they distract attention from other aspects of managing the business, and second, different points of view on how to address the problem can result in conflict. The severity of the conflict is in direct proportion to the degree that the partners see the cash-flow problems as an imminent threat to the survival of the business.

Difficulties with financial projections and cash-flow problems naturally lead to debt-service problems. Contributing to such deficiency is the partners' ability to convince lenders to provide more financial support than the business can carry. Ultimately, the business's collateral partnerships with banks become unstable as lenders get nervous about the company's ability to carry the debt. The pressure on the partners becomes so great that they became distracted from the business, and those tensions feed employee anxiety. This quickly becomes a vicious cycle that can soon lead to out-and-out business failure.

Employee Behavior

Employees are a mirror of a company's health. When problems persist, employees become anxious and express their anxieties in complaints that soon interfere with their work. Partners who then launch criticism, which will only exacerbate the problem, should try to build a product partnership with employees by helping them understand the nature of the problem and the company's efforts to find a solution. Employees should also be asked for their input; otherwise, morale will suffer and the problem will only worsen.

As tensions increase, all sorts of negative behaviors surface: increased irritability, less cooperation, more conflicts and complaints, secretive discussions behind closed doors, and more self-serving competition. These behaviors rapidly escalate when partners fail to take prompt corrective action. The relationship between partners also deteriorates as their anxieties deepen. As stress increases, the partners quickly begin to blame each other and their employees, which makes a bad situation intolerable.

PRODUCT DELIVERY

Partner differences on quality control are a common source of dispute. One partner may value minimal attention while the other may believe that strict standards should apply to ensure a successful collateral partnership with the customer. Partners are likely to disagree on how much resources to devote to quality control and to getting feedback from customers. They may also differ on the payment schedule for delivery of their product. In a service business, a prompt response is needed to prevent interruption of the customer's business. This problem becomes a prominent issue when one partner has to deal with customer complaints and the other does not. The difference becomes more serious when the focus shifts from the issue that must be resolved to an ongoing struggle for control in the relationship.

CHAPTER 19

Evolution of a Partnership Divorce

The term *business divorce* suggests failure, but failure is not necessarily the case. Partnerships change for various reasons, not just because the business fails. Those reasons include differences of opinion, boredom, and desire to pursue other interests. Actually, business divorces occur even in very successful businesses. Understanding how partnerships evolve and function will provide insight about how and why business divorces occur. Partnerships don't break up overnight; rather, dissolution takes place over time even when the breakup may appear precipitous. A business's chances for success are enhanced by a harmonious personal relationship between partners, but as is true in marriages, they can function even in the absence of harmony.

As shown earlier, partnerships are more likely to be successful when two parties have a clear understanding of each other's expectations and when that understanding is articulated in a formal partnership agreement. Less clear but no less important is the partners' emotional commitment to the relationship. The partners must be able to achieve a balance between individual and joint priorities in the relationship and to develop and maintain open and constructive ways of communicating.

As discussed earlier in the book, family businesses are often more casual in defining the partnership. This is unfortunate because the more ambiguity, the greater the likelihood that problems will develop in the resulting partnership. Often participants in family businesses do not enter into a formal agreement because trust between family members is presumed. This is especially the case when a family elder invites a son or other relative into a partnership.

A business divorce produces much the same emotional trauma that usually accompanies a marital divorce. Severing emotional and financial commitments is usually complicated and painful, especially when the relationship is longstanding. Separating business and personal relationships is possible in theory but not in practice. The path to a business divorce is often equally complicated. Understanding the process by which it occurs can help partners avoid it or effect a constructive resolution. Application of this learning improves the chances of not encountering the same problems again.

DEVELOPMENTAL HISTORY OF A DIVORCE

The seeds of a business divorce may be sown at any point in the relationship. In some businesses, they are sown at the very beginning when doubts about entering the relationship are relegated to the background as the partners are seduced by the challenge and the vision of success. Those self-doubts lie inert until aroused by chronic problems that are increasingly experienced as unresolvable. In other businesses, the relationship may be satisfactory for an extended period of time until the comfort level in working together becomes increasingly problematic. The seeds of divorce begin to germinate as differences on important issues remain unresolved or as hard feelings develop and go unattended. Chronic controversy gradually erodes the confidence gained from past successes in problem resolution.

A paradigm for business divorce contains 10 stages, which overlap and can be bidirectional. The path of divorce may stabilize at various points along the way and may even be interrupted by periods of improvement as the partners temporarily regain their ability to resolve problems. For most, this is a temporary respite, and the unresolvable problems recur. This cycle can go on until the partners learn to cope harmoniously on a more satisfactory and consistent basis or until they ultimately end the relationship.

Stage 1: Formation of a Partnership

The first point of vulnerability in a partnership involves the degree of compatibility between the partners' personalities and value systems. The mesmerizing effect of starting a new business can make it easy to overlook incompatibilities as partners observe each other through the lens of optimism and persuade themselves that offending characteristics will change over time. In much the same way, a man or woman may marry with the idea that he or she will be able to change any unattractive personality trait in the prospective partner. This approach works no better in a business partnership than it does in a marriage.

Example: Failure to deal with personality and value differences plays a significant part in the business divorces in the case examples described in Appendix A. In four of the cases—Management Consulting Firm, Textile Company, Furniture Company, and Insurance Company—the partnerships started with the partners' awareness of personality incompatibilities. With the exception of the management company, the partnerships were formed in spite of that awareness because of family ties and commitments.

Stage 2: The Business Start-Up

The climate in which business relationships are initiated varies from great enthusiasm and euphoria to more sober attitudes. For some, the start of a business relationship is so exciting and challenging that any anxieties are obscured. Any problems and disagreements that crop up are optimistically dismissed with the notion that something will be worked out. Indeed, euphoria at start-up can lead to feelings of invincibility and dampen any nagging concern about long-term outcomes.

For others, a business relationship begins with careful planning reflecting an awareness of all the considerations that provide the best chance of success. Vision and enthusiasm are tempered by recognition of these realities.

Example: The Management Consulting Firm partners were so entranced by their visions for their business that they minimized basic personality differences and values, only to have them resurface as major issues after a few months.

In contrast, the Nursing Home Company was founded on the basis of a sound business plan and careful attention to its implementation. The partners expressed cautious optimism for their business. They were doing well until they decided to expand their business. Under pressure of evolving events, they did not apply their usual careful attention to checking out the compatibility of prospective new partners. They soon learned that cutting corners has its price.

Stage 3: Awareness of a Serious Relationship Problem

Awareness of the possibility of a partnership, as in marriage, starts well before it is talked about. Once talking about it results in a partnership, only matters immediately related to starting the business gain attention. After the business is running well enough to permit time for reflection, the partners can turn to matters they had to neglect. First, they should take care of matters that carry the greatest prospect of solution, for successfully resolving them will enhance confidence in the partner relationship. The regular incidence of unresolved tension and mistrust will erode the partners' confidence that they can address their differences. Partners know they have a serious problem on their hands when attempts to resolve problems increasingly become more adversarial than collaborative, when their focus shifts from issues to blaming each other, when values that were once held jointly move in a different direction, when commonly held beliefs about matters related to the business yield to different evaluations, when it becomes more and more difficult to agree on priorities, when issues in a partner's personal life significantly interfere with fulfilling partnership responsibilities, or when the level of commitment to the partnership changes.

In these instances, caution and mistrust gradually replace camaraderie, and events that are normally dealt with readily become more difficult to manage. Often it takes more energy to accomplish less. Once fulfilled by being in business together, the partners feel stressed, avoid important issues, and may confront one another with hostility; awareness gradually emerges that the partnership is in deep trouble.

Example: The partners of the Textile Company, the Furniture Company, and the Insurance Company all started their businesses aware that their working relationships were strained. Finding solutions to their problems was often a more adversarial than collaborative process. They had difficulty agreeing on priorities because of value differences and their inability to deal with their differences constructively. In all three cases, the partnerships were formed when the brothers inherited businesses from their fathers; unfortunately, they had varying commitments to making the partnerships work.

The partners of the Construction Company, the Management Consulting Firm, the Sporting Goods Company, and the Nursing Home Company started with the expectation of good working relationships, and it would be months to several years before serious relationship problems began to surface. The Construction Company, the Consulting Firm, and the Nursing Home became aware of serious problems in about a year. The Sporting Goods Company's problems did not occur for several years because the partners' work commitments did not afford the partners the time needed to test their ability to work together.

Stage 4: Attempts to Resolve Relationship Problems

In healthy partnerships, the differences between partners are an asset. The partners recognize that a complementary benefit can accrue from personality and value differences, and they have confidence that they can merge their differences for the good of their business. They therefore address relationship problems as soon as they arise, and they learn to tolerate those times when the results are disappointing. Concern arises when unsatisfactory occurrences become too frequent, and the residual tension increases the likelihood that the experience will be repeated. Gradually, the partners begin to avoid facing issues that in earlier times they addressed quite comfortably. This process feeds on itself and only leads to increased tension.

Example: In the Construction Company example, Jerry and Ernie had a successful relationship until Ernie's son became involved in the business and undermined their relationship. Eventually, the threat of financial disaster enabled them to regain their former relationship. Only through financial crisis did Ernie face the disappointment and humiliation of his son's mismanagement.

The Medical Group Practice and the Law Firm are examples of partnerships that never develop the trust needed to resolve differences. In both cases, fundamental value differences in business management led to an early termination of the partnership.

Stage 5: Businesses with an Uncertain Future

Chronic difficulty in resolving differences clouds the future of the business relationship. Both partners may begin to wonder whether their relationship will survive, but in this period they do not acknowledge it to one another and at times not even to themselves. This felt uncertainty distracts them from business matters and further exacerbates the tension between them. This readily becomes a vicious cycle that, if left uninterrupted, will hasten the demise of the partnership.

The struggle to cope with unresolved tension often erupts into exchanging blame. The chance of a constructive resolution rapidly diminishes, as more energy is expended on the exchange of blame and less on constructive effort. Allowing such behavior to get out of control will undermine the business and compromise individual and business reputations. The situation gets more complicated and difficult when sale of the business is involved.

Example: The Sporting Goods Company found itself in a period of serious financial crisis, putting a great deal of strain on the partnership of father and four sons. The tension increased as the financial crisis grew and it became evident that the partnership would not survive. Relationships between the partners became so tense that they could not perform their responsibilities. Ultimately, the financial crisis forced three of the sons to leave the business.

A somewhat similar situation developed in the Advertising Company example. The partners had worked together for 12 years, during which the business was conducted mostly under conditions of a stressed partnership. Both partners had more and more doubts about the viability of their partnership, which were not alleviated by changing business conditions. Although they finally decided to terminate their partnership, they found they could not do so for a period of time because of standing commitments. Once they agreed on the terms for the divorce and the uncertainty of their situation ceased, they functioned more easily and showed more tolerance of their differences.

Stage 6: Unresolvable Awareness Differences

With the realization that differences cannot be resolved, anticipatory mourning of the relationship begins and plans are made to end the partnership. The specifics of when and how the partners will openly confront the fact that their partnership is in jeopardy is likely to be guided by efforts to gain advantage before raising the issue.

The divorce is amicable when one or more of the partners recognizes that their commitment to their business has changed so radically that it interferes with constructively continuing in the business. That change in commitment may be a statement about their relationship, the nature of the business, or both. Sharing an awareness of a shift in priorities as soon as the shift becomes obvious provides an opportunity to evaluate whether mutually acceptable ways can be found to continue or end the partnership, or whether a hostile divorce is more likely.

Attending to the business during this period can make an already stressful situation worse. Preoccupation with the possibility of divorce is likely to hamper judgment and to divert energy from current business activities. The business is likely to suffer, particularly as employees, sensing the tension between the partners, become distracted from their duties. Employees might be tempted to take advantage of this situation and seek financial incentives to ensure they don't leave the company in a time of crisis, or they may seek other employment if they feel their jobs are at risk.

Intermingled with concerns about coping with current issues are thoughts about the possible consequences of a terminated partnership. Whether those possibilities are seen as desirable or undesirable will influence how much energy a partner will direct toward resolution or, alternatively, toward pursuit of the divorce.

Example: When one of the partners in the Textile Company—the younger brother, Josh—recognized that the differences between him and his brother Mark were not going to be resolved, he began to develop other business possibilities for himself before confronting his brother with his conclusion.

The brother partners in the Insurance Company used another approach to this kind of problem. The younger brother, Sam, feeling disenfranchised when his brother was put in charge of the business, dealt with his feelings by developing outside deals and interests.

Stage 7: Unresolvable Differences as an Open Issue

Eventually, both partners will acknowledge the precarious status of their business relationship and will begin to confront their willingness to address the sources of tension, or they will decide how and when to terminate the relationship. Getting their concerns out into the open becomes a relief, but the relief is likely to be short-lived, lasting only until the next unresolved argument reminds them of the tenuousness of their relationship.

When partners view divorce as a very threatening prospect, the ability to focus on important issues is hampered. Such distraction is likely to become a self-fulfilling prophecy: the more the distraction occurs, the greater the possibility that problematic behavior will increase and the greater the likelihood of a business divorce. When the partner with these concerns feels helpless to influence evolving events, the impact of the distraction will only increase. Less effort will be expended on resolving differences when the partners view the business relationship with mixed feelings or when there is a rumbling desire to get out. Once alternatives to ending the business relationship became sufficiently attractive, termination will be hastened.

Example: The partners in both the Medical Group Practice and the Law Practice publicly proclaimed that their differences were unresolvable and as a result achieved speedy resolutions. In both cases, there had been insufficient acknowledgment of concerns and no good faith effort at negotiation, and so the partnerships came to a quick end.

A different outcome occurred for the partners of the Management Consulting Firm. When Gregory declared that his differences with his other partners were unresolvable, a period of open hostility began during which he accused his partners of ignoring his concerns. The result was a protracted period of stressfulness that permeated the entire staff.

Stage 8: The Decision to Divorce

Knowledge of when to end the struggle and institute the divorce proceeding occurs in stage 6, when the partners conclude that their differences are unresolvable, or in stage 7, when they become an open issue. Although many different reasons may account for the breakdown, the underlying one is that individual priorities have become sufficiently important to overshadow the commitment to shared priorities.

The considerations that influence the decision to get a divorce include the following:

- *Whether one partner buys out the other or there is a sale to a third party.* Partners who have animosity toward one another may have an easier time selling to a third party than in buying one another out. In this way neither one gains the benefit of the other's effort.

- *The meaning a divorce has for the partners—relief, shame, loss of an opportunity or vision, failure, and so on.* Facing the prospect of the negative feelings that accompany a divorce may lead a partner to put off implementing the divorce until the discomfort of staying in the relationship exceeds that of divorce.

- *Each partner's confidence in finding new business opportunities after the divorce.* Partners who have other viable business opportunities in sight have more incentive to pursue the divorce.

- *The partners' willingness to negotiate in spite of any personal animosities they may have toward one another.* Partners who are able to subordinate their personal struggles in service of effecting an acceptable divorce will be more willing to go the divorce route.

Example: In the Law Firm and the Medical Group Practice cases, Alex and Jean left their respective partnerships when their differences of opinion about compensation practices overshadowed their commitment to shared goals and values. This was also the case in the Advertising Company. Fred's commitment to the partnership was not as great as his growing displeasure over Kurt's gruff manner in dealing with disagreements. Eventually, Fred concluded that the benefits of the partnership were not worth the stress required to maintain it.

Conditions for Amicable Divorce

The way the decision to divorce evolves will determine whether the divorce is amicable or hostile. Divorce occurs amicably when the partners jointly recognize that their commitment to their business has shifted so much that they cannot constructively continue the partnership. This breakdown may occur because of the perceived irretrievable deterioration in the partner relationship, obsolescence of the business's product or service, the desire of one or more partners to pursue another business interest, or personal reasons such as health problems or changing family needs.

Promptly sharing one's awareness of shifting priorities with one's partner provides an optimal opportunity to evaluate whether the partnership can continue or should be ended or whether a hostile divorce is likely to occur.

Example: The decision to divorce was made relatively quickly in the Medical Group Practice, the Law Firm, and the Nursing Home Company cases, once it became clear that a major issue was not resolvable. In the Medical Group and the Law Firm, the issue was about distribution of compensation. The decision in the Nursing Home Company case came very quickly after the chief operating officer discovered a misallocation of funds.

In the Advertising Business and Furniture Company cases, the decision to divorce was a far more protracted one. It took the partners in the Advertising Business a long time to arrive at a decision because the level of dissatisfaction was more tolerable than the anticipated stress of dissolving a 12-year partnership. Eventually, the demands of managing the business on a day-to-day basis left too little time and energy for their business goals and they opted for divorce. A similar situation occurred in the Furniture Company.

Conditions for Hostile Divorce

The conditions that lead to a hostile divorce include the following:

- One partner may use the threat of divorce as an attempt to manipulate the relationship. This risky effort often backfires when the partner proposing it is not prepared to follow through if the other partner accepts the proposal of a divorce.
- Personality differences become incompatible.
- The divorce benefits one partner and not the other.
- One partner makes accusations of malfeasance against the other.

Stage 9: The Emotional Aspects of Divorce

Many conditions may impede the divorce process. Here are some of the more notable:

- *Difficulty reaching agreement to divorce.* A business divorce is difficult under the best of conditions. Coming to terms with the prospect of dissolution is made more difficult when a partner has a great deal of unresolved anger, when only one partner wants a divorce, or when there is resistance to ending the partnership.
- *Fear of the divorce process.* The process of negotiation involves a tumultuous series of offers and counteroffers that inevitably involves waves of frustration between the partners and between the partners and the lawyers. Interwoven periods of anger and rationality only add to the turmoil.
- *Free-floating anxiety.* Proceeding with a divorce can be very difficult when the anxiety surrounding it is free floating. Such anxiety may occur as a result of feelings of helplessness and vulnerability regarding the undesirable consequences of divorce, feelings of sadness over the ending of a long-held dream, or the felt absence of any viable financial opportunity after the divorce. The impact of such concerns keeps a person from defining and addressing the specifics involved in a divorce. The more a person remains subject to vague fear and its related anxiety, the more difficulty he or she will have effecting a constructive resolution.
- *Absence of viable alternatives.* Facing divorce is difficult when no viable job alternatives exist. Persisting in the business relationship may sometimes seem more

acceptable than the felt absence of options. The perception that the financial consequences of divorce are either uncertain or too great can prolong the partnership as long as possible, even though doing so may be more costly in the long run.

- *Anger.* The significant presence of anger in one or both partners, as well as blame, resentment, and shame, will interfere with reasoned attempts to accomplish the business divorce.

- *Facing failure.* Some people hang on to a bad business relationship in an attempt to avoid facing failure. The pain involved in confronting failure may override the compelling logic that the divorce must proceed. Characteristically, when the emotional discomfort reaches a certain level, cognitive behavior becomes subordinate to emotional needs.

- *Loss of a vision.* Facing the loss of a dream and the end of prestige and perks can be emotionally compelling reasons for resisting a divorce. People who cannot face such feelings are likely to persist in the fantasy that somehow things will work out. But that only delays the inevitable. People at this point tend to reach for easy solutions without adequate consideration and avoid considering consequences that can become emotionally and financially detrimental or even disastrous.

- *Impact of past history.* A history of handling divorce and other losses poorly will color the ability to cope with another loss. Those who have experienced painful and unresolved losses are likely to repeat those experiences. They tend to be quick to judge and to blame others for the impending divorce. They can also take the path of denial that anything is wrong until facing the problem that can no longer be avoided.

  Divorce negotiations are likely to arouse feelings of felt injustices in both the past and the present. These injustices may involve old issues that are being revisited or new ones that may or may not have been previously discussed. At the public level, partners may blame each other, their employees, the economy, government policies, and so on. Privately, they may blame themselves, their families, or any other source that might help alleviate their pain.

- *Divorce as unexpected.* Coping with the divorce process is more difficult if a partner's decision to divorce is unexpected. Under such a condition, a person needs time to deal with the pain of the impending loss, to explore possible solutions, to find time to prepare for the negotiations, and to consider postdivorce options.

- *Power of familiarity.* Familiarity is a powerful reason for continuing in a bad situation. Many people feel more secure dealing with a known difficult situation than with unknown situations.

- *Ambivalence about getting divorced.* When a partner has mixed feelings about ending the business relationship, he or she may at times focus on preserving the relationship and at other times on getting the divorce. That gives rise to frustrating divorce negotiations. Positions and feelings may change from day to day, creating great confusion for all concerned.

- *Conflict in the attorney-client relationship.* Relationship problems often develop between attorney and client as a result of either issues of substance in the negotiation or the overflow of tensions involved in the divorce process. A client tends to hold the attorney accountable when negotiations are not going well, either with or without a reasonable basis.

Some conditions facilitate the completion of divorce, such as the following:

- *Confidence in postdivorce opportunities.* Partners can define acceptable consequences that follow the business divorce on both business and personal levels.

- *Agreement on use of third parties.* Once partners have decided to divorce, their relationship is further tested as they seek to effect it in a constructive manner. If their relationship is too strained, they usually resort to third parties such as attorneys, accountants, mediators, and therapists. The use of third parties is a mixed blessing, however, for while it provides some objectivity, it also carries the potential for more stress in anticipation of an uncertain outcome. The involvement of a third party increases anxiety resulting from the feeling of diminished control of events.

- *Agreement on business management during divorce negotiations.* Agreement on how to cope with day-to-day business problems during the divorce process reduces the possibility of adding problems to ongoing negotiations.

- *Compatibility between partners and their lawyers.* The attorney-client relationship becomes a short-term partnership in service of accomplishing acceptable terms for a business divorce. Some of the same basic principles that apply to any partnership will determine the success of this partnership, namely, the necessity for open communication, including effective ways to deal with differences, understanding and agreement on expectations of one another, and a timely follow-through on commitments.

- *Recognition that the partnership is no longer viable.* An amicable joint recognition that there is no longer a desire to continue the partnership facilitates the negotiation of a divorce. The way to an amicable end is eased when the partners have a good working relationship and there are no significant outstanding unresolved issues.

Example: The partners in the Advertising Business had faced a number of difficulties in contemplating the divorce process and had vacillated on the necessity for a divorce for several years. Fred was very threatened by the negotiations necessary to get a divorce, and he was not very comfortable dealing with Kurt's anger. Both partners harbored lots of anger and resentment over issues that had not been adequately addressed. Moreover, both of them were disappointed that they had not achieved their shared vision of a profitable and creative business. Having gone through two marital divorces, Kurt was leery about going through a business divorce. On the positive side, both partners were confident that they would find alternative business opportunities if they dissolved their partnership. Fortunately, the business was sufficiently established that they had little difficulty coping with day-to-day issues during the divorce process. Encouragement from his wife enabled Kurt to pursue the divorce to completion.

The Sporting Goods Company faced a different set of issues in its pursuit of a business divorce. The economic pressures confronting this business forced a change in the partnership, which resulted in three sons leaving. The father, Paul, usually functioned under a great deal of anxiety, and the prospect of his sons leaving the partnership only deepened his anxiety. The divorce proved a great blow to him because it represented not just failure but the shattering of his vision of a family business that would outlive him. The business had been started decades before by his own father and grandfather.

Business divorces affect the partners' families, and families are themselves contributors to divorce when their needs compete with business needs. The degree to which families are affected depends on the kinds of changes, both good and bad, produced by the divorce, including changes in income, the partner's now greater availability to the family, reduced stress, loss of business perks, and uncertain future prospects.

With the tensions of the divorce, the partner will have less energy to devote to his or her family, thereby adding more strain to an already overstressed situation. And if family relationships were already difficult prior to the beginning of the proceedings, the situation can become intolerable. Thus things can go from bad to worse. When family pressures are strong enough, the partners may even be willing to endure their discontent and avoid the divorce or may sacrifice more than they would otherwise be inclined to do to satisfy family needs.

Example: Fred, a partner in the Advertising Business case, proceeded to initiate a business divorce in part because of pressure from his wife, Helen, who was increasingly upset over their deteriorating marriage. She blamed the partnership and convinced Fred that they would manage financially if the partnership ended. She urged him to follow through on the divorce, a process he had talked about doing for a long time.

The Sporting Goods Company faced a far more difficult situation. The survival of the business was at risk. And as a result, the three sons had to leave the partnership because it could no longer support all of them. This placed a heavy burden on family relationships. Far more damaging to the family was the discovery that the three brothers had not been privy to how the finances were being managed during the period that led up to the crisis. The revelation of that exclusion created a great deal of anger because the three were personally liable for business debts. One of the sons, Brad, was completely cut off from his parents, and as a result the relationships of his three children with their grandparents were shattered. All three sons who left the business suffered significant financial consequences following the breakup of the partnership.

Stage 10: Adjustment after the Business Divorce

The pain of divorce can be mitigated if acceptable job opportunities arise. However, a fractured relationship takes time to heal even if the partners part with respect for one another. Often, the trauma of a failed business becomes intertwined with the personal relationship, limiting the possibility of any future dealings. In difficult cases, professional counseling may be needed to help cope with the consequences of the divorce.

GUIDELINES FOR AVOIDING A BUSINESS DIVORCE

Partners can take the following steps to avoid resorting to divorce or to mitigate its negative impact if divorce is unavoidable:

1. Determine the compatibility of personalities before considering a partnership.
2. Regularly review the status of the relationship, much as a financial review would be performed, considering both positive and negative experiences.
3. Address problems that develop in the business relationship in a prompt manner. Delay takes energy away from the business and exacerbates existing problems, making solutions much more difficult.
4. In resolving differences, focus on specifics and not on general concepts that are subject to varying interpretations.
5. Express feelings, needs, and concerns frankly but in a constructive way even though it may provoke controversy. This provides an opportunity to know what the problem is. The greatest danger comes from failure to discuss problems.
6. Resolve differences by finding solutions acceptable to all concerned. Win-lose solutions ultimately lead to lose-lose solutions.

CHAPTER 20

Troubled Partnerships

Carl B. Israel and Marvin Snider

All business partnerships eventually run into difficulty; sometimes the difficulty is resolvable and other times not. Eventually, major unresolved problems end in divorce. A number of options may be considered when the prospect of divorce appears likely. In this chapter, we use a case study to illustrate how a partnership got into trouble and how the partners approached the options available to them in considering divorce.

PIEDMONT MARBLE AND GRANITE COMPANY

Harry and Fred formed a company for the purpose of selling marble and granite tile as well as customized kitchen and bathroom flooring, counters, and sinks. It is now 10 years later. Each owns a 45 percent interest, although each owns 50 percent of the voting stock. The company, called Piedmont Marble and Granite Company, originally signed a 20-year lease (10 years still remain), and both stockholders are personally guaranteed on that obligation of the company. In addition, the company obtained a $1 million line of credit from a local bank, which is presently in effect and is usually at capacity, and signed an equipment lease for $2 million worth of cutting and polishing equipment (of which approximately 50 percent has been paid down). Both of these obligations are also guaranteed by the two shareholders.

Harry, the chief executive officer and president, is 60 years old and has been in the marble and granite business most of his adult life. Fred, the treasurer and clerk, is 40 years old and is a great salesman. Harry has a 30-year-old son, Tom, who is an employee and has recently purchased 10 percent of the company, but his slice of the business is made up of nonvoting stock. Until recently, Tom was in sales under Fred's wing. The three of them make up the board of directors of the company.

The company recently decided to go into the wholesale business of selling large slabs of granite and marble to retailers and contractors. The wholesale end is very profitable because it is not labor intensive and has the potential of becoming a major portion of the business. Harry wanted to put Tom in charge of that part of the business, but Fred objected, viewing it as a potential threat to his position in the company after Harry steps down. However, Fred was outvoted by Harry and Tom, and Tom took over the wholesale division. Recently, the wholesale business has taken off, beating all expectations and overshadowing Fred's performance for sales on the retail side. Harry and Tom are plotting future expansion of the business but are not taking Fred into their confidences.

This year sales are way off in the retail division because of the ongoing economic recession. Harry is therefore leaning on Fred to either increase his end of the business or be prepared to take a substantial salary cut. The wholesale division, on the other hand, is still doing well, and Harry wants to give Tom a salary increase. Fred, unhappy with this turn of events, calls for a board meeting. At the meeting, Fred argues that all three of them—not just Fred—should take a salary cut, or alternatively he proposes that other tightening measures should be taken. All the same, Tom gets his increase and Fred is given 90 days to increase sales dramatically or receive the cut in pay. Fred leaves the meeting with knowledge that it is getting more and more difficult to deal with Harry and Tom.

Three months pass. The recession has deepened and retail sales are still down, at which point Harry puts Fred's pay cut into effect. In addition, Harry and Tom have begun discussing the possibility of splitting off the wholesale division and making it into a separate company and either giving or selling the stock at some minimal value.

Before approaching Fred with this idea, however, Harry and Tom consult with their personal attorney as to the viability of their plan. The attorney states that Fred will of course object to the proposal. Aware that the relationship between the three shareholders is breaking down, the attorney suggests that they prepare a formal shareholder agreement delineating procedures in the event of any shareholder's termination of employment either by death, disability, retirement, or voluntary or involuntary termination. The lawyer also proposes that all employees, including the three shareholders, sign noncompetition agreements in the event anyone should leave the company. The attorney advises Harry to discuss these types of agreements with the company's attorney and have them drawn up. When Fred learns of the suggested agreements, he becomes even more anxious about his position with the company and decides to consult with his own attorney to see if he has reason to be concerned.

In the interim, despite cost cutting, the company needs to increase its line of credit with the bank by almost double. The bank agrees to the increase but requires new loan documents and new guarantee forms to be signed by all three shareholders. Fred flatly refuses to sign anything until he settles his concerns with Harry and Tom. Harry and Tom are livid because the company needs the money immediately. Both sides contact their respective attorneys to discuss their next moves.

SELECTING AN ATTORNEY

Because Fred senses that the partnership might not survive this crisis, he decides to select an attorney experienced in managing business divorce, should that ultimate step become necessary. He considers what criteria to use in making his selection. Recognizing that initiating a collateral partnership with a lawyer warrants the same care one exercises in entering a business partnership, he adopts the following criteria for this selection:

1. His and the lawyer's personalities should be compatible.
2. The lawyer will be responsive to his phone calls.
3. The lawyer is available for consultation either by phone or office conference.
4. The lawyer is experienced in corporate and partnership law in general and in business divorces in particular.
5. The lawyer is an experienced negotiator.
6. The lawyer fully explains all fees in advance, and fees are compatible with his ability to pay.

Fred is fully aware that lawyers working with troubled partnerships often have to ask hard questions that may be embarrassing and may present him with difficult choices. From his research he knows that he must not take out his frustration and anger over the process on his attorney, for that would add to the problem. The discerning client quickly learns that the best way to proceed is to focus on how to make the best of the situation rather than getting into a blaming contest.

Fred understands that it is reasonable to expect his lawyer to handle the case without becoming reactive to it. He needs to be alert to signs that his attorney is uncomfortable dealing with his distress and should question whether he has a suitable fit with his lawyer. He accepts that a successful lawyer-client relationship requires that both be able to speak frankly about their respective concerns when a problem develops in the relationship. He acknowledges this is best accomplished when the client's feelings focus on issues and not on personal judgments—"I am angry at what you did or did not say or what you did or did not do," as opposed to, "How could you make such a statement," or "You don't know what you are talking about." A client and his attorney have enough problems to handle without letting personal differences undermine their working relationship.

Ending a business relationship, Fred thinks, especially one that is of long standing, is much like coping with marital divorce and death. A major adjustment will be required to handle the change, just as a mourning process is necessary in dealing with death. Mourning is a process for adjusting to change, even if the partnership experience was very unpleasant. It also becomes clear to Fred that his lawyer will need to know all of his client's problems and concerns, what issues are bothering him about his partners and why. Finally, the attorney will need to know as much as possible about his adversary. It's not always a rational business issue that drives a wedge between partners. Whatever caused the breakdown between partners, the attorney must become aware of it as quickly as possible in order to map out a successful strategy.

Consideration of these variables leads Fred to select Cecil Wise, an experienced corporate lawyer, as his attorney. After listening to Fred's account of what has been happening at the company, Cecil tells Fred he will have to review the Articles of Incorporation, the bylaws, the shareholder agreements regarding governance, and financials for the last three years. In addition Cecil wants to review the law relating to protection of minority shareholders even though Fred owns 50 percent of the voting stock. Cecil asks Fred what remedies he proposes and whether he can force a deadlock at the shareholder level. Cecil has some immediate advice for Fred. He urges him not to agree to sell the wholesale division or to sign a stockholder agreement at this time; he also advises him not to sign a noncompetition agreement or the new bank guarantee yet.

Cecil agrees that Fred's partners are probably plotting either to lessen Fred's say in the business or possibly to split the lucrative wholesale division off from the company and to sell or give Harry's son Tom a controlling interest for little consideration. Cecil also tells Fred that although he owns 50 percent of the voting stock, he can use that vote only to deadlock a stockholder vote. It has no effect at the board of directors level. At that level he is outvoted by his two other partners. Moreover, as president, Harry has control over the day-to-day operations of the company.

Therefore, the lawyer urges Fred to plan a strategy designed to stop his partners from lessening the value of the company or his interest in the company. Fred, he says, will have to be alert and attend all meetings that touch on the wholesale division. Finally, Cecil tells Fred to emphasize to his partners that no action relating to the sale of the division or refinancing will be tolerated without Fred's okay.

Cecil also asks Fred whether he might be willing to sell his interest to his partners, to which Fred gives an adamant no! The business is his life, and besides that he is much too young to retire.

When Fred returns to work the next day, Harry asks him when he is going to sign his guarantee and also tells him that the wholesale division has to be split off into a separate company that should be owned 50 percent by Tom and 25 percent each by Harry and Fred. When Fred refuses both, Harry and Tom consult with the company's attorney, Beatrice Fine, to let her know that there are some real storm clouds forming. Beatrice can see that this may very well be a matter that precludes her from taking sides. While she sympathizes with Harry and Tom, particularly with regard to the immediate need for the increased line of credit, she agrees to discuss matters with Fred. After talking to Fred, she meets with all three partners and announces that the three-way partnership is clearly no longer working.

SPLITTING UP THE PARTNERSHIP

The split could be handled in two ways:

- Harry and Tom could stay and Fred could leave. This would be a complicated process because Harry and Fred were jointly involved in a lot of financial commitments. Fred would therefore have to be bought out, which might require additional borrowing. Fred would want his name taken off the bank and lease guarantees, but Tom is not strong enough financially to substitute for Fred.

- Harry and Fred could stay and Tom could spin off the wholesale division. This option seems to be a more viable one since Tom already has been running the wholesale division. In addition Harry and Tom have not had much to do with the division, being much more comfortable with the retail business they have been handling for years. To make it easier for Tom to buy out Fred and Harry, Harry might give his interest to Tom as a gift.

After protracted discussion the partners agree with Bernice that Tom will handle the newly split-off wholesale division and that selling the division to Tom makes the most sense. She recommends that each side consult an attorney. Beatrice indicates that the following steps will need to be considered:

- An impartial valuation by one or more appraisers of both the retail and whole-sale divisions of the company needs to be made. This might be difficult to do because the wholesale company is only two years old. They should keep in mind that there is presently only one company, so the appraisers will have to allocate overhead and salaries as if there were two separate companies.

- Fred and Harry will be buying Tom's shares in the company. The company then will spin off its wholesale division by selling the assets of the wholesale division to Tom. Tom might also be assuming some of the liabilities.

- A decision will have to be made as to whether Tom can relocate his business or whether he can sublet space from the company.

- Fred and Harry need the approval of their bank before they can sell off a division. The bank might look for additional collateral from Harry and Fred to go along with the deal.
- The three partners should also consider signing noncompetition agreements between their respective companies and owners. Even though they agree in principle on how to break up the partnership, everyone recognizes that a number of issues need to be resolved.

There are three approaches to effecting a business divorce: adversarial, mediation, and arbitration. In the *adversarial approach*, each partner retains a lawyer in an attempt to accomplish an agreement that maximizes that partner's interests. This can involve protracted negotiations or wind up in court. The *mediation approach* involves the services of a disinterested third party experienced in resolving disputes. The mediator helps develop an agreement that is acceptable to both sides. The mediator's only power is that of a facilitator; he or she has no power to impose a solution. In *arbitration*, arbitrators act as a board, serving the same function as a court but without the formality, expense, and delay associated with court litigation.

FREUND'S APPROACH TO MEDIATION

James C. Freund (1997), an experienced negotiator, recommends a 12-step approach to mediation. Both parties are present for the first three steps:

Step 1: Set the ground rules for the mediation.

Step 2: Permit each party to air his or her grievances in the presence of the other party.

Step 3: Ask the parties to rehash their prior settlement negotiations (if any) leading up to the mediation.

Step 4: Listen to each partner complain in private about how difficult the other partner is to live with; and pose inquiries, the answers to which will be useful to the mediator in helping the parties determine the threshold questions of whether the situation is ripe for a divorce and, if so, what form it should take.

The following steps assume that the mediator and the parties have concluded that the best solution is to split up the business.

Step 5: Hold an additional separate discussion through which the mediator assesses the parties' differing priorities on the issues, decides which issues can and cannot be resolved, and prepares the parties for step 6.

Step 6: Invite each party to propose privately a fair basis for the split up and probe each proposal with that party.

Step 7: Develop the mediator's realistic expectation as to the basis on which the company might be divided.

Step 8: Present orally to each partner a proposal for splitting up the company and receive their individual critiques.

Step 9: Shuttle back and forth between the parties on specific issues—a mix of serving as bearer of each partner's position and offering the mediator's own evaluation of what is feasible. This will determine whether the parties can be brought into closer proximity.

The next step assumes that progress has been made.

Step 10: Present the parties with a written agreement in principle, which serves to record their agreement on those issues that have been resolved, along with the mediator's recommendations for handling the matters still in dispute.

Step 11: Conduct the final rounds of negotiation to enable the parties to reach agreement in principle.

Step 12: Help the parties turn their agreement in principle into a binding agreement and close the deal.

One statement of Freund's is quite debatable. He writes:

The guiding principle for the mediator is never to lose sight of rationality. The situation is often highly emotional, sometimes containing a degree of bitterness akin to that in a failed marriage. The mediator's job, however, is to make the parties realize that what is at issue here, after all, is a business. They have to put their emotions behind them and work out rational, commercially reasonable outcomes. (p. 520)

Although people may well have the capacity to "put their emotions behind them," emotions often are so strong that they quite overpower intellect. That is the case when a person in the guise of behaving rationally sticks to a given position beyond the point supported by the data. A more satisfactory outcome is likely to result if emotional issues are addressed before attempting to tackle the business issues.

Freund defines the crucial ground rules for dispute resolution as laid out by the CPR Institute for Dispute Resolution (366 Madison Ave., New York, NY 10017, 212-949-6490):

1. Mediation is a voluntary, nonbinding process from which the parties can withdraw if they are not satisfied—but at least they will refrain from making war while they are engaged in the mediation.

2. The mediator is permitted to meet separately with each party and to determine whether meetings should be joint, separate, or a little of each.

3. The mediator will not pass along information received from one party to the other party (or to any third party) unless authorized to do so by the party providing the information.

4. The mediator may express his or her views on the issues in the dispute and can also suggest appropriate resolutions.

5. The entire process is confidential. Nothing is usable in evidence if the parties go back to court. The mediator cannot act as an arbitrator (unless both parties later consent) or be called as a witness, and the documents in his or her possession are not subject to subpoena.

The choice of how to approach the resolution of issues was relatively easy for the partners in the case example. Since they had a reasonably good working relationship, they all agreed that mediation would be the best way to proceed.

WAYS TO DISSOLVE A PARTNERSHIP

As they explored the process of dissolving a partnership further, Harry, Fred, and Tom learned that they had options in the way they could dissolve the business.

One Partner Sells His or Her Interest to the Other Partner

This is the most common solution to the problem and depends on one partner being willing to leave the business and the other having both the desire and wherewithal to buy out the departing partner's interest. This solution is particularly useful if the departing partner no longer wishes to stay in the business.

Resolution becomes much more problematic if the departing partner wants to stay in a similar business and compete with the company. This will likely happen only when the departing partner's prospects for success offset the lower buyout price that the remaining partner is willing to pay. Certainly, the remaining partner will not be willing to pay for a business that is not fully realized because of competition from the departing partner. He or she might be willing to do so if other compensation is possible, namely, real estate or ownership of products with future potential.

From the selling partner's standpoint, the most important issues usually relate to how much he or she will be receiving for his or her interest, over what period of time it will be paid, and what security ensures payment of the outstanding amount. Other issues may relate to restrictions on the selling partner's future activities (e.g., noncompete clauses) and outstanding liabilities for which the selling partner may be personally obligated (e.g., bank loans).

Aside from any financial considerations, selling out to a partner can produce the feeling of losing, no matter how advantageous the deal. This feeling can arise even if the partner is happy to get out of the business. Letting one's creation go is somewhat akin to giving up your child for adoption. Frequently, a partner in this situation goes through a difficult period until he or she becomes accustomed to the idea of being out of the business.

One Partner Buys Out the Other Partner's Interest

Here the buyer's focus is completely different from that of the seller. The buying partner is concerned with how much he or she is paying for the selling partner's interest. He or she also will want to structure the deal in a way that will minimize his or her tax liability. In addition, the buyer may want to make sure that the seller doesn't open the same type of business around the corner, selling to the same customers, in which case the buyer may end up paying for nothing. The buyer therefore may want to insist on a broad noncompetition agreement as part of any buyout package.

Buying out a partner can be done in different frames of mind. At one end of the scale, the partner is thrilled; at the other end, the partner might be filled with apprehension about whether he or she can carry the business off by him- or herself. Being thrilled carries with it the presumption of confidence in the buyer's ability to run the business by him- or herself or confidence of finding another partner. Though this point is obvious, it is often overlooked. As in marital relationships, people make the same mistakes when going from one relationship to another simply because it is difficult to face why the relationship failed.

At the apprehensive end of the scale is the challenge to make sure such feelings do not interfere with the buyer's managing the business on his or her own. If the plan is to get a new partner, the buyer needs to be careful not to let his or her vulnerability and eagerness for a new partner blind him or her to finding a good fit. The prospect of getting that good fit will be enhanced if the new partner is chosen on the basis of what the buyer learns from the last partnership.

One Partner Sells His or Her Interest to a Third Party

Occasionally, the breakup is resolved by having one of the parties sell his or her interest to a third party. Technically, if a partner leaves a two-person partnership and another takes his or her place, the old partnership is terminated. This is not the case in a corporation. In addition, selling shares does not affect a corporation's legal status.

Even if no legal obstacles block transferring an ownership interest to an outside third party, attracting a third party to come into an unhappy business partnership and pay money to do so is not very realistic. It usually works only when the outside third-party buyer is currently working at the company with either little or no ownership in the company. To be a realistic alternative, however, it will need the remaining partner's blessing. How a partner reacts to the idea of selling his or her interest to a third party depends on how the remaining partner feels about it, the partner's reason for doing it, and how he or she feels about leaving the business.

If leaving the business occurs under amicable circumstances, then the selling partner's only problem is adjusting to the change of not being in the business. If leaving the business is not by choice, there is the added problem of coping with being forced out. In that case, selling to a third party can be a bitter experience. This problem can be all the more difficult if the departing partner feels the business was his or her creation. This would not be the same if the seller initiated the sale.

Sale of the Business to a Third Party

Selling the business to a third party can be an effective way to work out what is usually the most difficult aspect of any buyout: determining the price. When the focus is on one partner buying out the other, valuation of the selling partner's interest is the key issue, and it is fraught with problems of conflicting interests—particularly if the parties have not already worked out in advance a valuation formula for the buyout.

A good way to establish the fair market value of a business is through the bid of an interested legitimate outside third party, and preferably more than one outside bidder. Often irreconcilable business differences fade away when a healthy bid comes from an outsider. A common problem is getting the parties to agree to sell to an outsider before their dispute rips their business apart and drives it into the remaining alternatives. The attitude taken to selling to a third party depends on the selling price, the circumstances under which the business is sold, the relationship between partners, and whether more than one alternative is available.

Feelings of relief are likely to be present if getting out of the business is viewed as a positive step, especially if the partners share that sentiment and the relationship is intact. The situation is likely to be quite different if selling the business is not being done by choice. In that case, the adjustment will be painful and even more so if the sale is significantly related to the partners' incompatibility. Having another business opportunity in mind can make the transition easier.

In our case example, Harry and Fred bought out Tom's interest, which was acceptable to all concerned. The situation would have been far more difficult if Harry and Tom had squeezed Fred out of management and had forced him to sell them his interest.

The discussion about business divorce led Harry and Fred to anticipate what they should keep in mind should they come to a point when dissolving their partnership might be desired or necessary. They were told that it does not make financial sense to break up a partnership by way of an orderly liquidation and dissolution when the business is still profitable. That rarely occurs because an orderly liquidation and dissolution will not usually bring the highest return. Under normal circumstances, one partner wants to take over running the business, or if not, both parties will sell it to a third party rather than liquidate it. However, if the business's future prospects are dim and no goodwill remains, an orderly dissolution of the business and liquidation of the assets can make good sense to both partners. Investing more capital or taking on the risk of borrowing is not sensible just to keep a doubtful business going. In this situation, economic self-interest should outweigh most internal disputes between the partners.

An orderly liquidation or dissolution presumes that there are at least as many assets as there are liabilities, that creditors are paid what they are owed, and that the partners may even be able to walk away free of debt, if not with something in their pockets.

Ending a partnership for any reason can be difficult. The task is eased when the partners' relationship is viable and they can jointly experience the mourning process. When the partnership is marked by animosity, the mourning process is greatly complicated, as is the dissolution process.

PROCESS FOR RESOLVING DISPUTES

Partners should provide a mechanism for resolving disputes in the event terminating the partnership becomes desirable. Harry and Fred recognized from their earlier discussions that mediation was the preferred way to resolve conflicts. However, they felt that the process could be improved by developing a game plan and agreeing on the rules to be followed in accomplishing it.

Prearranged Agreement to Resolve Buyout Disputes

Much as a couple signs a prenuptial agreement in anticipation of marriage, business partners can try to avoid costly and antagonistic disputes when their relationship breaks down. Such agreements should cover methods of coping with death, disability, retirement, and voluntary or involuntary departure of a partner. They can also establish a value for the departing partner's interest in the business or a procedure to determine its worth. These agreements may also address issues of payout terms, including the number of years the buyer has to pay for the seller's interest, whether there will be interest on any unpaid balance in the event of an installment sale, and whether the seller will have security in the event of nonpayment. They may also address the question of whether life or disability insurance should be purchased to facilitate the payment for a deceased or disabled partner's share.

Taking the time and effort to draw up such an agreement can alleviate the grief that comes with negotiating the end of a business partnership under stressful conditions. At that time, the stress and anxiety leading to termination can handicap one's ability to make prudent decisions.

There is an emotional contradiction in talking about negotiating the end of a relationship before it has started. At that time, it is easy to skimp on the details of this kind of agreement. It is useful to provide for the worst scenario and stipulate how to cope with the death, disability, retirement, and voluntary or involuntary departure of either partner. Engaging in this exercise has one added benefit: prospective partners get to know each other under challenging conditions that either reinforce the wisdom of choosing the partner in the first place or become a cause for concern. In the latter case, it is prudent to reevaluate whether proceeding with the partnership is warranted.

Agreement to a Bidding Process

Commonly, partners do not sign or even consider a prearranged agreement for the buyout of a departing partner. Moreover, when the partners are discussing an impending breakup and how to handle it, they are usually in their most emotional and antagonistic states of mind. Nevertheless, it is up to the partners and their advisors to arrive at some mutually acceptable method of dealing with the breakup.

One method for deciding who will remain in the business is to conduct a bidding process whereby the high bidder is chosen. This method assumes that both parties want the business. First, the ground rules have to be established, such as the terms for payment. Will payment be all cash, or will it be an installment sale? If an installment sale is involved, what period of time, what interest rate factor, what security for payment, and so on are involved? Once all the terms but the price are agreed upon, the rules are established for the bidding. One way to keep everyone honest is to have each party submit his or her bid in a closed envelope. The high bid gets the business. The secret bid assures the parties of getting the very highest bid, as opposed to conducting an auction in which a partner might hold back depending on how high the other bidding partner is willing to go.

This bidding option is attractive to a person with a gambling instinct and a comfortable sense of what the business is worth. The challenge in any such bidding situation is to determine how much the bidder wants the business and how much he or she is willing to risk to get it. One consideration in formulating a bid is the resultant feeling if the offer is too low. The objective is to get the business at the lowest price. Which is more important—paying too much for the business or bidding too low and losing the business?

Another consideration in making the bid is to examine how each partner would feel if the other got the business, all other considerations aside. If the partnership relationship has been hostile, one partner might be tempted to make an unrealistically high bid in order to ensure that his or her partner doesn't get the business. The thought of the other partner walking away with all that was invested in the business over the years would be intolerable. When emotions are strong enough, they can short-circuit business logic and create a disastrous economic situation for the "winning bidder."

One Partner Sets the Price, the Other One Selects

This option presents an interesting challenge. For it to be a viable option, the partners have to be willing to go either way—to buy the business or to leave it. One partner sets the price as low as possible in the event he or she buys it and high enough if he or she is bought out. In return, the other partner decides who buys and who sells. This process yields a realistic price on the business.

Agreement to Sell to a Third Party

The key words "agreement to sell" assume that the parties have decided to sell to a third party, either an outsider or someone presently in the business who is not an owner. The parties should consider having the business evaluated prior to placing it on the market, particularly if it is either unique or is not commonly sold using some standard formula in its industry. The parties usually have a better chance of achieving their goal if there is some rational foundation for the asking price.

Another consideration is whether to use a business broker or whether to handle the sale personally. If confidentiality is important, a business broker can be extremely helpful in preventing premature disclosure of the desire to sell the business. Otherwise, there is the risk of losing employees or frightening customers or suppliers through rumors that the business is for sale, as well as leading competitors to circulate rumors designed to hurt the business.

In addition to business brokers, businesses are often sold through the use of accountants, banks, investment brokers, and others in the same industry. Newspaper ads are also used. If confidentiality is a concern, it is prudent to use a phone number other than the business number.

A sale to a third party is acceptable unless one of the selling partners is being unduly influenced by too attractive an employment offer by the buyer. If this is the case, it represents an increase in the purchase price paid to one of the selling partners at the expense of the other selling partner. Even if the employment offer to one of the selling partners is at standard rates, it means that one selling partner is receiving something in addition to the purchase price that the other selling partner may not be receiving. Such an occurrence should be fully disclosed to all the selling partners in advance of the sale, and in that way the divorcing partners are kept in line.

This option minimizes the possibility that emotional entanglements between the partners will get in the way of making the best possible business decision. One problem that may still occur derives from a history of competition for control of the partnership. Identifying who has the greater influence in negotiating terms for the sale may be as important to the partners as any other consideration. Problems also arise when one partner has real value to the buyer while the other does not.

Another problem will remain if sale of the business was forced by one of the partners. The resentment felt by the other partner could get expressed in difficult negotiations regarding terms of the sale. All such rancor can be avoided if the partners work out their differences before putting the business on the market. That approach will be to their mutual advantage both for purposes of the sale and their relationship afterward.

Agreement to Dissolve and Liquidate

If the parties are contemplating a dissolution and liquidation, it means they have usually determined that there is no purchaser for the business or no bid worthy of consideration. The parties have also decided that the liquidated value of the assets either exceeds or is about even with the liabilities, so that all the creditors will be paid either what they are owed or what they will accept. Some businesses hold going-out-of-business sales, others bring in auctioneers, and still others sell their businesses piecemeal over an extended period of time. Each situation is different, but the final result is the same. The business comes to an end, the creditors are paid, and the partners split the remainder—usually in accordance with the laws of liquidation and dissolution. In brief, the laws usually provide for the following order of payment: all third-party creditors (secured creditors first, then unsecured); amounts owed to partners as creditors (i.e., loans to the business); repayment of capital; and profits in proportion to ownership interest. According to the laws in most states, the business, if incorporated, will continue to have a life for a short period of time even after dissolution and liquidation. This protects unpaid creditors or others who are making claims against the business. If it was a partnership, the individual partners will remain liable for those unpaid creditors and claimants.

Forcing a Dissolution and Liquidation

In some cases, the parties cannot reach agreement on which direction to take and at least one party will want out of the business. If the business is a partnership, a partner can usually withdraw and demand a dissolution, a liquidation, and an accounting. It is an entirely different story if the business has been incorporated. In that circumstance, most jurisdictions have mechanisms for forcing a dissolution and liquidation, but it may require not only a deadlock of the board of directors and shareholders, but also evidence that the business cannot economically survive if the deadlock continues. In many cases, the business continues to operate profitably despite the deadlock, and the courts may therefore be very reluctant to force a liquidation and dissolution, leading the parties back to square one. That is why cooler heads must try to come up with some agreed-upon method to accomplish the business divorce.

The partner who chooses to force a liquidation must be prepared for a rough time, whereas the partner who wishes to continue the business is likely to feel betrayed and undermined. This will be all the more of a problem if such action puts him or her in a precarious financial situation or under emotional pressure. Whatever good feelings existed between partners will be at risk.

The partner seeking liquidation should be sure that the remaining partner understands that this action is not frivolous but has been necessitated by personal financial or emotional need. The remaining partner will need to understand that it is not in his or her interest for the business to continue under such conditions.

The situation of the partner wanting out has its own difficulties. Facing the loss of a business in which he or she has invested a great deal financially and emotionally can weigh heavily. Moreover, leaving a partner of long standing and losing that relationship may be difficult. The situation will be quite the reverse if the relationship has been problematic.

As indicated earlier, the partners in our case example agreed to use mediation as a means of dissolving the partnership involving Tom. The partnership between Harry and Fred continued, with adjustments made to account for Tom's departure.

BANKRUPTCY

If their business had not been solvent, Harry, Fred, and Tom would have had to consider a different set of options, as follows.

Involuntary Bankruptcy

Involuntary bankruptcy is likely to occur if the dispute between the partners has been long drawn out and expensive, and therefore has negatively affected the viability of the business. In this scenario, the company cannot pay its bills as they become due, or it has more liabilities than assets, or both. The real concern, therefore, moves from how much one's interest in the business is worth to how many personal obligations are involved if the business fails. If the company begins to head in this direction, the attorneys for the partners must make sure their clients are placed in the hands of experts in bankruptcy, before the situation becomes a total disaster. Briefly, there are alternatives to bankruptcy such as making an assignment for the benefit of creditors, whereby unsecured creditors are treated the same but usually end up with less than 100 percent on the dollar. Bankruptcy is voluntary when the debtor files and involuntary when the creditors file and force the debtor into bankruptcy. Both are under the auspices of the bankruptcy court. Therefore, there are more formal procedures, which are usually more expensive than an assignment for the benefit of creditors.

Significant differences exist between a corporation and a partnership going into bankruptcy. A corporation is a legal entity, and it is separate from the owner and stockholders. The shareholders don't necessarily go into bankruptcy when the business does. But they might also be forced into bankruptcy if they were guarantors on the corporate obligations and neither the business nor the shareholders can pay those obligations when due. When a partnership needs to file for bankruptcy, all the partners file as well, since all the partners are *jointly* and severally responsible for all the debts of the partnership. The partner need not guarantee the debts of the partnership since, by law, he or she is fully liable for the debts of the partnership.

Bankruptcies are very difficult procedures and prove embarrassing when they are viewed as a failure of the partners. Added to the private sense of failure is the public disclosure of it. Attempts to cope with the discomfort lead the partners to blame the other as the cause of the problem. The challenge to partners is to put their energies into ways to fix the problem and get out of the bankruptcy, if that remains an option. Where the bankruptcy forces the termination of the business, the focus is on how to manage the mourning period.

Voluntary Filing of Bankruptcy

When the parties have agreed to end their relationship as partners by ending their business, the business is insolvent. It either has fewer assets than liabilities, or it cannot pay its debts as they come due. One way to avoid being forced into involuntary bankruptcy is the first-strike action of filing for bankruptcy. This will prevent creditors from forcing bankruptcy. At such times, the help of professionals specializing in this area to guide one through the pitfalls is recommended, particularly if the business has not been current with the payment of payroll taxes or if the partners are personally liable for other debt. As noted earlier in this chapter, there are significant differences between corporations and partnerships when it comes to bankruptcy.

Nonbankruptcy Procedures

A nonbankruptcy procedure such as an assignment for the benefit of creditors may also fit the situation. The key here is for the parties to face reality as soon as possible in order to ward off personal bankruptcy. This alternative is not easy when there is a lot of discord among the partners or when there are personal guarantees on obligations of the business that cannot be paid. Hopefully, the parties can set their differences aside and act for their personal good. Partners do well to take the peremptory step of initiating the action themselves, giving them some sense of being masters of their own fate.

SETTING A VALUE FOR THE BUSINESS

Once the partners have decided that a divorce is unavoidable, the next consideration is to determine the value of the business as a whole and the value each owner has in the business. In many cases, a process for effectuating the divorce cannot be started until the parties know what the business is worth. Furthermore, no matter which process is finally chosen, the owners must have clear knowledge of the value of the business.

Determining this value can be tricky and complicated. The more straightforward approach is to determine it based on standard procedures that deal solely with numbers. More difficult to evaluate are intangibles such as goodwill and the impact of the partners' personalities on the business profits. Partners may have a hard time dealing with an arm's-length assessment of their business's value when these other considerations do not get the attention they think appropriate. The way to accomplish this is to hire an outside evaluator.

In some cases, the choice of the evaluator is predetermined through an agreement between the owners, as part of a "prenuptial agreement." Such agreements are called buyout or stock redemption agreements. Life is simplified when the parties have already agreed on these matters before temperatures run high. However, most business partners don't execute such an agreement, and so they are forced into making this evaluation when there is diminished trust among them. At such times, the prudent will obtain their own evaluator regardless of the process selected for the divorce. Each one must feel that he or she is receiving advice on the value of the business from a totally independent agent. Utilizing a resource free from conflict of interest eliminates one source of stress and potential conflict. It also assures the partner that his or her interests are getting the best possible protection.

Inside Comptroller/Chief Financial Officer

If all parties are confident that the company's comptroller or chief financial officer (CFO) can arrive at an unbiased fair value, that person may be a good choice for the evaluator. This is especially so if the type of business in question is normally valued by relying heavily on its fixed assets such as inventory, real estate, equipment, and accounts receivable, as opposed to intangibles such as goodwill or an approach that relies on comparisons with the sale of other businesses in the same industry.

Accounting Firm Servicing the Business

In many buyout or redemption agreements between business partners, the accountant who is servicing the business is designated as the person who will determine the value of the business. Even if no agreement is in place prior to the divorce negotiations, the accountant may still be the appropriate person. He or she is likely to be in a better position than the inside CFO to provide comparisons of what similar businesses are selling for, especially if the accountant is servicing clients in the same type of business.

The caveat here, as well as when the inside financial officer is being used, is that if you are the selling partner and the accountant or insider financial officer hopes to stay on with the company, there is a built-in conflict. Obviously, in that situation the selling partner should be aware that the accountant or CFO will naturally want to please the buying partner who will continue the business and, the accountant or CFO hopes, continue using his or her services. However, if the playing field is level and both partners are looking to sell to a third party who has his or her own accountant or CFO, much less of a problem arises as long as the accountant or CFO has sufficient knowledge to perform an evaluation of the business.

Outside Business Evaluator

For many businesses, industry valuations and guidelines have become the customary way to arrive at the sale or market price. In those situations, an evaluator with a good reputation in the specific industry in question is recommended. This brings immediate credibility to the evaluation. In situations where there are two co-owners of the business, they can choose a process whereby one of them will buy out the other. In order to arrive at a price, each party may bring in his or her own industry expert. When these experts are close enough in their evaluations, the two parties can split the difference and arrive at an accepted value for the business.

Independent Accounting Firm

If the business is not in an industry that has its own unique valuation process and the company's accountant is expecting to stay on to service the company, the selling partner should seriously consider hiring his or her own independent accounting firm to advise him or her on the valuation of the business. One reason for doing so is that there are generally three typical approaches to valuing a business: market-based, asset-based, and income-based. Within those three approaches several factors need to be considered. Deciding which approach to emphasize or which factors are most important can be somewhat subjective. It is not an exact science, and therefore the values that are ultimately arrived at can diverge widely.

The selling partner will be in a better bargaining position if he or she has an evaluation that rationally adopts the approach that would place the highest possible value on the company. The independent accountant can also prove very useful to both sides if he or she comes back with an evaluation that agrees with either the value being used by the company's accountant or another valuation being used by the buying partner.

Combination of Methods

In certain industries, it is not unusual for the seller and buyer to use different methods for evaluation. The selling or buying party will want to take an approach that is most advantageous to his or her position regardless of what may be "traditional." In that situation, one party may be using an outside industry evaluator, while the other is using an accounting firm. The challenge for the attorneys is to keep the parties talking even if one side feels the evaluation being submitted by the other is way out of line.

Placing the Business for Sale to a Third Party

The parties need to understand what their business is worth in order to effectively sell it to a third party. In most instances, the parties are working together as opposed to each trying to arrive at the evaluation separately. Furthermore, the parties' agreement on the value of the business does not mean that an outside third party is willing to purchase the business. In this instance, the valuation is not the basis of an agreement between the parties but merely a guideline for effectively selling the business to a third party. The business may sell for more or less than the appraisal depending on market conditions, the needs of the third-party buyer, and the needs of other selling partners.

As indicated earlier, once the business is up for sale to the public at large, the parties are usually satisfied that they are receiving the fair market value from the third-party buyer, unless it is considered a forced sale. In this scenario, it is usually possible to avoid wrangling over whose accountant or appraiser provided the true and correct valuation of the business.

Other Methods

Another method of arriving at valuation is to hold an auction, usually private, but it may be public as well. Sometimes the private auction method is confined to the owners only. In this way, the highest bidder gets it, but since it is not a secret or a sealed bid, the competing parties can pace themselves. This may be an acceptable method, but it doesn't always ensure that the highest value will be placed on the business. Bidding can also be limited to a select group of third parties who have indicated a desire to purchase, or it can be limited to a combination of owners as well as outside third parties. Here again the owners should try to obtain an evaluation before putting the business up for auction in the event they want to start the bidding at a certain price. The auction could be "with reserve" so that if a minimum is not reached, the owners can withdraw the business from the auction. In addition to valuation, the terms of the purchase should also be agreed to before the auction begins so that everyone is on a level playing field.

The discussion Harry and Fred had with the company's lawyer about what is involved when a business is dissolved led them to appreciate the importance of having a buyout agreement before this became an issue. This discussion led them to put this agreement in effect. They learned that such agreements are useful in the following ways.

First they had to understand that the terms *buyout agreement, shareholder redemption agreement,* and *cross-purchase agreement* all connote some type of agreement that the partners/shareholders of a business enter into so that they can establish ground rules in advance in the event a partner/shareholder leaves the business.

Eventually, every business partnership relationship, no matter how successful, comes to an end. The termination may be caused by the death or retirement of a partner or, more commonly, by a partner leaving the business or being asked to leave for any one of myriad reasons.

Unlike a prenuptial agreement that must be entered into prior to the marriage of the signatories, so-called buyout agreements can be entered into at any time prior to the breakup. It makes good business sense for the partners to decide how to deal with various breakup events early on in their relationship. Like prenuptial agreements, the parties to them can predetermine the disposition of the business between them in the event of a breakup and thereby save the enormous time, energy, and expense that are typically needed when the parties have not signed that type of agreement.

BUYOUT AGREEMENTS

Events Included in a Buyout Agreement

Death of a Partner

All buyout agreements should cover the death of a partner. When asked the question "Do you want your partner's spouse or children to inherit his share of the business and become your new partner when he dies?" invariably the answer that comes back is an emphatic "No!" Interestingly enough, when a partner is asked if, after his death, he would feel his family would be sufficiently protected without a buyout agreement of the deceased's interest in the business, the answer is yet another emphatic "No!" The family of a deceased partner is usually looking for liquidity to pay bills, taxes, and so on, and will not necessarily want to continue to retain its interest in the business. Under ordinary circumstances, both sides usually agree that the surviving partner or partners will carry on the business and that the deceased partner's estate will be bought out of its share. Obviously, there are exceptions whereby the deceased's spouse and family continue in the business, but that is not the topic of this discussion.

Death as a breakup event can be insured against and therefore can be easier for the business partners to deal with, especially if the subject comes up when they are young, healthy, and insurable.

Once the partners have ascertained the desirability of buying out a deceased partner, they have to determine how to arrive at the value of the deceased partner's interest and when and how that will be paid.

Disability

The disability of a partner, especially permanent and total disability, is a breakup event like death, which most business partners can agree should be the subject of a buyout agreement, at least with regard to the active, working partners. Unlike death, the concern here is to clearly and unambiguously define what is permanent and total disability. Many people are not aware that a business can arrange through insurance for a lump-sum buyout, just as in the case of death, for a disabled partner. This kind of insurance should not be confused with a disability income insurance policy that provides the insured with an income in the event of temporary or permanent disability. The income protection–type policy is often a benefit that a company provides to its executive employees, regardless of whether they hold an ownership interest.

If one partner holds an ownership interest strictly because he or she has provided needed capital or loans to the business (i.e., he or she is an investor partner as opposed to a working partner), the need to buy that partner's interest out in the event of his or her permanent and total disability may not be a factor.

Retirement

The retirement of a partner is clearly a breakup event, and while the business cannot insure against it, as it can for death or disability, over the course of the partner's employment it can provide various retirement-type funds that can be factored into the price agreed upon for purchasing his or her interest in the business. Eligibility for retirement should depend on what is normal for similar businesses, what the tax code may allow for drawing down from retirement funds without penalties, and what deferred compensation plans stipulate.

Another consideration with regard to retirement is whether it would be beneficial to either the business or to the retiree, or both, to consider having them enter into a consulting agreement for a period of time after retirement. That may give the business the benefit of the retiree's knowledge and the ability to deduct the payments for his or her services. Since the business cannot deduct for the payments it makes to buy out the retiree's interest, it could provide the retiree with a consulting arrangement that would keep him or her partially employed for a period of time rather than fight over whether the buyout amount for his or her interest in the business might be unreasonably high. The idea is to be as creative as possible within the confines of the law and good business sense.

The business will also want to consider putting some restrictions on the retiree resurfacing as a competitor after announcing his or her retirement. Certainly, if the retiree is getting paid for his or her percentage of the fair value of the business, the remaining partner will not want to see the retiree come back as a competitor and undermine the value of the business by taking away clients or accounts. That would amount to double payment.

Voluntary or Forced Departure

Whether a partner wants to leave voluntarily or is forced out, the parties can provide for all types of alternatives and work out a buyout of the departing partner's interest. One alternative is to require the business to purchase the departing partner's interest. The drawback to this approach is that the remaining partner may resist being forced to buy the interest of the departing partner, depending on how the business is being valued and the timing of the departure. This may be particularly so if the partner leaves at a highly profitable stage in the business's history that may never be duplicated. Furthermore, a requirement that the business purchase a departing partner's interest places the control with the departing partner, not with the business or remaining partner.

A better alternative for the business and the remaining partner may be to give them the option to purchase the departing partner's share on the date of departure or for some period after departure. This method shifts control of when and if to buy out the departing partner's interest to the business and the remaining partner. Another alternative is to use the right of first refusal, which gives the business or remaining partner the right to match any offer that the departing partner may receive from an outside third party for his or her interest in the business. Unfortunately, a less-than-100-percent interest in a nonpublicly traded business is difficult enough to sell; giving a right of first refusal to the business or remaining partner effectively and utterly destroys the departing partner's ability to sell his or her share to a third party. The parties often resolve the control issue by looking at the reasons for the departure and determining which party made the decision.

If a partner is being asked to leave because the personality fit isn't right, because the partner's vision of the business's future has changed, or because he or she is no longer productive, the business should be required to buy his or her interest. On the other hand, if a partner decides to leave on his or her own accord, whether or not he or she intends to compete, the business should have an option to purchase or have a right of first refusal and not be forced to buy out the departing partner's interest.

Valuation of the Business

Regardless of which breakup event occurs, or whether the remaining or departing partner can trigger the buyout, all buyout events require that a methodology be worked out for arriving at the value of the departing partner's interest and a period of time in which to pay the value. Both the value of the business and the length of time for payment may be influenced by the reason for the departure. If a partner leaves voluntarily and goes into competition with the business, the valuation of his or her interest, as well as how long the business has to pay him or her, may reflect that fact. To punish the partner, the business may purchase his or her shares at a very low value to be paid over many years. This approach discourages a partner from leaving and competing.

On the other hand, the agreement should reflect the remaining partner's willingness to pay full value to the departing partner if he or she is being asked to leave, or if the departing partner is relocating at some noncompetitive distance or entering a different type of business. Payments should be made over the shortest period the business or the remaining partner can afford without jeopardizing their financial stability.

The actual methodology used to arrive at the purchase price can be quite varied; there are no general rules of thumb. The Internal Revenue Code has rules for valuing businesses for estate tax purposes. In addition, there are customary valuation rules in many industries or business fields, and the parties and their legal, accounting, and financial advisors may be helpful in coming up with a figure or formula that everyone can agree upon.

If the agreement uses a fixed monetary amount, the parties must carefully review that amount at least once a year to make sure it reflects the current value or must build in flexibility. Thus, in arriving at a figure, the parties are not forced to use a stale number that no longer reflects the actual value of the business. Without flexibility it can be a crapshoot, at best, as to who might benefit, and at worst, the parties will be litigating. Flexibility can be built into agreements by requiring the parties to arrive at a new figure within a fixed period of time after the end of the tax year. Another way is to value the business at the time of the breakup incident, assuming the last valuation is more than six months old.

Using a formula instead of a fixed number gives the parties more flexibility and may not require them to agree on a valuation once a year. In any event, the parties should review the agreement often in order to make sure that any life or disability buyout insurance purchased is still sufficient to cover the purchase of a deceased or disabled partner's interest. Even if the partners don't wish to purchase additional insurance, they should at least know how much additional money will be needed beyond the insurance proceeds so that no unpleasant surprises await when the buyout agreement is finally instituted. The formula itself should be reviewed because it may become outdated. For example, businesses in a certain segment of industry may sell at two or three times earnings before taxes, but for many different reasons may later be selling for only one or one and one-half times earnings before taxes. One reason that a business sells for less may be that the profit margin in that industry may have declined; a second reason may be that competition has driven the prices down; and a third may be a pessimistic outlook for the future. To understand this last concept one need only look at the value of local pharmacies or hardware stores over the past 10 to 15 years. Regardless of whether the partners agree on a formula or a fixed amount, they have to determine over what period of time the business or other partners have to pay the agreed-upon purchase price.

If insurance is involved in the buyout and it fully covers the agreed-upon price, the business may be able to pay the purchase price in one lump sum. However, if the insurance is not sufficient, or if the breakup event is not insurable, such as a voluntary or an involuntary withdrawal from the business, then the payout period becomes extremely important to both the remaining and the departing partners.

The remaining partners will want to ensure that they have sufficient capital to operate the business and to address the cost of replacing the departing partner. They will be more likely to favor a prolonged payment period even if they are required to pay interest on the unpaid balance. From the standpoint of the departing partners, the concerns will be focused on replacing lost income from wages or perhaps on whether the business will be viable enough in the future to make the buyout payments. In fact, the parties often discuss security to insure full payment of the buyout price.

Restrictions on Transferability

One other reason for entering into a buyout agreement when the business is operated out of a corporate shell is to cover restrictions on the transferability of shares owned by the shareholders/partners. The restrictions usually cover the gift, sale, pledge, or other transfer of stock to a third person or entity from the original shareholder. The restrictions are meant to prevent unwanted transfers from occurring without the opportunity for the business or remaining partners to buy out the transferring partner's interest.

In the case example, the partners also learned that dissolving a partnership can become a bit complicated when it comes to sorting out who has what liabilities. They were interested in seeing how that might apply should they decide to dissolve their partnership.

Outstanding Liabilities for Consideration by the Exiting Partner

The exiting partner's success in negotiating his or her deal will be measured not only by how much he or she got for his or her share of the business but also by how much relief was achieved from personal obligations. All too often the euphoria of exiting with a "good deal" minimizes the direct or indirect liability obligations of the exiting partner.

The partner in a general partnership context as opposed to a corporation is personally liable for all business obligations as well as for the negligent or wrongful acts of copartners. When a partner is bought out, the existing partnership comes to a technical, if not legal, termination that involves liquidation, dissolution, payment of all debts, and an accounting between partners to divide profits or, if insolvent, to divide the indebtedness. If one is exiting from a general partnership, the person or persons who are going to carry on the business should notify the world at large that the exiting partner is no longer involved. This becomes a major concern if the exiting partner's name is still being held out to the public as part of the firm. If an outside third party can reasonably assume that the exiting partner is still involved with the business, then the exiting partner can still be liable for the debts of the partnership.

The partners' personal assets are on the line for partnership debts. Therefore, if there are not enough assets to pay the business debts, the partners must personally pay for them; all of their personal assets are subject to being taken for payment. In a general partnership, partners do not sign personal guarantees for the debts of the partnership, because they are already liable for them.

A more common scenario is that of the exiting shareholder in a corporation. A corporation has important advantages over a general partnership, such as limited liability for shareholders. Under ordinary circumstances, therefore, the shareholders are liable up to their investments only in the corporation and not for all of a corporation's debts. This is because a corporation under the law is considered to be an independent person, albeit an artificial one created by law. In addition, a corporation has continued existence and does not terminate when a shareholder leaves. A shareholder of a corporation can also transfer his or her shares to others without causing dissolution of the business. These factors permit an easier exit from the business.

The shareholders of a corporation may sometimes be asked to personally guarantee the obligations of the business. A common example occurs when the business wants to borrow money from a bank. The bank may ask the corporation to sign for the loan and to supply collateral for the payment, which could take many different forms, including having the shareholders personally guarantee the obligations of the corporation. In addition, if the corporation is either new or relatively young, the landlord may ask the shareholders to guarantee the corporate lease. Vendors may ask shareholders to guarantee the debt of a new or financially struggling corporation before supplying product. An exiting shareholder must protect him- or herself from these obligations, just as he or she must make sure that the value being offered for his or her interest is a fair one.

One of the biggest mistakes made by new or relatively new prospective entrepreneurs is too great a casualness about the consequences of commitments to personal financial vulnerability. It is all too easy to slide by the full impact of personal signatures. Although the concept may be clear enough, it is hard for the full implication to be perceived on an emotional level, especially when one is blinded by the excitement and potential rewards of the new venture. Time pressures and other demands do not leave much opportunity for contemplation. The problem is not resolved for those who fully appreciate the implications of making such commitments. The belief that "It will never come to the point of having to fulfill it" can lull one into complacency about making the commitment.

Another consideration when partners are being asked to make personal commitments is to recognize that the partners may have significantly different personal assets. The partner with little to lose can be more eager to make the personal guarantee than the partner with more responsibilities and assets. The partner with the greater risk will do well to consider personal guarantees under worst-case scenarios. When banks call in personal guarantees to cover debts, they go after whoever has the needed assets. Of course, they are more likely to start with those who have the greatest assets. Each partner should therefore take that into consideration before committing to any business relationship.

The shareholder has the potential for greater protection in a corporation; on the other hand, this person does not have any control over what happens unless he or she is an officer, director, or major shareholder. A large shareholder, such as an investment fund, may exert significant influence on the management of a public company.

Protecting against Outstanding Liabilities

The first step in protecting an exiting shareholder from future liability on a guarantee is to require that his or her name be taken off the obligation. This may be accomplished by paying off the obligation in full, paying it down sufficiently so that personal guarantees are no longer required, substituting another's guarantee, or perhaps merely requesting a release of the exiting shareholder's personal guarantee. This may work in many instances but not in all. In some circumstances, for instance, the bank or landlord relies heavily on the exiting shareholder's assets in agreeing to the loan or lease to the business and therefore is not prepared to release the exiting shareholder.

This scenario may require the parties to rethink the viability of the buyout. Assuming, however, that the corporation and exiting shareholder are still willing to go through with the buyout, the exiting shareholder should now be concerned with protecting him- or herself in the event the business defaults on its obligation to the bank or landlord. Under those circumstances, the exiting shareholder should try to obtain indemnification from the corporation as well as the other shareholders in the event he or she is forced to pay on his or her guarantee. In other words, if the exiting shareholder becomes liable for his or her guarantee, he or she can try to collect from the remaining shareholders and the corporation. Unfortunately, by the time the exiting shareholder is being sued on the guarantee, the business is often already in dire financial straits, as may be the remaining shareholders as well.

The exiting shareholder may want to back the indemnifications of the corporation and the remaining shareholders with collateral, such as a security interest on the assets of the corporation or the remaining shareholders. However, as an example, one needs to determine whether there are any assets not already encumbered by a security interest by the bank.

At the very least, one should try to negotiate some protection for those personal obligations that will continue once the shareholder is bought out.

The complications that can derive from personal guarantees underscore the importance of giving very careful worst-case consideration before making such a commitment. Such consideration includes being able and willing to risk living with it happening. Even when that is done, there is no guarantee that it will work out as planned. There may be no way to eliminate risk. This risk is part of the package of being an entrepreneur. The best that can be done is to minimize it, which is accomplished through cold realism about the viability of the business opportunity, the relationships needed to sustain it, and the risks involved.

Steps to Limiting Liabilities

1. Have all obligations on which the exiting partner/shareholder is liable paid off or paid down at the time of exit so as to allow for his or her release from those obligations.

2. If obligations cannot be paid off or paid down sufficiently at the time of exit, obtain the release of the exiting partner/shareholder from any responsibility for the obligation.

3. If a release cannot be obtained and the exiting partner/shareholder still wants out, obtain indemnifications from the corporation and the remaining shareholders or, in the case of a partnership, from the partners who are continuing the business. If possible, obtain security for those indemnifications.

These possibilities may not be a problem in a viable business. However, a common reason for wanting to exit a business venture is the perceived risk and a desire to protect against it. Attempting to protect the risk in a business that is in financial straits is likely to be a very difficult, if not impossible, process. The difficulty happens because there are insufficient corporate or personal resources to get proper indemnification because the creditor refuses to grant a release. The best way to avoid such a situation is to ensure that the opportunity to exit is adequately considered at the point of entering such an arrangement. The absence of a satisfactory arrangement for that purpose should put the wisdom of participating in the venture in question.

REFERENCE

Freund, J.C. (1997). Anatomy of a split-up: Mediating the business divorce. *Business Lawyer* 52(2), 479–530.

CHAPTER 21

After the Divorce

A relationship ends when its benefits are outweighed by its deficits or when external pressures such as involuntary bankruptcy occur. A valuable learning opportunity will be lost if the grief surrounding the divorce is permitted to prevent a review of how and why it happened. It is equally important not to let the negative aspects of the experience overshadow an appreciation of the positive aspects. Engaging in this process helps to heal wounds and to integrate learning that comes from both successes and failures. When done adequately, the evaluation, or mourning, process can provide confidence, rather than pessimism, in approaching future partnership opportunities.

COPING WITH THE LOST PARTNERSHIP

Undesired and unexpected losses in business follow a process of adjustment similar to that which one goes through upon the death of a loved one. The process commonly referred to as mourning characteristically involves a number of stages: disappointment, shock or panic, anger, guilt, blame, and eventual acceptance and replacement with a new experience. Coping with the undesired or unexpected ending of a partnership involves some combination of these experiences, depending on the individual circumstances. The length of time needed to accomplish mourning depends on the meaning individuals attach to ending the relationship and on the quality of future prospects. In very difficult situations, a person can become fixated at any step in the process. A person who loses a business may never recover—that is, he or she will never be able to risk engaging in another business relationship and exposing him- or herself to the disappointment that could result. The consequences of such a loss are even more damaging when it undermines one's self-confidence and willingness to trust. This effect may be expressed in the attitude that losing a relationship is so painful that it is better not to engage in one. One may never get past the anger at the loss or the felt guilt for its occurrence. The successful conclusion of each step in the mourning process is essential to the productive resumption of one's life.

Example: George, a partner in the Furniture Company, never came to grips with the breakup of the partnership. His initial sadness and bitterness over the need to end the partnership continued without cease until his death 15 years later. Even though he was never very fond of his partner—his own brother—he regretted that they had not been able to carry out their father's legacy.

The Sporting Goods Company's partnership was dissolved three years ago. All of the partners, a father and four sons, are still coping with the consequences of that dissolution. The way the partnership ended had a great impact on all of them financially as well as in their interpersonal relationships. For example, Robert, the third-oldest son, continued to harbor anger and resentment toward his father and brother. The result was a complete emotional cutoff from the family: he asked his parents never to call or visit again, or even to see their grandchildren.

Those in family businesses have the most difficulty coming to terms with a lost partnership because the partnership may end but the family relationships usually continue, with ongoing contact between members serving as a bitter reminder of the past. This situation prolongs the mourning period, especially when the end was an acrimonious one.

REFLECTION ON THE CAUSE OF DIVORCE

Whenever we suffer a significant loss we tend to speculate on the precipitating cause and wonder whether the loss could have been avoided. What events caused the change, and could we have prevented them? A common early reaction is to blame someone else for it because generally that is easier than to consider one's own contribution. In either case, a range of feelings from anger to guilt affects the ability to go through the mourning process successfully and greatly complicates closure following the divorce.

Example: A range of reasons caused divorce in the examples considered earlier and in Appendix A. Some are listed here:

- *Construction Company.* Mismanagement of finances by Marshall, Ernie's son, excluding his uncle, Jerry, from participation in major financial decisions, and Ernie's failure to take corrective action on Jerry's behalf.

- *Medical Group Practice and Law Firm.* A partner's departure because of the felt imbalance between work productivity and compensation.

- *Management Consulting Firm.* Gregory's development of mental health problems, which interfered with his ability to relate to his partners constructively.

- *Sporting Goods Company.* Financial mismanagement by Paul and his son, Ethan, to the exclusion of the other sons in financial matters.

- *Nursing Home Company.* Jeff's malfeasance in managing the company.

- *Advertising Business.* Kurt and Fred's chronic incompatibility.

- *Furniture Company.* George's incompatible relationship with his older brother, Manny, Manny's refusal to sell his share in the business, and George's agreement to let Manny buy him out.

- *Insurance Company.* Sam's anger and lackadaisical attitude toward his responsibilities in the company and his resentment of his brother's position.

HOW THE DIVORCE OCCURRED

Whether the divorce occurs voluntarily or involuntarily will affect how it is handled.

Divorce by Choice

Divorce may be precipitated by either partner or by their joint agreement. Although the partners may share many of the feelings that led to the divorce, their feelings about how it came about may differ markedly. A partner who is forced to end a relationship that he or she feels could have become workable is likely to be angry and resentful over the forced termination. The strength of these feelings will depend on many considerations, including the following:

- Whether the partner is able to continue the business by buying his or her partner's share of the business or finding a new partner, or both, as was the case in the Furniture Company.

- Whether the divorce was precipitated by conflict in the relationship or simply by shifting interests, as was the case in the Advertising Company.

- Whether the exiting partner made an apparent good faith effort to find ways to continue the relationship, as was the case in the Insurance Company.

- The way the partner's behavior precipitated the divorce. In the Furniture Company case, destructive behavior precipitated the divorce, whereas in the Medical Practice and Law Firm cases, the divorce was effected in a constructive manner.

- The way the partner not wanting the divorce will be affected financially and professionally. In the Nursing Home Company example, Jim was not seriously affected either financially or professionally when he was forced out of the partnership.

When both partners agree to the divorce, they can focus their joint attention on effecting it. Their attitude in accomplishing the divorce will of course be colored by how they arrived at the decision. If the quality of their relationship was not the issue, then they will have to look at the other possibilities, such as their diminished interest in continuing the business, either in order to pursue other interests or close the business whose viability is in question. Whatever the case, making the decision brings comfort. The only lingering issue may be their remaining differences as to how to terminate the business.

Example: Three companies—the Management Consulting Firm, the Sporting Goods Company, and the Furniture Company—were involved in a divorce by mutual consent. In all three cases, the divorce was finalized only with great difficulty. In both the Management Firm and the Furniture Company cases, the divorce was mainly the result of personality clashes. In the Sporting Goods Company case, financial problems forced the partners to recognize that the partnership as originally defined was no longer viable.

Sometimes both partners want to continue their relationship, but outside considerations force an end to it. For one thing, financial statements may lead bankers to question the viability of the company and to impose restrictions on available loans or on operating procedures, which ultimately means the demise of the company. In addition, a partner's work responsibilities often seriously interfere with his or her marriage and parental commitments, particularly when a large amount of travel is necessary, work hours are long, or the stresses of this existence adversely affect family relations. Alternatively, a partner may decide to leave the business for health reasons—either his or her own or those of a spouse or children. A spouse's health problems or a child's special emotional or physical needs may require more parental support and involvement than the partner's business responsibilities will allow. At worst, a partner's spouse who is significantly handicapped or who dies will most likely require the partner to leave the business.

Imposed Divorce

An imposed divorce means that ending the business relationship is no longer the partners' option. Such a divorce is independent of the quality of the partners' relationship or their interest in continuing the business. Dissolution occurs when the bank recalls loans, creditors press for bankruptcy, or the business or service has become obsolete.

IMPACT OF THE DIVORCE

The effects of a business divorce are felt over a long period of time. The impact starts with the first awareness that the divorce might occur, and it continues for some time after it happens. The length of time involved and the degree of impact are a function of the resulting positive and negative consequences and the business opportunities that follow.

The ending of a business relationship is usually followed by varying intensities of positive and negative feelings depending on the circumstances associated with the divorce. These feelings will diminish with time as the businessperson's attention gradually shifts to developing other career opportunities, attending to family and other personal matters, and accumulating new experiences. The period of adjustment will be markedly shortened if new experiences quickly become more important than the past ones. If that is not the case, past disappointments may lead to negative, self-fulfilling prophecies. Fear of failure will lead to diminished performance and an increased likelihood of repeated failure.

Review of the positive experiences gained in the business might include an appreciation of the information and skills that were learned over the years; nostalgia about lost positive, satisfying relationships; and relief from no longer being subject to negative relationships. Negative feelings, on the other hand, might include anger over lost opportunities, mistakes made on the job, injustices experienced, and recollection of failures and the resulting embarrassment. The intensity of such feelings depends on the degree to which they left permanent scars; those viewed as transient experiences that led to maturity are viewed in a positive light.

The weight a partner gives to the combination of positive and negative recollections determines whether he or she leaves a business divorce with self-confidence. Such confidence is a major determinant of how a person approaches the next step in his or her career.

When the business experience affects a person's health, the affected partner will be constantly reminded of the lost partnership. When feelings about the partnership are largely positive, the limitations may be viewed as the downside of a productive experience. When they are negative, each experience of a limitation may heighten one's awareness of the health problem and one's anger at its impact on the partnership. A secondary problem comes into play when such feelings affect family relationships and future work experiences.

Leaving the company may alternatively have a positive impact on health. Release from all the stress of the business often leads to quick recovery from any transient health problems that the work precipitated. Often, a partner will not even become aware of the impact of the partnership experience until he or she gets some distance from it and, with time, learns more appropriate behavior for the next work experience.

Leaving a company results in a variety of desirable and/or undesirable effects.

Examples:

- *Construction Company.* Ernie was embarrassed when his neglect led his son Marshall to put the business in jeopardy. Ernie was pleased that he and his brother were able to salvage their partnership. Jerry felt good about his efforts, which saved the business and their partnership.

- *Medical Group Practice and Law Firm.* Both Peter and Jean were pleased that they had extricated themselves from an unfavorable situation once it became clear their point of view was being ignored.

- *Management Consulting Firm.* Gregory's reaction to the divorce was complicated by the fact that his emotional breakdown precipitated its occurrence. He didn't know how much blame to attribute to his illness and how much to his relationships. His illness required brief hospitalization at the time it became clear a divorce was necessary. Shortly thereafter Gregory was able to participate in the divorce. Contact with him was lost after the divorce was completed.

    The other partners, though shaken by the surrounding emotional events, felt they had learned from the experience, particularly as regards the importance of compatibility between partners.

- *Sporting Goods Company.* John and Paul, father and son, felt embarrassed and guilty because they had mismanaged the finances and had failed to involve the other brothers in financial decision making. However, they did not publicly express their feelings or take responsibility for their actions. Instead, they developed a rationale to justify their behavior, which further stressed their partnership with the other sons. The brothers who were forced to leave the company felt betrayed, angry, and guilty for not having been more aware of what was happening.

- *Nursing Home Company.* When Jeff, upset that his concerns were not being addressed, left the company, he felt abandoned by his longstanding partners and unappreciated for his contributions. All the same, he was relieved of pressures, and his self-confidence remained undaunted. The remaining partners were embarrassed by their failure to more closely monitor the performance of their new partners. Jim, the managing partner, left the partnership feeling misunderstood and falsely accused and returned to his former work situation outwardly undaunted.

- *Advertising Business.* Fred was relieved that he had pressed for the divorce so strongly and was annoyed only that he had taken so long to do it. Kurt regretted that Fred chose to leave the partnership but had no problem in continuing on his own.

- *Furniture Company.* George was relieved that he was finally free from the struggle with his brother. The divorce affected neither George's business confidence nor his relationships. In retrospect, he felt that the emotional pressure of dissolution took a greater toll than it should have. Manny, happy to be free of pressures from his brother, felt energized and eagerly looked forward to running the company the way he felt it should be run.

- *Insurance Company.* Sam, angered by his brother Bill's mistreatment, was now free to pursue his own interests. Outwardly, he was optimistic about future opportunities, but privately, ever mindful of his brother's accusation that he lacked the ability to follow through, he was anxious about his ability to pursue his interests. Bill, on the other hand, was pleased that he would be able to devote more energy to managing the company.

Impact on Family Relationships

The impact of divorce on the family begins even before the partnership officially ends. The partner going through the business breakup is likely to be less available and more stressed than usual, thereby exacerbating any preexisting family problems. Going through with the divorce presents a new set of challenges. Will the person's greater availability now be applied to improving family relationships? Will feelings about the loss of the business simply add to family problems? If some of the newly available time is not, at least temporarily, spent with the family, the family members will conclude that they have low priority and could stop allowing latitude they allowed because of the pressure of work.

The newfound time provides the divorced businessperson an opportunity to redefine family relationships that had suffered during the demanding work commitments. The person's efforts might not meet with the desired response, not because the family has no interest in bettering the relationship, but because they are protecting themselves from reengaging in a relationship that they feel would revert to form once new employment is found.

Efforts to relate to family become more challenging when the business results in significant loss of income. Doing without material benefits that were taken for granted will test a family's ability to redefine its relationships and lifestyle. The challenge is to work together and to avoid allowing adverse circumstances to add to dissension between family members.

When the person experiencing the business relationship breakup is also a wife and mother, the consequences may be somewhat different for her and for her male counterpart. Her presence at home will likely have greater impact when the termination is viewed with relief; the newly acquired time will lead to more time for family involvement. When she feels the business loss as a deprivation, her negative feelings are likely to get expressed both in nonverbal and verbal cues that the return to homemaking is nothing but a burden.

Finally, termination can allow the businessperson to rekindle or reestablish relationships with friends. It also provides the opportunity to redefine his or her marital relationship and address the feelings and problems that resulted from the business relationship. Lack of time to nurture the relationship and the spouse's feelings of being an only parent and feeling low on the businessperson's list of priorities can be corrected. This occurs when the marital couple are able to jointly redefine their lifestyle.

The same applies in the relationship with one's children. It becomes easy for children to get absorbed in their own world, especially when a parent is absorbed in a career that leaves little time for parenting and the child doesn't feel he or she can compete with the parent's career. Termination provides the parent an opportunity to reestablish the parent-child relationship in a way that is meaningful to both.

Example: Business divorce has its most acute impact when the partners are related to each other, especially when relationships between the family members involved are already strained:

- *Construction Company.* Ernie and Jerry's relationship was already strained when a well-functioning partnership was allowed to deteriorate. This happened when Ernie's son mismanaged the company to the point of near bankruptcy. Only by taking legal action could Jerry get his brother's attention.
- *Sporting Goods Company.* John and his son Paul mismanaged finances, thereby creating a major rift with the families of three of the sons who were forced to leave the partnership. The third son was unhappy but was emotionally unable to address his feelings.
- *Furniture Company.* The divorce added tension to a relationship that was already very stressed. Contact between the families was minimal and, at best, civil when circumstances brought them together at the same event.
- *Insurance Company.* The mother, Ann, was caught in the cross fire between her two sons. She tended to identify with her younger son, Sam, which only intensified the brothers' conflict. It also strained her relationship with her older son, Bill, and his family.

Impact on Finances

The negative consequences of a terminated partnership can be mitigated when financial rewards and enhanced confidence and self-worth follow. The exception is the termination that is so painful that any positive consequences are at least temporarily obscured.

The negative impact of business divorce on the family's financial status creates great stress for all family members. The person involved now finds it harder to adjust to his or her triple loss of the business relationship, financial status, and family stability. The situation becomes even more precarious when considerable debt or the risk of bankruptcy is the case. The combination of such events undermines self-confidence and adversely affects any resources that are available for future business ventures. In turn, it makes it more difficult for the family to adjust to necessary lifestyle changes. Making future plans becomes clouded by uncertainty. A marriage that was already in trouble before the termination may not survive the added stress.

Example: Termination was financially devastating for three of the businesses in the case examples:

- *Sporting Goods Company.* All five partners were pushed to the brink of bankruptcy by the conditions that resulted in the breakup of the partnership. Three of the partners almost lost their homes. The three brothers who left the company were forced to adopt a lifestyle that was far inferior to the one they had enjoyed earlier. Private schools, two-car families, and expensive vacations all became luxuries of the past. The uncertainty of their economic future only added to the dire picture.

- *Nursing Home Company.* The near bankruptcy resulting from Jim's mismanagement created a period of great uncertainty. The company was able to escape unscathed only through Sheldon's determination, personal resources, creativity, and reputation for financial negotiations.

- *Furniture Company.* Gregory did not fare well after the divorce. His desire to distance himself from his brother Manny led him to agree to sell the company to him under terms that he would regret for years to come. With his departure from the partnership, Gregory's new cars, country club membership, and expensive clothes soon disappeared to become replaced by a very modest lifestyle.

Impact Outside of Career and Family

For many people, managing a business leaves little time for other interests. The termination of a business relationship means that at last they can pursue neglected interests and seek other opportunities which often helps them adjust to the loss. The person who never had other interests, however, finds the postrelationship adjustment more difficult.

Example: In the Insurance Company case study, Sam, the disgruntled partner, increasingly turned to racing cars as his disappointment over his place in the company grew

The Business Divorce–Marital Divorce Parallel

Business divorce has consequences comparable to those of a marital breakup. First, let's look at the positive consequences and the negative consequences of a business breakup.

Positive Consequences

- Knowledge gained from the business experience
- A network of colleagues useful in the pursuit of future ventures
- Freedom to pursue new business interests
- Not having to be accountable to a partner
- Decrease in responsibilities

Negative Consequences

- Loss of the enjoyable aspects of the business and partner relationship
- Loss of a dream and a challenge
- Lost perks
- Need to start over

- Negative impact on reputation or professional image
- Lost time
- Loss of valued relationships

Now let's compare those with the consequences of a marital divorce.

Positive Consequences

- Knowledge gained from the marital experience
- Expanded network of friends
- Not having to be accountable to a spouse
- Freedom to pursue new relationships
- Decrease in responsibilities

Negative Consequences

- Loss of companionship
- Loss of a dream
- Loss of positive aspects of lifestyle
- Having to assume added responsibility for managing lifestyle
- Need to start over
- Lost relationships

LESSONS LEARNED FROM THE EXPERIENCE

A forcibly terminated business relationship leads to many negative experiences that are painful and costly in both material and emotional ways. The accrued benefits from knowledge gained from the ordeal can be lost if the pain of the experience interferes with the ability to learn from it. When efforts to identify the learning trigger negative associations, the prospect of repeating mistakes is greatly heightened. Conscious effort is needed to resist the temptation to follow familiar paths.

The learning that takes place on the business level has a parallel on the personal level.

Making a careful assessment of personal gains from the business experience can produce considerable benefits, including gains in knowledge and experience, understanding of the needs of others, new skills, emotional maturity, communication skills, and conflict resolution skills.

Example: In the case examples, Marshall and Fred learned valuable lessons from their respective business experiences.

- *Construction Company.* Marshall learned that remaining passive when dealing with important matters can be disastrous. He discovered that he had waited much too long to take aggressive action after he gleaned the direction in which his nephew was taking the business. Both Marshall and Ernie learned it was a mistake to mix family relationships with business.

- *Advertising Business.* Fred learned that because he was reluctant to adequately take care of a situation that was not good for him, he subjected himself to much needless frustration and discomfort.

PART III

Types of Partnerships

CHAPTER 22

Basic Partnerships

Partnerships fall into two categories: basic and collateral. Basic partnerships are those involved in some form of business enterprise; basic partnerships comprise active, silent, corporate, professional, family business, and product partnerships. Collateral partnerships are those that in one form or another provide support to active partnerships; they are partnerships with professional entities, banks, one's family, and consumers. Basic partnerships are considered here using the dimensions of partnerships described in part I. Collateral partnerships are discussed in chapter 23.

ACTIVE PARTNERSHIPS

The most demanding form of business partnership is one in which both partners actively participate in the daily operation of the business. These partners have joint ownership that may or may not involve equal shares. Ownership contributions may take any combination of financial resources, time, expertise, ideas, special skills, and other characteristics. It is difficult to determine the ownership portion when the contributions to any of the dimensions that define the partnership are not equal.

Partners share risks, responsibilities, and rewards. The division of labor in managing responsibilities and the distribution of rewards are ongoing challenges in a partnership. Success in a partnership is heavily dependent on managing these issues in a manner satisfactory to both partners. Specifically, partners are liable for each other's behavior, and both partners likely have to sign personally for any loans in all but well-established businesses.

Dimensions

The care with which a partnership is launched determines its probability of success. A sound business plan with compatible partners and appropriate resources gets this partnership off on the right footing

Values, beliefs, and goals define the superstructure of the partnership and function as its compass. A value is a statement that defines what should happen, whereas a belief reflects the perception of what exists; a goal is an operational statement necessary to achieve the partners' vision. In the absence of compatibility between partners on values, beliefs, and goals, too much psychic energy will be devoted to resolving conflicts—energy needed to launch and pursue business objectives.

Power refers to the ability of one person to influence the thinking, feeling, and behavior of another. When used wisely, it is essential to the success of a partnership; when abused it becomes destructive both to the partnership and to the partners individually. Efforts to influence need to be directed in pursuit of maintaining a healthy partnership and a successful business. Influence that is used merely for personal needs at the expense of partnership objectives will undermine both the business and the partner relationship.

The lifeblood of a partnership is the availability and appropriate application of needed *resources* to accomplish its human, material, and financial goals. A successful partnership depends on knowledge of what resources are needed and having access to them. This knowledge starts with the partners' assessment of their personal resources, of what is needed, and of how to access those resources they do not possess.

Decisions are most productive when they are the product of sufficient information and when adequate time and resources are devoted to evaluating data. Rarely, however, does one have all the information one needs and adequate time and knowledge to evaluate the data. Nevertheless, it is important to remember that postponing a decision until conditions are more favorable often carries greater risk than making a decision based on limited information. Under these circumstances, one should strive simply to learn from the experience and to try to minimize the times when decisions have to be made under adverse conditions.

As noted earlier, it is essential that partners are able to *resolve differences* in a manner that is acceptable to both. A disagreement becomes a conflict when resolution seems problematic. A set procedure should be in place that will help the partners to cope with conflicts that reach an impasse. Allowing an impasse to go unresolved can put both the partnership and the business at risk by draining energy and attention from matters of business to personal struggles for control and vindication.

Delegation properly utilized contributes to increased productivity; delegation inappropriately used will have the opposite effect. When partners are unrealistic about how much they can do, unfulfilled commitments, short tempers, and conflict are too frequently the result. Another result of unrealistic attitudes is the assumption that delegating will make the partners more productive. Often overlooked is the time it takes to train and supervise delegatees. Improper supervision reduces the time the partners gain from delegating responsibility and can be disruptive.

Conditions in a business environment are never static. Partners must be able to *manage transition;* that entails the ability to anticipate and adapt to events, maintain stability, and manage the termination of events. Essential to this ability is the application of learning from past experiences, something assumed to be obvious that often doesn't happen. Business conditions frequently require flexibility in adapting to change. Managing the transition of terminating a partnership, whether by choice or forced, presents an intellectual and emotional challenge. Emotional investments in ideas and projects often cloud one's judgment as to whether an idea or project is not working. Managing termination when it is beyond one's control, as in a bankruptcy, is particularly hard, especially when embarrassment is involved and when the future is uncertain.

Effective *communication skills* are key to a successful partnership; this requires effective listening and speaking skills. This depends on possessing a thorough understanding of managing assumptions and the relationship between verbal and nonverbal communication. Partners who lack effective communication skills place an added burden on their relationship. Coping with day-to-day issues becomes far more complicated when problems result from misunderstandings or assumptions that are not checked out. Conflict resolution becomes more elusive when the partners are unable to articulate their views or listen to each other with understanding. This situation worsens when communication limitations are expressed in personality conflicts.

Knowing and applying the difference between being a *leader* and a *manager* will significantly impact on the success of a partnership. Successful businesses need both leaders and managers—leaders are needed for their vision and ability to inspire others, and managers for their ability to implement the vision.

Understanding the dynamics of a *business culture* in relation to its environment contributes to the success of a partnership. Partnerships do not operate in a vacuum. They define a business culture for their employees in the context of how they need to interact with their customer base and other parts of the community—bankers, lawyers, the public, and more.

Keeping the partnership healthy is essential to achieving business goals. The healthy business starts with a thoughtful business plan and its implementation. Also needed is an ongoing program to watch for signs that it might be running into difficulty. Prompt attention to an evolving problem will forestall a full-blown crisis. This early-warning system will keep a partnership functioning at its most productive level. One practical component of such a system is regular review of the partnership and business relationships.

The life of the partnership will depend on maintaining a positive *cost-benefit ratio*—to ensure that the benefits gained from the partnership are worthy of the costs of getting them. When the costs of obtaining benefits are reasonable in comparison to the benefits, the relationship can endure the inevitable trials of business. When the partners begin to question whether the benefits are worth the costs, however, the partnership is on shaky ground. Under such conditions, a partner would want to end the partnership.

Finally, active partners need a flexible definition of a compatible *division of labor*, which will enable them to modify their responsibilities as circumstances warrant.

SILENT PARTNERSHIPS

A silent partnership is not formally acknowledged and in many cases is not public information. For one reason or another, the silent partner does not want his or her role to become public knowledge. A silent partner is not involved in the daily operation of the business; rather, his or her role can vary widely from solely financial participation and advice to close involvement with the ostensible entrepreneur/manager. The silent partner's involvement in the business may be time limited; an investor, for example, may participate in helping a business get started for just a specified time period. Although a silent partner usually benefits financially from the relationship, the exception would be the parent or friend who helps another engage in a business venture.

Transient Silent Partner

As the name *transient silent partner* indicates, this partner may be involved for a limited time, perhaps simply to help a business get started and stabilized. The partnership may be informal, as when formed with a close friend, or formal, which will depend on trust and on whether the silent partner becomes financially responsible for any of the business's obligations. If there is a formal agreement, it is likely to be a much less detailed one than it would be in an active partnership. The major considerations will probably be to protect the silent partner's equity and to limit his or her financial exposure to debts of the business.

The transient silent partner is likely to be concerned with the *values, beliefs, and goals* of the partnership to the extent that it affects his or her investment. The transient silent partner is likely to defer any *power* concerns to the active partner, reserving his or her power to withdraw anytime he or she becomes unhappy with any aspect of the partnership. His or her only concern will likely be the availability of adequate *resources* to conduct the business. At best, he or she will be only minimally involved in resources concerns.

While the transient partner is generally not involved in day-to-day *decision making,* he or she may well have some input in major decisions. The partnership agreement should clearly define the nature of that involvement.

As for *conflict resolution capability,* there is not likely to be much need for the transient partner to resolve conflicts since he or she has a finite interest in the business and is not involved in its day-to-day workings. Conflict becomes a concern only if there is a threat of business failure. The transient partner is not likely to get involved in *delegation* issues except in an advisory capacity.

Management of transitions will be relevant at the start of the partnership and at its ending. At other times the active partner may ask for help in managing a major transition such as initiating or terminating a product or managing a crisis. Also of less relevance to the transient partner are matters such as *communication skills, leadership issues,* and *quality of the business culture.* They will be of concern to the extent they affect the transient partner's investment. The transient partner will be interested in supporting any effort that contributes to *keeping the business healthy.*

The importance of the *cost-benefit ratio* in this type of partnership depends on the reason behind entering into the silent partnership. If return on investment is the reason, than the ratio will need to be favorable for the partnership to continue. If other reasons are the basis for the partnership, such as helping a family member or friend, then the importance of the financial return will be tempered by the importance of the relationship. The *division of labor,* that is, how the partners' time and energy are committed to this form of partnership, needs to fit the silent partner's other commitments for the partnership to be viable.

Investment Silent Partner

Sometimes a silent partner is involved solely to make an investment and does not participate in the operation of the business. A person who is involved in an investment will want to have a formal partnership agreement that fully details the conditions of his or her investment. The investment silent partner is not likely to make the investment unless he or she is comfortable with his or her partner's *values, beliefs, and goals.* He or she will exercise *power* in negotiating the initial agreement and when the management of the business is being conducted in a way that may threaten his or her investment. The investment partner will want to make sure that the necessary *resources* are available for conducting a profitable business but will generally defer *decision making* to the active partner unless the partnership agreement specifically states how and when he or she should be involved in certain areas of decision making.

It is prudent for the partnership agreement to define a procedure for how to *resolve conflicts*. *Delegation,* however, is left to the active partner. *Management of transitions* is likely to be of most concern at the beginning and end of the partnership relationship; the investment silent partner may provide assistance in managing a crisis. The degree to which *communication skills* are important will depend on the degree to which the investment partner is involved in the affairs of the business. The investment partner is likely to be concerned with *leadership* issues when he or she perceives they have an impact on his or her investment. Defining the *business culture* will be of concern to the extent it is perceived to affect the success of the business. In addition, procedures will be established for monitoring the business to ensure that it continues to be *healthy* and profitable.

Finally, both *cost-benefit* and *division-of-labor* considerations will have the same importance for the investment partner as for the transient partner, with the added importance that there is enough return on investment to warrant continuing the relationship. Other reasons for being in the partnership are likely to have less weight for a long-term involvement.

Covert Active Partner

A covert active partner is one who is not visible in the operation of the business but plays an active ongoing open-ended role behind the scenes, unlike the transient partner, who is involved for a limited period. This partner might be a spouse, a trusted friend, or a colleague. For one reason or another, the covert partner does not want public knowledge of the relationship and keeps the relationship informal. The covert active partner shares the *values, beliefs, and goals* of the active partner to a degree sufficient to enable a working relationship. The issues relating to *power* are similar to those that apply in an active partnership except that only the visible partner makes an overt effort to influence others. Similarly, decisions about the allocation and management of *resources* are a joint process, but they are implemented only by the visible partner. Major *decisions* are made jointly, and day-to-day decisions are at the visible partner's discretion.

The covert partner must have the same ability to *resolve conflict* as is the case in an active partnership. The covert active partner of necessity *delegates* to the active partner performance of any action that requires public exposure. Decisions about *managing transitions* may be made jointly but are carried out by the active partner unless the covert active partner is able to perform his or her duties without public exposure.

Communication skills are just as important as they are in an active partnership, with whatever limitations the covert partnership might impose by definition. Overt *leadership* has to come from the active partner, although guiding leadership might well come from the silent partner. Such a partner is colloquially referred to as "the man behind the throne." Both partners share in the definition and implementation of the *business culture* within the definition of their partnership.

The responsibility for *keeping the business healthy* necessarily falls to the active partner. The evaluation of the *cost-benefit ratio* is similar to what it is an active partnership. One difference is that due to its covert nature, the partnership might carry a higher emotional cost than if it were public, and it would likely require an adequate increase in benefits to offset the trials of having to function covertly. *Division of labor* is of necessity muted because of the covert nature of the partnership.

CORPORATE PARTNERSHIPS

A closely held corporation functions as a partnership does in practice and can be defined as follows:

- This partnership applies to closely held businesses in which partners are actively engaged in the daily operation of the business.
- It requires two officers with legal responsibility.
- Liability is limited to investment in the corporation.
- The corporation survives a change in partners.
- The partnership is governed by laws pertaining to corporations.

Senior management has multiple partnerships; this includes partnerships between the chief executive officer and his or her board, the CEO and his or her reporting subordinates, and the CEO and his or her executive committee. Managing these multiple parallel partnerships so that they don't conflict with one another is a challenge to leadership.

Dimensions

The corporate partnership is different from all others in its basic structure and operation because it is subject to laws pertaining to corporations. There may be less pressure to scrutinize a potential partner because unlike in other partnerships, in this one liability is limited to the corporation and does not extend to individuals. This partnership is implemented much like an active partnership within the requirements imposed by the legal requirements of a corporation. People choose this form of partnership to protect personal liability and to gain the benefits available from a corporation but not from a legal partnership.

Values, beliefs, and goals are similar to those of an active partnership. The legal requirement of having officers gives the partner holding the president or chief executive position legitimacy in the exercise of *power* both with the other partner or partners and in the eyes of the employees. The same applies to the board of directors in relationship to the CEO. The partnership that requires officers poses a potential power imbalance in the partnership. The title of president carries a message to the outside world about power in the business. That may not be a problem in a mature and healthy partnership, but it can present difficulty in a partnership that has shifted to a less comfortable position.

The management of power in corporate organizations is more complex because of the legitimate power granted to one holding an office. A CEO has to manage his or her partner relationships with each of the board members individually and as a group. The CEO also has to be aware of the power relationships between board members and relate to them in a way that will permit him to pursue the mission as he or she best sees fit.

Available resources concerns are similar to those of an active partnership. Only officers have the formal authority to *make decisions*. However, in closely held small companies, the decision-making process may function as it does in an active partnership. *Conflict resolution* is similar to that of active partnerships except officers have the ultimate authority to make a decision without requiring the consent of others. They must exercise that authority in a manner that doesn't alienate those who are not in agreement.

Delegation is accomplished as in an active partnership unless the corporate partners agree to function by the formal structure of a corporation. *Managing transitions* is also similar to the process in an active partnership with the added complexity that more people are likely to be involved in when and how transitions are managed. This raises the potential for more conflict and thus may make managing transitions more cumbersome than when just two partners are involved. A good example is the stress and conflict that occurs when companies downsize. The resulting stress, tension, and conflicts reverberate through the whole company as roles and responsibilities are redefined. Added stress occurs from the uncertainty of who will be next.

Communication needs are similar to that in an active partnership. *Leadership* needs are like those involved in an active partnership. The formality of being a corporation is not likely to have any impact in a strong partnership, although the formal title might give added leverage in managing leadership differences in the partnership. *Keeping the relationship healthy* and recognizing *signs of trouble* carry the same challenge as in an active partnership. The board of directors has the benefit of providing perspective on the health of an organization based on its distance from day-to-day operations. Defining the *corporate partnership culture* is more complex because of legal requirements and input from the directors and their various perspectives. The *cost-benefit* considerations are the same as in an active partnership. Adding to the benefits is protection from personal liability unless banks require personal signatures. The *division of labor* is similar to that of an active partnership, with any differences resulting from duties related to positions of president and clerk.

PROFESSIONAL PARTNERSHIPS

Members of professional partnerships, unlike those of active partnerships, operate primarily in parallel on individual cases rather than collaboratively on a single objective. Law firms and medical group practices are examples of professional partnerships. These partnerships often have multiple partners. In other respects, however, professional partnerships are guided by business principles similar to those that steer active partnerships.

Dimensions

Professional partnerships are implemented in the same way as active partnerships. New partners are incorporated as defined in the bylaws, and the primary criterion for acceptance is their potential economic contribution. Unlike in a small two-person business partnership, partners may leave without terminating the partnership.

The success of the partnership depends in large part on the partners' ability to share *values, beliefs, and goals* as defined in the bylaws, based on the needs of the particular practice. The pursuit and use of *power* becomes more complicated when multiple partners are involved. Subgroups of partners often form alliances on particular issues that can result in competition for power. This becomes a serious problem when these subgroups become entrenched and power struggles evolve between subgroups. Professional partnerships sometimes fail more from internal struggles than from external ones.

Among the incentives for multiple partners is the benefit of the different *resources* each partner brings in terms of both his or her expertise and the other resources such as finances, contacts, and ability to generate clients. Part of the value of a large firm is the diversity of services it offers a client. That reduces the probability of losing a client who has to go to another firm for services a given attorney, for example, doesn't provide.

Partners *make decisions* as a group. When that approach becomes too unwieldy, however, operating decisions are delegated to a managing partner or an executive committee, or both, subject to review by the partners as a group. The partnership needs to develop established procedures for *resolving conflict* to avoid undue investment of psychic resources in inter-partner competition. Attending to this process in the partnership bylaws can minimize this problem.

Each partner manages his or her own *delegation* within the guidelines defined in the bylaws or through the authority delegated to the managing partner and executive committee. In addition, each partner manages his or her own transitions involved in his or her practice. The exception would be *managing transitions* that affect the practice as a group. Management would guide those transitions. Partners' different styles come into play in *managing conflict*.

The bylaws set the standards for *communication*, which are implemented by practice management. The need for frequent communication is diminished because each partner manages his or her own clients. It is a different situation when partners work collaboratively or on issues that affect the entire practice. Each group of collaborating partners evolves its own communication style. Interpersonal relationships are enhanced when the bylaws include a code of ethics as a guideline for partner communication.

In small firms, management problems are similar to those involved in an active partnership. In larger firms, *leadership* is generally provided by a managing partner with the assistance of an executive committee. Informal leadership evolves from the unique personalities of opinion makers whose views are respected by many partners; such informal leadership can significantly influence practice management.

Primary responsibility for *keeping the relationship healthy* resides with management and with the partners as individuals. Management should be sensitive to detecting and addressing evolving problems before they get difficult to manage. This is particularly relevant for large partnerships, which can be difficult to manage because of their size.

The primary responsibility of management is to be vigilant for *signs of trouble*. That is best accomplished when partners are educated in the early detection of warning signs of incipient problems. This knowledge can also help the partners avoid reinforcing evolving difficulties.

The *partnership culture* is defined by the qualities of the partners, the nature of their product or service, their clients, and the business climate in which the partnership functions. No partnership functions in a vacuum; its success depends on how it is viewed by the community it serves. To gain this desired impression requires considered effort in presenting services in a manner that invites clients. The partnership will achieve this when it is seen as contributing to the community's quality of life. The partners' contribution may include donating money to local social service agencies, donating time and energy, and doing pro bono work. Contributions have more impact when services are tailored to community mores— for example, by observing local customs or having personnel who speak the dominant language of the community.

Partners remain in a professional partnership as long as they are satisfied with the *cost-benefit ratio*. They have great mobility because they always have the option of leaving for a more lucrative practice and taking their clients with them.

The *division of labor* within professional relationships is pretty clearly defined by the practice culture, which sets guidelines for what is expected of a partner besides service to his or her clients.

FAMILY BUSINESS PARTNERSHIPS

Family business partnerships occur either when a parent starts a business that involves a child or children as they come of age or when two or more relatives form a business. The vision behind such a partnership involves passing the family business from one generation to the next. Unfortunately for some entrepreneurs, the offspring may not share that vision.

The family business often functions with an informal business plan that evolves over time. The presence or absence of accountability is usually managed by the founding or managing partners. Problems develop when different standards of accountability apply to family members than apply to nonfamily members. Indeed, problems frequently develop when family members are unable to separate family relationships from business relationships. This usually results in family conflicts that are expressed both in the business and in the family. Contributing to such conflicts are ambiguous job descriptions. While unrelated employees would expect and get job descriptions, family members may be presumed not to need them.

Businesses that fathers and sons start will develop more like active partnerships than family businesses. However, the way they define the partnership will be influenced by their family relationship history. A major determinant of how the partnership evolves is the balance of resources, that is, what money and experience each brings to the partnership.

Resentment often develops among nonfamily employees when family members gain positions of responsibility and perks based on relationship rather than on merit. Similarly, family businesses often have difficulty keeping talented personnel because ownership and senior positions are reserved for family members even when they are less qualified. Moreover, it becomes difficult, if not impossible, to fire family members because of conflicting commitments between business and family and pressure from noninvolved family members, particularly if the complainant is a partner's spouse.

Family relationships present yet another problem. When the time comes for senior partners to yield the reins of authority even to a well-qualified child, they may find it difficult to do so. They make great speeches about the pleasure of handing over the business to the next generation but invariably manage to find reasons to postpone it. Confronting the end of one's career is difficult in any setting, and it becomes especially difficult in a family business. The emotional connection readily overshadows rational commitments.

Dimensions

More than any other form of partnership, family businesses are guilty of not developing formal partnership agreements. The notion of trust in family relationships is thought to preempt the need for such formality, but in so doing it provides the seeds for future conflict. Different perceptions come into play as to who said what to whom about the terms of the partnership. The most common areas of conflict are compensation, promised responsibilities, and ownership.

When a parent has formed the business, the *values, beliefs, and goals* are of course established well before the children reach the status of partners. A considerable period of time elapses before the children of partners are able to influence the values, goals, and beliefs relevant in the business. The case of two relatives starting a business will be more like an active partnership with regard to how they evolve a common set of values, beliefs, and goals. This process will be influenced by the relative status of the partners. An older brother, for example, may have greater influence because of his seniority.

Power in family partnerships is often a function of age, experience, and access to resources—especially money, contacts, and reputation. Other family members become powerful sources of influence by virtue of their place in the family. In the case of a parent-child partnership, a spouse, usually a mother, may have special and informal influence. The mother often becomes an advocate of the adult child more on the basis of her parental role than the child's qualifications.

Personal conflicts between husband and wife in a husband-and-wife partnership may spill over and affect the business relationship. A wife partner, for example, plays out her anger at her husband by championing her employee son's issue over her husband, ignoring the merits of her husband's rationale for opposing the son on a particular issue.

Partnerships of peers, especially brothers, are likely to share their *resources* for the partnership. In contrast, partnerships of parents and children will depend on the parent to provide the necessary resources until the child partner is able to bring the needed resources to the partnership in his or her own right.

In a two-generation partnership, *decision making* is usually dominated by the senior generation, at least until a partner of the younger generation gains enough experience and expertise to compete for power. Decision making between partners of the same generation will function more like an active partnership and will be influenced by their family history. Problems develop when sibling competition is involved. Unresolved issues or competitive history can readily influence siblings' business behavior. The ability to *resolve conflicts* will be a product of the partners' family history, their position of power in the business, and their social skills in managing differences. Also relevant will be the respect they have for one another's abilities and judgment.

Generally *delegation* will be from the senior member to the more junior member. Commonly, in a two-generation relationship, responsibility is delegated to a younger partner by an older partner. But as noted earlier, the senior partner may profess the desire to delegate responsibility but often has difficulty in relinquishing control. A talented junior partner will ultimately bolt the partnership if his or her need for more influence in the partnership meets with frustration.

Senior members in a two-generation partnership manage *transitions* until the junior partners gain the necessary maturity and experience to manage them. This would include aiding the junior member in his or her transition from junior to senior partner. The way in which partners *communicate* is largely influenced by patterns of communication carried over from family relationships and is modified as partners gain experience and maturity in the business. It becomes difficult to separate family ways of communicating from those required in the family business.

In two-generation partnerships, *leadership* is primarily the domain of the older generation. That may be modified as a younger partner demonstrates leadership ability and the older partner is comfortable making room for sharing leadership.

The ability to maintain a *healthy partnership* will depend on the partners' ability to regularly review the status of their relationship. Partners need constant vigilance to keep family relationships from unduly affecting business relationships, and they need the ability to give and accept critical feedback in a constructive manner. In a two-generation partnership, the partners must be able to communicate in a manner different from the way they relate in the family context. A case in point is the father who can accept the expression of anger from his or her son without invoking the standard of respect that applies in the family context.

Signs of trouble that affect constructive communication in a family business include such behaviors as diminished tolerance for different points of view, heightened criticism, less positive acknowledgment, less willingness to express constructive suggestions, less empathy, subpar performance, and diminished interest in the business.

A key element in the success of a family partnership is the partners' ability to develop a *partnership culture* that integrates their individual values, beliefs, and goals. In both a one- and two-generation partnership, that involves relating to one another for the good of the prospective business—without any complications from their prepartnership relationship. An added complication can occur when a younger partner attempts to influence the partnership with the views of his or her generation and the added perspective that results from his or her education, which may either threaten an older partner or be welcomed. Friction between the generations develops when the older generation has difficulty adapting to societal changes and shifting values, especially in matters of dress, values about commitment to work, and respect for elders.

At least three things influence the cost-benefit ratio for the parents: pride and pleasure in turning over their creation to another generation, which in a multigenerational business has a pleasing quality of immortality about it; joy and frustration in being able to enjoy one's children in ways that would not otherwise be possible; and the satisfaction of being able to ensure the economic well-being of one's family, particularly when one observes the economic struggle that children in other families face.

The complementary benefits the children receive are financial security and the luxury of not having to face the trials of the alien workplace. Sometimes, however, children pay a dear price when they feel compelled to enter the family business and do not really have a choice in the matter. In addition, they may find themselves working in an environment in which they feel criticized and underappreciated.

The *division of labor* in the family business partnership tends to be more informal than in other types of partnerships; this is especially the case in small businesses where family relationships and competition for power complicate the situation. It can be difficult for a second-generation member to get the needed range of experience that would more readily be had in a business other than a family business. This becomes a subtle way that the senior members have of maintaining control.

PRODUCT PARTNERSHIPS

The product partnership involves a joint collaborative effort for the benefit of both employer(s) and employees rather than ownership. This partnership occurs when partners develop a working environment in which employees feel they are partners in the joint effort. Unless employees are encouraged to make creative contributions, no collaborative partnership takes place. As a result, employees give less than their capability and will tend only to meet the minimum requirements to keep their job.

The product partnership is defined informally. The work relationship becomes a partnership only when management encourages participatory involvement that employees welcome. Employees become vested in the success of the company outside of their personal compensation, with personal satisfaction and success becoming identified with company success.

Employees share ownership only when owners unilaterally grant equity as a reward for services rendered. For example, one businessman gave deserving employees small amounts of equity instead of bonuses in the belief that that would encourage better motivation and commitment and lead them to think and act more like owners. That approach worked well for all concerned, beyond what would have been realized through bonuses, when he sold his business. Some companies utilize profit to encourage development of a product partnership mind-set without involving equity ownership. The product partnership is based on an individual relationship between partners and an employee, and it can apply to all employees who demonstrate a vested interest in their work that goes beyond meeting minimal requirements and are able to provide creative input.

Dimensions

The quality of the product partnership will be enhanced when employees are welcomed to participate at a creative level and there is a specific understanding of what each party expects of the other. Contributing to this accomplishment are realistic job descriptions and the accountability of all parties for their behavior.

The *values, beliefs, and goals* of the product partnership are defined by the employer's ability to consider his or her employees' values and beliefs. Managing this possibility is a key element to the success of a product partnership. Product partners exert *power* through reward and discipline; some tools used are compensation, promotion, profit sharing, and in some cases granting equity. Employees exercise power through their initiative, commitment to their work, loyalty, and the way they represent the company.

Partners provide the physical environment for conducting the partnership, financial resources, the business concept, management, and the quality of the work environment. The employer and employees together provide the cognitive and emotional *resources* necessary for a successful partnership. Key to this success are the employees' creative input to the company's product and the employer's acknowledgment and rewarding of that input.

Employees need to feel they have appropriate input in *making decisions*, especially those that affect them—such as decisions about working conditions and personnel practices. The product partnership benefits when employees understand the basis for decisions, particularly when their input cannot be honored. Partners are responsible for providing appropriate mechanisms for *resolving conflicts* relating to employee grievances and concerns. That requires showing respect for differences and providing solutions that reflect the interests of both partners and employees.

Appropriate use of *delegation* to employees works to the benefit of both owner and employees, making maximum use of their abilities, adding to their expertise, and enhancing the quality of the product partnership. Partners have the primary responsibility for managing business *transitions;* they also assist employees in their work transitions. For their part employees contribute to managing transitions by showing initiative and cooperating in both helping management through business transitions and getting help in managing their own transitions. Examples of transitions include promotions, a change in a product, moving to a new location, and organizational restructuring.

Communication is enhanced when both partners and employees develop common standards, including always verifying assumptions, respecting one another's differences, using good listening skills, and being sensitive to nonverbal messages.

Product partners provide *leadership* by motivating others in the pursuit of their vision through modeling and by respecting the contributions of subordinates. Also needed is the ability to train subordinates to lead in their respective domains. Employees can show an indirect form of leadership by taking advantage of training, showing initiative, and providing constructive feedback

Partners will help *keep the product partner relationship healthy* by maintaining open communication, positively acknowledging one another, and ensuring that they are able to express concerns safely. Also important are respecting differences and being committed to resolving them in a way that reflects the needs of both partners and employees.

Prompt attention to any *signs of trouble,* such as any negative changes in the partnership, will ensure continuation of a healthy product partnership. In such a partnership employees share responsibility for detecting signs of trouble. A product partnership also benefits from the diverse backgrounds of employees who have an impact on defining the *partnership culture.* This culture is not static; rather, it needs to adjust to changes in employee backgrounds and changes in the marketplace and community in which the partnership functions.

The product partnership will thrive as long as the cost-benefit ratio is acceptable to both employers and employees; this partnership will cease to be viable when that ratio becomes unacceptable to either party. That will occur when the parties lose their joint commitment to having a partnership that works for all concerned. Sacrifices are required by both parties to maintain this parity. The productive product partnership also provides for flexibility in the *division of labor.* In such a partnership, both partners and employees are able to adapt to changes as long as constructive, open communication and the means for resolving difference are possible.

CHAPTER 23

Collateral Partnerships

COLLATERAL PROFESSIONAL PARTNERSHIPS

Collateral professional partnerships are relationships between partners and professional service providers—lawyers, accountants, and others—as dictated by special needs. Such providers are not involved in ownership, nor do they have any financial responsibility or accountability for the functioning of the partnership. They share the goal of helping the business to succeed, they function in an advisory capacity within the limits of their respective professional ethics, and their functions are clearly defined. Accountants participate on a regular basis, whereas lawyers participate on an as-needed basis, as do other consultants.

Dimensions

A written understanding of what expectations each party has of the other will minimize misunderstandings and improve the prospects for achieving a mutually satisfactory partnership. Collateral partnerships with lawyers and accountants will have a greater chance of being success-ful if the *values, beliefs, and goals* for the working relationship are shared. This involves checking compatibility before any agreement is made. Chemistry in the working relationship is as important as technical compe-tence, as is clarity in the partners' mutual expectations.

The collateral professional partnership derives its *power* from the consul-tant's desire to have the company as a client. This power is in part deter-mined by the importance that the partnership holds in the professional client base. A high-profile client will of course receive more attention than a low-profile one; a large company is more likely than a smaller company to be attended to by a senior partner.

One consideration in a partnership's selection of lawyers or accountants is that they have the requisite expertise, *resources,* and range of skills and preferably have experience in the partnership's area of performance. Compatibility in working style and temperament will assuredly promote a good collateral relationship. No partnership likes to pay to educate its consultants in the nature of its business.

Decisions are usually made jointly by the professional making recommendations and the partners. The recommendations are either accepted or an alternative is negotiated that is acceptable to both parties. Exceptions to this occur when the partnership defers to the judgment of the professional or when a consultant is given the authority to make decisions based on faith rather than on the partners making informed decisions.

Mutual respect and a commitment to honor differences within legal and ethical bounds will generally result in a comfortable relationship, giving the partnership a feeling of trust. *Conflicts* are likely to occur when the partners want their consultants to do what the consultants consider unwise. Such conflicts should be managed as part of negotiating their relationship. The occurrence of chronic conflicts may indicate a problem in compatibility in this partnership. The partners *delegate* to their consultants services they cannot or prefer not to do themselves. That may include giving an accountant or lawyer the power of attorney to negotiate with the Internal Revenue Service or with banks.

Partners share responsibility in managing *transitions* in their working relationship and in legal and accounting matters, such as when they deal with outside third parties in contracts and suits, adapt to new regulations, or cope with outside agencies such as the IRS or other governmental agencies.

Open and frank lines of *communication* need to be defined and maintained; dealing in subtleties and acting on assumptions damage the relationship. Partners need to take the reins of *leadership* in clearly stating what is needed from their professional consultants. In turn, the consultants are expected to take the lead in informing the partnership about matters that affect it.

To *keep the collateral professional relationship healthy,* the partnership depends on its professional consultants to apprise it of any events in their domain that might affect their relationship adversely, whereas the partnership should let its consultants know of anything happening in the business in which the consultants should be involved. Prompt awareness and reporting will heighten the consultants' potential helpfulness. The collateral partnership is best served when both parties—partnership and consultants—inform each other at the first *sign of trouble* in either their working relationship or in any matter affecting the business.

The *partnership culture* will be productive when the compatibility of the parties' backgrounds and interests is reflected in their defined expectations of one another. That includes a suitable means for managing accountability. The partners will be satisfied with their consultant relationship as long as they feel they are being well served. They will face a precarious period if the *cost-benefit ratio* shifts to the point where it is no longer clear that the benefits of the relationship are worth the hassle involved to keep it going. This period of uncertainty is fed by the prospect of the disruption and inconvenience that accompany changing consultants.

Division of labor will not be a problem if mutual expectations are clearly delineated at the onset of the partnership. Changing circumstances may require renegotiation of expectations.

COLLATERAL PARTNERSHIPS WITH BANKS

Although one does not think of being in partnership with a bank, that is in fact what happens. An entrepreneur and bank agree to collaborate to the mutual benefit of both. Oftentimes, this relationship may not feel like a partnership, since it seems that the bank unilaterally defines the terms of the partnership. Often, there is little room for negotiation of terms. However, understanding the dimensions that define a partnership may help to make the collateral partnership with a bank more comfortable and productive.

Banks share a common goal with owners, that is, profit. A bank becomes involved in the business's operation in two ways: at the time of granting a loan and in the event the bank perceives a potential threat to its investment. The bank may have an indirect impact on business operations when it refuses to grant a loan for purposes that might put the bank's investment at risk. The bank has clear expectations of accountability—timely payment of debt service and the provision of financial records as required.

Dimensions

A collateral partnership with a bank is implemented when the terms set by the bank for granting a loan or providing other services are accepted by the partnership. A bank that enters into a collateral partnership needs to have confidence in the *values, beliefs, and goals* of the partnership, and vice versa. However, the partnership may not be in a position to demand that the bank share its values if obtaining necessary financing is a problem.

Power in the bank-partnership relationship lies primarily with the bank, which has the power to grant the needed financing and to call the loan at whatever time it begins to lose confidence in the viability of the partnership. The partnership has little leverage inasmuch as it needs the bank more than the bank needs to lend the money—unless the bank has some special reason for granting the loan. For example, it might want to demonstrate its commitment to diversity.

The bank's primary concern is that the partnership has the necessary *resources*—finances, business management, sound product, good business plan, and necessary personnel—to meet its responsibilities. The bank's *decision-making* function includes determining the viability of the partnership, the amount and terms of the loan, and the partnership's possession of adequate know-how and personnel to accomplish its objectives. The partnership's decision-making function involves determining that the terms of the loan are viable and ensuring that the debt service obligations are met in a timely manner. There is little room for *conflict resolution*, however, once the bank determines that the loan is no longer viable. Nor is *delegation* a relevant consideration in a collateral partnership with a bank. The one exception lies in the partnership's decision to have its lawyer or accountant negotiate on its behalf.

A bank can help the partnership make the *transition* of getting started and help it deal with short-term crises outside of its control, as long as it is satisfied with the partnership's management of the problem. This requires that the partnership keep the bank informed of all matters affecting the bank's trust. The bank can also help ease the transition involved in new purchases of property or equipment.

As noted earlier, good relations with the bank depend on *communication* that keeps the bank informed of any circumstances that could adversely affect the partnership's ability to honor its debt service commitments. Any inkling that the partnership is being less than forthright with the bank can undermine the bank's trust in the partnership. Letting a bank know a partnership is in trouble and how it is managing it will invite a more sympathetic ear than would be the case if the bank were to find out on its own. That will arouse the bank's mistrust in the partnership and make future dealings more difficult.

The bank demonstrates its *leadership* by defining the loan in such a way as to meet the partnership's needs and by helping the partnership cope with problems that may arise. The partnership demonstrates its leadership by successfully managing the business and meeting its debt service obligations.

Keeping the relationship healthy is primarily the responsibility of the partnership, with the help of the bank, especially in managing financial crises. Both the partnership and the bank should be sensitive to any *signs of incipient problems*. The bank will be especially alert to debt service payments that do not occur on the prescribed basis. In that case the bank will likely become involved in determining the source of the problem.

The partnership culture may impact how the partnership conducts its business. For example, the bank may not wish to grant a loan to the partnership to buy property in an area it considers would put the business at risk. Partnership culture is also sensitive to the current economic conditions. A robust economy and low interest rates will have a great impact on how the partnership culture is defined.

A bank participates in this partnership as long as the *cost-benefit ratio* is favorable to it and the active partnership doesn't make unrealistic demands on bank services. Partners engage in an agreement with whatever bank will provide the services relative to cost involved. This choice may be tempered by special considerations such as willingness to extend additional credit or to change financing terms. The *division of labor* in this partnership is clearly defined and is not especially subject to change.

COLLATERAL FAMILY PARTNERSHIPS

The unsung heroes behind the successful entrepreneur are his or her family, for with the family's support, the entrepreneur can concentrate on his or her venture. Without their support, he or she would have a far more difficult time and would, so to speak, be fighting a war on two fronts at the same time.

Unlike in a family business, in which family members actively participate, family members in a collateral family partnership are not actively involved in the business. In fact, in this partnership the family commonly does not know very much about the partnership and its operation. Family members enter into this partnership out of the desire to support the partner's effort to succeed in his or her business. There must therefore be an understanding as to when the financial needs of the business take precedence over family needs and activities, and when one should be willing to help out in the business when needed. The collateral family partnership frees up the partner's psychic energy to attend to his or her business, energy that would otherwise have to be expended on dealing with family conflict arising from business demands.

Dimensions

The collateral family partnership starts off in difficulty if a family member imposes this relationship on the family. A successful partnership is best achieved when the entrepreneur consults with family members about what is being asked of them as well as the benefits to be gained from their contribution. Recognizing their anticipated sacrifices is helpful in gaining their cooperation. It is also helpful for the family to know that at times it will be a priority.

The potential for success will be enhanced when the family participates in the definition of *values, beliefs, and goals*—only then will the partnership be meaningful and have the support of the whole family. Family members exert *power* in their support or hindrance of the partner's attendance to the business partnership. The partner exercises power through the attention he or she pays to family needs and the appreciation he or she shows for their efforts. Spouses play a particularly important role through the emotional and physical support they provide and through their ability to act as both parents when the business demands require it. The partner also shows power through rewards that come from a successful business.

The *resources* needed from the spouse involved in the business partnership include emotional support, understanding, and tolerance; he or she should realize that the demands of the business put a heavy burden on the family. The non-partner spouse also needs to be consulted on matters that affect the family and should know that at times his or her needs can be a priority.

Family members, as appropriate, need to have a say in *making decisions* that affect them; at the very least, they need to understand why they are being made. Involving family members in finding *solutions to conflicts* that arise from business requirements will yield more constructive results than unilaterally expecting the family to accept whatever is being asked of it. Being part of a solution makes it much easier to accept unpleasant circumstances.

The partner needs to negotiate with the spouse on how to *delegate* responsibilities that the partner's work involvement does not permit him or her to always perform. This may involve training family members to perform these duties in his or her absence; it may also require educating the spouse in how to supervise unfamiliar activities.

Managing *transitions* during a business start-up is stressful for all concerned; attention should be paid to how all family members are affected, and appropriate accommodations should be made. Parents need to work together to help the family make the various transitions that may result from partnership activities. That may include coping with shifting responsibilities in maintaining the family; coping with the partner's absence from the family, especially when traveling is required; having to manage on less income than was historically the case; and so on.

Open and forthright *communication* between family members will contribute to a workable family partnership. Family partners need to be aware of problems that result from operating from assumptions; they need also to be aware of the implications of nonverbal communication. The partnership will work best when family members are kept informed of changes that affect them and when their input is sought to the extent that their concerns might influence the outcome.

A successful collateral family partnership requires *leadership* from both spouses, although the primary leadership will need to come from the partner in business. The spouse can exercise leadership by anticipating what is expected and by behaving in a supportive manner as long as he or she is kept duly informed. The spouse also leads by providing a positive model for others to follow.

A *healthy collateral family partnership* will prevail when problems are addressed as soon as they arise. It is helpful to approach each problematic situation with the attitude of fixing the problem rather than getting into a complaining or judgmental mode. Otherwise, it becomes too easy to let concerns drift until they reach the crisis stage, which makes resolution all the more difficult.

The most obvious *sign of trouble* is visible when communication begins to break down and when stated needs are ignored either overtly or by inattention. Other indications are evidenced in behavior: more and more arguments go unresolved, school or work problems develop, chores don't get done, and the family mood shifts from upbeat to depressed.

A successful *partnership culture* will result when the needs of the personal cultures of family members are considered and the lifestyle of the family is designed with those concerns in mind. Also needed is a clear definition of what family members expect from one another.

The family members can improve the *cost-benefit ratio* in this partnership by making sure that the family as a group attends to the needs of each family member in an equitable way. Properly managed, this collateral partnership can be a win-win one; otherwise, it can become a loss for all concerned. Family members can also ensure a favorable cost-benefit ratio by balancing personal needs with the needs of the partnership. The best way to do so is through open and constructive communication that deals with both positive and negative concerns.

Success in the collateral family partnership depends on a *division of labor* among all family members. The division of labor needs to be flexible enough to accommodate changing circumstances that are likely to occur with a start-up business and a growing family.

COLLATERAL CONSUMER PARTNERSHIPS

Rather than thinking of producers and consumers as being in a partnership, one is more likely to view them as adversaries. Consumers often feel exploited and badly treated by producers of goods and services. However, there are conditions under which producers and consumers do function in a partnership. One might wonder what the impact on goods and services would be if collateral consumer partnerships were made a meaningful part of every business.

Customers participate indirectly in formulating the concept of the company's product through market research, focus groups, and other groups. In this way, they share the goal of providing a product that meets consumer needs. Consumers influence partners when they act in sufficient numbers to affect the company's profitability. Consumer partnerships can exist only when company and customer establish a dialogue in which customers' concerns are acknowledged and have influence.

Dimensions

A partnership between partners and consumers is implemented only when the two parties develop a mutually satisfactory form of interaction. This occurs when partnerships are receptive to consumer feedback and concerns and respectfully respond to them. The consumer helps to develop the partnership by purchasing the company's product. The partnership becomes a reality only if the producers invite consumer participation.

Consumers have little input into the *values, beliefs, and goals* of the producers of the products they purchase. They can have an impact only through their views being solicited or through purchasing power. The values and beliefs of producers and consumers are not necessarily shared. The entrepreneur must know and understand the values and beliefs of potential consumers if he or she is to be successful in selling his or her product. The reverse is true only when the consumer needs to communicate with a business to have his or her concerns addressed. Having some idea of the values, beliefs, and objectives of the company can gain the most responsive hearing from the company.

A business's major mechanisms regarding interaction with consumers are sales, market surveys, and focus groups, all of which focus primarily on the quality of the product rather than on the quality of the relationship between consumer and company. Customer relations departments normally act as agents for the company in handling consumer complaints. This puts distance between management and the consumer, which limits the possibility of developing an effective, collaborative consumer partnership.

The producer exercises *power* by defining the product and how it will be marketed. The consumer's power comes in his or her choice of product to purchase. The consumer can express power only through his or her pocketbook. But a real effect is felt only when it is done as a group either in a boycott or through a class-action suit.

Producers have the *resources* to market their product and to educate consumers on the merits of a product or service through advertising in radio, television, sports events, and newspapers. Consumers, however, have limited resources with which to get their views heard. Their frustration in not getting an adequate hearing may lead to seeking recourse through better business bureaus, government regulatory agencies, and direct complaints to the producer.

The partnership exercises *decision-making* powers primarily in matters relating to how to produce its product or provide its service. Regulatory agencies exert considerable power on behalf of the consumer when violations occur. The consumer's primary decision concerns whether to purchase the product or service. Consumers also make decisions about how far they wish to pursue providing feedback to a partnership and whether to seek support from regulatory agencies.

Conflicts with consumers are resolved when producers feel it is in their best interest to do so. Consumers have recourse only through regulatory agencies when the complaint falls within their purview. The only other option is legal action, which is often prohibitively expensive in terms of energy and time as well as money.

Delegation is involved when the consumer delegates pursuit of a conflict with a producer to a regulatory agency or an attorney. The entrepreneur manages the life cycle of his or her product or service through a series of *transitions.* The process starts with anticipating consumer needs and is followed by the design and production of the product or service. Once a satisfactory product or service has been created, effort shifts to maintaining quality and supply. The decision to withdraw the product will be made when it ceases to be profitable.

The consumer undergoes a parallel process of anticipating whether a given product will serve his or her needs and will continue to support the product as long as it continues to meet those needs. At some point, the consumer may conclude that this is no longer the case and his or her interest in the product will end.

The primary mode of *communication* is through advertisement by the entrepreneur. Face-to-face communication between producer and consumer usually revolves around complaints. Focus groups are an exception—in that venue, producers test out consumer needs or reactions to the use of a product. The consumer's only communication option is through written or telephone communication with the business. That usually becomes a frustrating and laborious process, which in effect discourages such communication. Such an effort is also hampered by the series of automated responses that test a consumer's resolve when he or she contacts the company by phone. Interest rapidly gives way to frustration when a consumer is unable to talk to a live person. The company's attempt at greater efficiency therefore becomes an obstacle to satisfactory resolution of any problem, or it may be a calculated effort to avoid being accountable to consumers.

The capacity for *leadership* in this partnerships lies primarily in the producer's hands. Consumers on occasion exercise leadership by forming interest groups in support of a particular product, and they exercise some potential for limited leadership when they are consulted through questionnaires and focus groups. Yet they have no power to enforce their views except through some form of collective action.

Maintaining a *healthy relationship* with the consumer is primarily the responsibility of the producer because the consumer has very limited means for doing so. The company keeps the relationship healthy by producing a product or service that meets consumers' needs and that they can afford and by being available to respond to complaints.

Signs of trouble can be detected when the quality of the product or service deteriorates or when consumers cease to need a given product or service. Insensitivity or lack of attention to the consumer's needs marks the nonexistence of this partnership. This often occurs in the form of hostile responses to complaints, failure to follow through on commitments to explore complaints, or ignoring complaints.

The *consumer partnership culture* is defined by shared values, beliefs, goals, standards, and any defined means for communicating between the involved parties. Banks, other community institutions, and various governmental regulatory agencies influence the consumer-producer partnership to the degree that they affect the company's product. Other social institutions may have an impact to the degree that the company's product is of concern to them. For example, a religious or parent group may take offense with the advertising for a given product or service, such as tobacco or alcohol.

This partnership will cease to exist when either party finds that the *cost-benefit ratio* is unsatisfactory—the benefits no longer warrant the cost of having them. There is little room for loyalty in either direction. The *division of labor* is primarily the responsibility of the producer. Consumers contribute to the extent they that purchase the company's product or are able to give the company feedback regarding the quality it provides.

APPENDIX A

Case Studies and Interview Findings

The ten dimensions of partnership dynamics were derived from social and psychological considerations and case studies of nine partnerships. Those case studies are presented in the first section of this appendix. The next step in that exploration—seeing how those dimensions applied to a range of partnerships—was accomplished by interviewing partnerships of various sizes and types. The findings from those interviews are discussed in the second section of this appendix in two ways: how the dimensions of partnerships relate to the success of the partnership and the unique characteristics of different types of partnerships.

The sample of case studies is not large or representative enough to generalize conclusions, but this preliminary study does provide some useful insights into how partnerships function and why they succeed, are flawed, or fail. Three criteria that guided the selection of partnerships for the case study were size, type, and availability. The types of partnerships interviewed include active, silent, corporate, professional, family business, and product, as well as collateral partnerships with banks, families, and consumers.

CASE STUDIES

Construction Company

Jerry and Ernie inherited equal shares of a construction company from their father. They were successful in business and got along well for many years, and as they got older they began to bring their children into the business. Eventually, Ernie's son, Marshall, became the general manager and began to consult and make decisions with his father to the exclusion of his uncle, Jerry. Jerry became increasingly alienated. Marshall and Ernie, who were absent too much of the time, began running the business down to the point of near bankruptcy. Jerry hired counsel to try to work out the sale of his interest to Ernie or, alternatively, to buy Ernie out or sell the business to an outsider. Marshall, who had few assets of his own, wanted to buy Jerry out, but his father, Ernie, did not want to borrow the necessary money and become personally liable on a guarantee to the bank. The company's accountants began to shift from their original position of favoring Ernie to favoring Jerry when they saw how mismanaged the business was with Marshall in charge. The showdown came when Jerry was asked to sign personally on additional borrowing from the bank. He refused to do so without Marshall's removal. Jerry convinced Ernie that Marshall was the problem. Ernie fired his son, Marshall. Jerry and Ernie regained the management jointly and promptly returned the business to profitability. Two years later they sold the business to a third party.

Medical Group Practice

The practice was started with little or no discussion as to how it would operate and, in particular, how the profits would be carved out. The practice involved just two partners, Alex and Peter. Both worked hard, but Alex put in many more hours with his established patients, whereas Peter spent more time in management and marketing for new patients. At the end of the first year, Peter expected to split the profits evenly. Alex, on the other hand, expected to receive significantly greater compensation because of his billed and collected fees, and he was extremely upset when Peter couldn't see his side. To deal with the numbers after the money had already been distributed on a 50-50 basis created an intimidating situation for Peter and a very frustrating one for Alex. Unfortunately, before they could seek legal counsel, they exchanged unpleasant words and split up along mutually agreed-upon terms.

Law Firm

The practice was started with little discussion about how it would operate. The partners had very different work ethics, which led one of them to split with the other three lawyers. Jean was the workhorse but was receiving only 25 percent of the profits based on an even split among the four equal shareholders. Eventually, she worked out a separation from the practice so that she could practice her specialty on her own.

Management Consulting Firm

Three businessmen, Gregory, Jeffrey, and Michael, formed a partnership to provide organizational development consulting services. Their shared enthusiasm led them to disregard the details of how their partnership would be managed. The three partners had quite different personalities and personal value systems, though they all wanted to have their own office building and a large cadre of consultants. Although they managed to acquire both, in their enthusiasm they didn't pay enough attention to business practices and to managing their different views. Gregory began to find it increasingly difficult to cope with the cumulative pressures of business and unresolved conflict with his partners, which ultimately resulted in a nervous breakdown and a buyout of his share of the business. Jeffrey and Michael continued to run the business for a few years, when financial difficulties led to selling the business to a third party.

Sporting Goods Company

This sporting goods company was a family business managed by third- and fourth-generation members. The business was started by the grandfather of the third generation. The father, John, continued the business as a small neighborhood store in much the same way that his father had run it. John's son, Paul, joined him in the business when he graduated from high school and enjoyed the business. After a few years in the business, his father made him a partner, but no formal partnership agreement was drawn up. Paul gradually proposed a major expansion of the business, which his father quickly vetoed. Ten years later John became ill and was confined to a nursing home, giving Paul the opportunity to pursue his vision. Following in his father's footsteps, Paul formed a partnership with his four sons on an informal basis. For several years the business flourished. The original store was greatly enlarged, and other stores were added. Paul had a special relationship with his son Ethan, who had majored in business in college, and eventually Ethan was made president of the company. Paul and Ethan managed the company's finances with little input from the other three sons, and they quickly incurred more debt than the business could support. This development, coupled with higher salaries for the partners than the business could support, led them to the brink of bankruptcy after an economic recession set in. Pressure from the bank led to drastic reorganization and termination of executive positions. As a result, the other three sons were forced to leave the business. The split was accompanied by considerable bitterness when they realized that their father and brother had shown poor judgment and had not apprised them of what they were doing. Personal bankruptcy was narrowly avoided. As a result of the conflict, however, relationships were fractured beyond repair.

Nursing Home Company

A group of five partners established a group of nursing homes in two states. Three of the partners had worked together successfully in another business, which they sold before getting into the nursing home business. The dominant partner, Sheldon, was charismatic and creative and also had the largest financial resources. He was committed to working with his partners with respect and fairness. The three partners brought in two new partners who had experience in the nursing home business. The more senior of these partners, Jim, was given responsibility for daily management of the company. Shortly after opening their first two homes, one of the original partners, Jeff, seriously disagreed with the way the business was progressing. He was constantly critical, which resulted in a very stressful period in the partnership. Failure to resolve those differences led Jeff to sell his interest to the other partners. Although the company did well for two years, their business gradually deteriorated. At first, Sheldon and the other remaining original partner, Howard, didn't understand why the business was getting into serious financial trouble. Following their investigation, they learned that Jim was grossly mismanaging the finances, and so he was summarily forced into selling his share in the business. The remaining partners were able to restore financial stability. Two years later the business was sold, and the partnership was dissolved.

Advertising Business

Two partners with very different personality styles started an advertising business. Kurt was very assertive and was often insensitive to how his behavior affected others, particularly subordinates, whereas Fred was laid back and more conciliatory in his manner. Nonetheless, they complemented each other: Kurt's assertiveness and imagination were useful in building the business, whereas Fred managed the quality of the work product quite effectively. Fred, however, became increasingly unhappy with Kurt's brusque approach to the employees and blamed his manner for the frequent staff turnover. Employees clearly feared Kurt, which resulted in low morale. Kurt dismissed Fred's attempts to address the problem as being too soft, and in the end, Fred always capitulated because he was uncomfortable dealing with conflict. Gradually, however, Fred became less tolerant of Kurt's dominant ways and increasingly began to challenge Kurt. Each time Kurt would agree to be more considerate, but his behavior would change only briefly, and he would quickly revert to his old ways. Fred finally confronted Kurt on his lack of follow-through, and the upshot was sale of the business.

Furniture Company

Two sons inherited the business from their father. Although they had very different personalities, they got along at least while their father was alive. Once he died, however, the tensions between them began to mount. George, the younger brother, was personable and conscientious, fair, and very attentive to the business. Manny, the older brother, was dour and more casual about his business responsibilities. In addition, he was often aloof and curt with his customers and regularly violated the partners' agreement not to put personal expenses through the business. Manny was often noncommunicative with George, and when he did converse, it was usually to criticize. George's sense of loyalty to his father's memory and his felt obligation to his brother led him to overlook his grievances with his brother for a time. But ultimately, George was so deeply bothered by his brother's behavior, on both a personal and a business level, that he sold his share of the business to him.

Insurance Company

A woman inherited her husband's business upon his unexpected death. She did not work in the business, but her two sons did. The older son, Bill, was more competent and committed to the business than his brother, Sam. Intense sibling rivalry over the years had made their relationship more difficult. Their mother, who knew little about the business, found it difficult to cope with her unexpected and newfound responsibility. She put Bill in charge of the business, but at the same time she was very concerned about how Sam would react to her favoring his brother. Not surprisingly, Sam was angry and spent much of his work hours on personal deals unrelated to the business. Sam ultimately left to pursue his interest in racing cars, but not before the brothers' relationship was fractured beyond repair.

INTERVIEWS

Interviews were conducted with two-person, institutional, corporate, collateral bank, and product partnerships, partnerships of more than two persons, and family businesses to determine what contributes to a successful partnership. The interviews revealed that a successful partnership does not necessarily mean a successful business, although that is usually the case. The converse also applies: a troubled partnership does not necessarily result in a failed business, although it usually does.

Two-Person Partnerships

Three two-person partnerships were interviewed: a mental health practice and two law firms. The mental health practice and one of the law firms were both very successful, and the partners were very pleased with their relationships. In both cases, the partners knew each other well before entering into partnership and scored positively on all 10 dimensions of partnership.

The third partnership, a law firm, failed because the partners had little history prior to entering into the partnership and, most important, had incompatible personalities. One partner was domineering and confrontational, and the other was submissive and averse to dealing with conflict. They also had different values and goals and experienced chronic difficulty in resolving differences.

Partnerships of More Than Two Partners

There were four partnerships in this group: a small hotel company, a financial advisory group, a law firm, and a mental health clinic. Three of the four were successful partnerships on both a personal and a business level. The fourth was quite flawed, however.

The hotel company had six partners at the outset. Two of those partners had a 10-year history in another very successful partnership, and one of them was charismatic and functioned as the informal leader in the partnership. They functioned in an egalitarian manner and had a strong showing on the 10 dimensions of partnership.

The financial advisory group consisted of four partners. The senior partner in the group had been in two prior partnerships with mixed success. All of the partners were compatible and felt very comfortable in the partnership. They were strong on the critical dimensions of partnership and were adequate on the others.

The law firm consisted of 25 partners and was governed by a managing partner and an executive committee of three members, including the managing partner. These lawyers worked primarily on parallel tracks, with each partner servicing his own clients. Partnership issues centered around compensation and maintenance functions, which included support staff, management of the law library, and other legal support services. Associate lawyers were invited in as partners by a vote of the partners as a group and were consistently financially successful. They did moderately well on values and beliefs, communication, control, and conflict resolution and were strong on the other partnership dimensions.

The mental health practice consisted of four partners: two psychiatrists, one psychologist, and a businessman. The partnership had started with one of the psychiatrists and the psychologist, who were an unlikely match, but they shared a common interest in a particular method of psychotherapy and a vision of what an ideal practice would be like. Their personalities were marginally compatible, as were their values outside of their shared clinical interest. The partnership got more complicated when the businessman proposed building a clinical facility, which involved adding him and another psychiatrist to the partnership. None of the four partners knew each other very well and they had little experience in testing out the compatibility of personalities. The partnership failed after a short time because it was flawed on most dimensions of partnership.

Family Businesses

Six family businesses were interviewed: a software company, an art gallery, a clothing store, a container company, a motel, and a real estate company. Two of them comprised valued relationships and were financially successful. Three of them were significantly flawed, and one was very flawed.

Partners in the software company and the art gallery—both husband-and-wife partnerships—were happy with both their work and their marital relationship. The software company partners had been married several years before becoming business partners.

The art gallery couple had no trouble defining and integrating their marital and business relationships. Both couples were able to keep their marital relationship separate from their work relationship, which contributed to their success. They both scored strong on the 10 dimensions of partnership.

The clothing store involved a father and three sons, who superficially had a comfortable relationship and an acceptable division of labor. Although they all were equal partners, the father and a favored son managed the business finances. They borrowed beyond their capacity and ultimately drove the business into bankruptcy. The two other sons were not privy to the financial dealings and were suddenly confronted with the financial disaster inasmuch as all four were personally responsible for the loans. The result was a fractured partnership, and ultimately the two sons not involved in financial management were forced out of the business. This partnership had glaring deficiencies on the dimensions of communication, abuse of power, decision making, and conflict resolution.

Two brothers were partners in the manufacture of various forms of containers. They had a comfortable relationship and a successful business. Eventually, the son of one of the partners was brought into the business. He performed well, and after a few years they elevated him to a managerial position; this fit with their increasing desire to begin to move toward retirement. The son, however, didn't have the maturity and experience to manage the responsibility. The business deteriorated in a short period of time, requiring an infusion of cash that required the brothers' personal signature. The uncle refused to sign unless his nephew was removed from his position. The father agreed to his brother's demand when he recognized that the business would be in jeopardy without his support. The partners showed major deficiencies on the dimensions of unrealistic goals, communication, abuse of power, decision making, and conflict resolution. This case illustrates what happens when family relationships come in conflict with business management.

The motel company was financially successful but a disaster as a partnership. Two brothers and a sister inherited this family business and were incompatible in their values, beliefs, and goals. The older brother had wide and successful experience in a number of other business ventures, whereas the younger brother and sister were neither skilled nor motivated managers. The older brother wanted to sell out his share of the partnership, but a sense of loyalty as well as fear that the business would consequently fail kept him involved in an unpleasant and frustrating partnership. They were weak on all dimensions of partnership.

A mother and two children inherited a family real estate business on the death of the father. Both the son and daughter had been working in the business prior to his death, but the mother had only modest knowledge of the business. After her husband's death, the son took over as chief executive officer. The daughter, feeling she was more qualified for the position, resented being passed over. As a result she became lackadaisical, which created chronic conflict between them. The mother, unable to cope with the conflict between her children, deferred to her son at the expense of her daughter's resentment. At times, however, she advocated for her daughter, only to add to their problems, solving nothing. This is another example of a successful business and a flawed partnership. This partnership was weak along most of the partnership dimensions.

Institutional Partnerships

Institutional partnerships are nonprofit organizations whose goal is to provide a service. Two interviews were conducted, one with a minister and one with the dean of a school in a university. Of the two, the religious partnership was significantly more complex, as is probably typical of any religious community.

The rabbi or minister and the chief executive officer share at least one responsibility: they deal with coordinating multiple partnerships. A cleric has partnerships with his or her board of directors, professional staff and administrative staff, and congregation as both a group and individuals, and also has relationships with his or her peers and the community. However, the cleric faces a more complex situation than the CEO in that the cleric at times has to deal with one person in multiple partnerships. For example, the cleric may have to relate to one person who is a board member, a congregant, a parent of children the cleric educates, and a person in need of counseling in times of crisis on very personal matters; plus the cleric may officiate at weddings, funerals, and other ritual events in which the person is involved.

Each of these partnerships has different requirements, and the cleric must therefore be mindful of how one will affect the others. Management of multiple partnerships can become particularly difficult when the relations in one partnership can conflict with those in another. The cleric's role as educator may conflict with his or her partnership with board members or with professional or administrative staff. To be successful, the cleric has to function well along most dimensions of a partnership in each relationship. Managing relationships that involve both strong cognitive issues and emotional issues requires deft management of many skills.

The minister interviewed for this study was quite successful in managing the dimensions of partnership in his multiple relationships. At times he had to be careful not to unduly exercise the power of his position. Occasionally, he ran into trouble when his behavior in one partnership created problems in another. For example, his conflict with his assistant minister became known to a member of his board of trustees, creating a problem between the minister and the trustees.

As an added complication, the security of a cleric's position is dependent on managing all of his or her partnerships in a manner acceptable to a majority of the board and congregants. That management has the further difficulty that the criteria for success are far less clearly defined and are subject to debate among different factions of the congregation. In contrast, a CEO must abide by a far less ambiguous definition of success—have a good bottom line, maintain a good relationship with his or her board of directors, and be an effective manager of people.

The university dean's situation was similar to the cleric's in that she, too, had to manage multiple partnerships, but unlike the cleric she did not have to deal with the same person in different partnerships. The dean's challenge was how to manage a partnership that was hierarchically defined. She reported to the provost of the university and could negotiate for whatever she wanted, but the ultimate decision was his. The dean was in turn in a hierarchical position with her faculty and students and needed to deal with her partnerships in such a way that dealing with one did not conflict with another. The challenge for both the dean and the provost was to exercise authority in a way that would enhance achieving the objectives of the partnership. This dean was quite successful in managing the dimensions of partnership in multiple relationships.

Corporate Partnership

Interviews with the chief executive officer of a $75 million publicly traded company dealing in home products showed that his situation was similar to the university dean's situation. Both were in hierarchical partnerships in which the partner was both subordinate in one and dominant in the other. The CEO was a subordinate in the partnership with his board of directors and dominant in the partnerships with his subordinates. He had multiple partnerships with those who reported to him. He needed to manage those partnerships so that they did not conflict with one another or with his partnership with the board. He also had to manage his partnerships with the major investors who regularly monitored the company's performance. This face-to-face management occurs when institutional investors periodically visit to monitor their investment. This CEO's mastery of the dimensions of partnership is reflected in the financial success of his company and in the high esteem he has attained through all his dealings.

Collateral Bank Partnership

A manager of a large bank was interviewed to gain a perspective on a collateral partnership. The partnership was hierarchical. The terms of the partnership were unilateral and defined by the bank. The partnership would continue from the bank's view as long as its conditions were met. There was very limited wiggle room for modifying the partnership. The bank defined the value and belief system that guided the partnership and determined how both parties should behave in relation to one another. It did not offer leadership to its customers and was very clear as to the kind of communication expected from its lendees. The bank provided the financial resource when it was confident that the lendee had the necessary resources to meet its obligations. Decision making and management of conflict was largely determined by the bank. The bank would remain in the partnership as long as the lendee met his or her obligations. Delegation was not relevant in this partnership, and the division of labor was clearly defined.

Product Partnership

This interview involved a large dental practice. The dentist's relationship with his office staff of five was a product partnership in that they worked collaboratively on the best way to provide patient care. Staff members were regularly consulted on how best to provide service to patients. Their job descriptions were defined jointly and tailored to reflect individual needs when that did not compromise quality of patient care. Communication problems were readily addressed in an issue-focused basis and rarely became personalized. Decisions were made by the dentist that reflected input from those who would be affected by them. Division of labor was appropriate and well defined, and creativity was welcomed and acknowledged.

Product partnerships occur in the intimate environment of a small group, as in the case of the dentist, and they can also occur in a large company, as in the public company discussed earlier. The chief executive officer manages his or her relationships with staff as does the dentist. Employees are encouraged to take the initiative and are appropriately acknowledged for their contribution. Expectations are realistic and clearly defined. Employees have input in decisions that will affect them.

DISCUSSION

The objective of conducting the interviews was to determine how conceptual considerations regarding types and dimensions of partnerships are useful in understanding a partnership's success or failure. Partnerships are a fact of life and cannot be avoided. One selects the kind of partnership to enter and the conditions under which one will enter, knowing that the relationship will require one to commit personal resources, particularly psychic energy. One makes this investment with the consideration of what resources will be needed to make the partnership successful and how entering a given partnership will affect other partnerships. A common example is the entrepreneur who wants to start his own business. He has to consider how the venture will affect his ongoing partnerships with his wife, children, and extended family, and how it will affect any other partnerships to which he has committed himself. The success of the new venture will likely depend on this evaluation.

Excluded from the interviews were casual relationships in which one person provides a service to another without requiring any other contribution. An assembly line worker, bus driver, and clerk, for example, perform their required duties within a defined time period with little or no interaction between parties. You do your job, put your time in, and go home.

It was evident from the interviews that a successful relationship depends on constructive collaboration between the involved parties. This leads to the question of how to account for differences in partnerships. This study was limited to business partnerships, although the concepts will apply to any partnership.

The various partnership dimensions described in chapters 2 through 11 do not have equal importance. A review of the interviews reveals that four of the dimensions were critical for a successful partnership: values, beliefs, and goals; quality of communication; conflict resolution capability; and cost-benefit balance. All of the flawed partnerships were deficient in these dimensions. Of the four badly flawed partnerships, all were low on all of the four critical dimensions. Three of those turned out to be very dissatisfied family partnerships that were continuing to function only out of family loyalty or because leaving the partnership was more threatening than staying. Seeing no viable alternative they stayed intact, trapped within the family business.

The dimensions were a useful tool in evaluating partnerships, serving much like a physical examination. The state of a partnership is a composite of all behaviors working in concert. Poor communication interferes with effective decision making and conflict resolution, and it also affects one's ability to reach goals, the cost-benefit balance, and so on. Being able to identify a weak dimension facilitates taking corrective action.

The review of small partnerships suggested that their chances for success were enhanced when partners had a prior history; were temperamentally compatible; shared values, beliefs, and goals, as well as tools for dealing with difference; and were able to pursue individual goals within the framework of partnership goals. The success of a long-standing partnership, such as a law firm, is enhanced when new partners are able to fit in with the established culture.

An interesting contrast between small and large partnerships emerged. Small partnerships tended to be more susceptible to change. The larger partnerships possessed such complex infrastructures and established procedures that change was more cumbersome. All the large partnerships (corporate, university, church, and collateral with bank) had a multitude of varying levels of interlocking partnerships.

The interview with the cleric demonstrated how complicated multiple partnerships can become, especially when they are held with the same person. An added complexity occurs when the partnerships change in a multiple-person partnership. A manager in a company develops partnerships with a variety of people within the company. If he or she gets promoted, his or her standing partnerships will have to be redefined, requiring adjustments for all concerned. For example, when two managers develop a partnership as peers, one of them may later get promoted so that the other manager now becomes the promoted one's subordinate. Quite a lot of redefinition will have to take place, depending on the nature of changes involved.

As noted earlier, family partnerships present an example of what happens when managing multiple partnerships that have major components of both cognitive and emotional issues. This is also true of clergy partnerships. Both of these partnerships have to cope with these dual issues in a more complicated way than is the case in solely business partnerships.

The interview findings suggest that enlarging an existing partnership may complicate communication and decision making, change partners' ability to influence, and so on. Attention to these variables is likely to be useful in making decisions about considering new partners. A useful additional dimension would be for the partners to be equally capable of adapting to change. This would involve the ability to see the need for change and have the wherewithal to implement it. One reason partnerships get into difficulty is their inability to adapt to changing circumstances—in the economy, in the marketplace, in technology, in competition, and more.

Application of the partnership dimensions discussed in this book can help monitor the health of a partnership. Such monitoring should be done on a regular basis to ensure that the partnership is functioning effectively. This evaluation will do for the management of relationships what a financial audit does for the financial health of the partnership.

APPENDIX B

Schedule for Monitoring Partnership Health

Partnerships are not static. To maintain a healthy partnership, the dynamics that define it should be monitored in a manner similar to a financial audit.

The following guidelines that derive from material in this book provide an approach to monitoring partnership health. Background on each of the guidelines is found in the appropriate chapter. As partners conduct their evaluation, they should pay as much attention to achievements as to problems and should focus on the learning to be gained from both considerations.

These guidelines are offered as an example of the principle that an effective monitoring procedure is an important contribution to achieving and maintaining a successful partnership and business. The guideline will be most useful when adapted to the needs of the particular business.

Performing this evaluation every six months or annually is likely to be sufficient. More frequent reviews may be indicated in times of crisis or major impending changes.

1. Values, Beliefs, and Goals

   Monitoring of values, beliefs, and goals will be more effective if the partners commit to writing down the values that will guide their partnership and the beliefs (experience) upon which they are based. The same applies for short- and long-term goals. Each review period will provide an opportunity to update values, beliefs, and goals.

   A. Have there been any changes in values since the last review?

      1. Are any changes needed at this time?

      2. Are there any disagreements about values that guide the partnership?

    B. Have there been any changes in partners' beliefs since the last review?
       1. Are there any disagreements in beliefs?
       2. Are any changes needed at this time?
    C. Are goals adequately defined in measurable behavior?
       1. Are there adequate methods for assessing outcome?
       2. Have there been any changes in short- or long-term goals?
       3. Are any changes warranted at this time?
2. Leadership
    A. Are any changes warranted in the partners' vision for the partnership?
    B. Are employees at all levels appropriately motivated?
    C. What changes are needed?
3. Communication
    A. Have there been any chronic problems resulting from untested assumptions?
    B. Have there been any problems resulting from lapses in accountability for behavior?
    C. Have there been problems related to management of feelings?
    D. Have there been problems related to active speaking or active listening?
    E. Are there behaviors that facilitate or interfere with effective communication?
4. Use of Power
    A. Are there any problems in the exercise of power between partners or between partners and employees?
    B. Are employees being appropriately monitored and rewarded for achievements and constructively guided when their behavior needs to be improved?
    C. Are constructive methods being used that have a positive influence on behavior?
    D. Have there been any destructive uses of power?
5. Resources
    A. Are psychic energies being allocated in a balanced way among priorities?
    B. Are cognitive resources adequate for achieving stated goals?
    C. Are the emotional resources available to accomplish goals?
    D. Are the necessary organizational resources available to reach stated goals?
6. Decision Making
    A. Is there a timely process for making decisions?
    B. Are decisions based on having adequate information?
    C. Is adequate attention paid to evaluating the data on which decisions are made?
    D. Are decisions evaluated for their quality based on information available at the time the decisions were made or based on postdecision information?
7. Conflict Resolution
    A. Is the priority of partnership goals placed ahead of personal goals when they conflict?

    B. Is there adequate commitment to resolve differences in a manner that is acceptable to both partners?

    C. Are the partners able to keep differences focused on issues and not on personality?

8. Cost-Benefit Balance

    A. Is there a clear understanding of the benefits and costs in the partnership?

    B. Is the cost-benefit balance where it needs to be for both partners?

    C. If not, what can be done about it?

9. Delegation

    A. Is delegation used constructively to make the best use of personnel in service of productivity and training?

    B. Is the method of delegating responsibility causing any relationship problems between partners or between employees?

10. Division of Labor

    A. Do both partners feel the division of labor is equitable and acceptable?

    B. Do partners agree that they have a satisfactory way to monitor and implement changes as needed?

11. Defining Partnership Culture

    A. Has adequate attention been paid to those areas that can affect the success of the business: employees, unions, customers, government agencies, and other organizations or entities in the community?

12. Transitions

    A. Is enough attention paid to anticipating partnership needs?

    B. Is there adequate capacity to adapt to changing events, especially when they are not anticipated?

    C. Are there adequate means for maintaining an effective and efficient level of functioning over time?

    D. Are terminations and closings adequately anticipated, prepared for, and implemented?

    E. Are procedures adequate for incorporating the learning of past experiences?

13. Managing External Relationships

    A. Are outside consultants used appropriately?

    B. Is the partnership evaluating them properly?

    C. Are relationships with community resources, professional organizations, government agencies, and competitors used to best advantage?

    D. Is a good working relationship being maintained with the bank or banks?

    E. Is investment in pro bono efforts used to advantage?

    F. Has adequate consideration been given to Internet opportunities?

14. Stages of Development

    A. Is the business vision current?

    B. Does the partnership agreement need to be reviewed?

    C. Does the business plan need to be updated?

    D. Is there a good balance between strategic and tactical behavior?

E. Does the organizational structure need modification?

F. Is the physical plant satisfactory for current needs?

G. Is staffing adequate?

H. Are job descriptions realistic and up-to-date?

I. Do our personnel practices need to be reviewed?

15. Keeping the Partnership Healthy

A. Is there an adequate procedure for monitoring business operations and quality of the partnership?

B. Are meetings managed in a cost-effective manner?

C. Are performance reviews used to best advantage?

16. Signs of Trouble

A. Is there an early-warning system for identifying incipient problems?

B. Are there any problems developing between partners, between partners and employees, between employees, or between the company and customers or clients, consultants, government agencies, or any entity in the community?

C. Are there any incipient problems in the management of finances?

Bibliography

BUSINESS DIVORCE

Freund, J. C. (1997). Anatomy of a split-up: Mediating the business divorce. *Business Lawyer 52*(2), 479–530.

COMMUNICATION

Birdwhistle, R. L. (1962). An approach to communication. *Family Process 1*(2), 194–201.

Lazarus, A. (1984). *In the mind's eye: The power of imagery for personal enrichment.* New York: Guilford Press.

Leathers, D. (1976). *Nonverbal communication systems.* Boston: Allyn and Bacon.

McKay, M., Davis, M., & Fanning, P. (1983). *Messages: The communication skills book.* Oakland: New Harbinger.

McLagan, P., & Krebs, P. (1995). *On the level: Performance communication that works.* San Francisco: Berrett-Koehler.

CONFLICT RESOLUTION

Edelman, J., & Crain, M. B. (1993). *The tao of negotiation.* New York: Harper Collins.

Hargrove, R. (1998). *Mastering the art of creative collaboration.* New York: McGraw-Hill.

Nierenberg, G. I. (1995). *The art of negotiating.* New York: Barnes and Noble.

Putnam, L. L., & Roloff, M. E. (1992). *Communication and negotiation.* London: Sage.

Scott, G. G. (1990). *Resolving conflict with others and within yourself.* Oakland: New Harbinger.

Skopec, E.W., & Kiely, L.S. (1994). *Everything's negotiable.* New York: American Management Association.

Tjosvold, D. (1993). *Learning to manage conflict.* New York: Lexington Books.

DECISION MAKING

Zey, M. (Ed.). (1992). *Decision making.* London: Sage.

IMPLEMENTING BUSINESS RELATIONSHIPS

Fisher, M. (1996). *The ideafisher: How to land that big idea and other secrets of creativity in business.* Princeton, NJ: Peterson's.

Kaufman, R. (1986). *Identifying and solving problems.* San Diego: University Associates.

Rawlinson, J.G. (1983). *Creative thinking and brainstorming.* Guildford and King's Lynn, England: Biddles.

Silver, S. (1995). *Organized to be best.* Los Angeles: Adams-Hall.

KEEPING THE BUSINESS HEALTHY

Langer, E.J. (1989). *Mindfulness.* New York: Addison-Wesley.

Rossi, E.L. (1991). *The 20 minute break.* New York: Putnam.

LEADERSHIP, MANAGEMENT, AND MANAGING RELATIONSHIPS

Bennis, W. (1989). *Why leaders can't lead.* San Francisco: Jossey-Bass.

Bennis, W., & Townsend, R. (1985). *Reinventing leadership.* New York: William Morrow.

Eicholz, M. (1997). *Business relationships: The dynamics of teamwork.* Kirkland, WA: MECA Profiles.

Hickman, C.R. (1990). *Mind of a manager, soul of a leader.* New York: Wiley.

Kotter, J.P. (1996). *Leading change.* Boston: Harvard Business School Press.

Kuhn, R.L. (1988). *Handbook for creative and innovative managers.* New York: McGraw-Hill.

Lipman-Blumen, J. (1996). *The connective edge.* San Francisco: Jossey-Bass.

Shefsky, L. (1994). *Entrepreneurs are made not born.* New York: McGraw-Hill.

Snider, M. (2001). *Human relations management in young, growing companies.* Westport, CT: Quorum.

PARTNERSHIP

American Bar Association. (1997). *Uniform Partnership Act.* San Antonio: National Conference of Commissioners on Uniform State Laws.

Bell, C.R. (1996). *Customers as partners.* San Francisco: Berrett-Koehler.

Bell, C. R., & Shea, H. (1998). *Dance lessons: Six steps to great partnerships in business and life.* San Francisco: Berrett-Koehler.

Davidson, R. L., III. (1992). *The small business partnership.* New York: Wiley.

Davidson, R. L., III. (1993). *The small business partnership kit.* New York: Wiley.

Heenan, D. A., & Bennis, W. (2000). *The power of great partnerships.* New York: Wiley.

Melohn, T. (1994). *The new partnership.* New York: Wiley.

Wyman, J. & Wyman, E. (1999). *Married in business.* Scottsdale, AZ: Doer.

POWER

Boulding, K. E. (1989). *Three faces of power.* London: Sage.

Cialdini, R. B. (1993). *The psychology of influence and persuasion.* New York: William Morrow.

French, J. R. P., Jr., Cartwright, D., & Zander, A. (1968). The bases of social power. In D. Cartwright & A. Zander (Eds.), *Group dynamics* (3d ed.). New York: Harper and Row.

Lucas, J. R. (1998). *Balance of power: Authority or empowerment?* New York: American Management Association.

Pfeffer, J. (1992). *Managing with power: Politics and influence in organizations.* Boston: Harvard Business School Press.

Wrong, D. H. (1980). *Power: Its forms, bases, and uses.* New York: Harper and Row.

TRANSITIONS

Kubler-Ross, E. (1979). *On death and dying.* New York: Macmillan.

Lazarus, A. (1984). *In the mind's eye: The power of imagery for personal enrichment.* New York: Guilford Press.

VALUES, ATTITUDES, BELIEFS, AND GOALS

Helzel, L. B. (1995). *A goal is a dream with a deadline.* New York: McGraw-Hill.

Rokeach, M. (1968). *Beliefs, attitudes, and values: A theory of organization and change.* San Francisco: Jossey-Bass.

Rokeach, M. (1980). Some unresolved issues in theories of beliefs, attitudes, and values. In H. E. Howe Jr. (Ed.), *1979 Nebraska Symposium on Motivation.* Lincoln: University of Nebraska Press.

Index

About the Author

MARVIN SNIDER is an organizational consultant in Waban, Massachusetts. His clients have included hospitals, school systems, banks, law firms, public agencies, and an insurance company. He is the author of *Human Relations Management in Young, Growing Companies: A Manual for Entrepreneurs and Executives* (Quorum Books, 2001).